# WRITING *the* FICTION SERIES

## THE COMPLETE GUIDE FOR NOVELS AND NOVELLAS

### KAREN S. WIESNER

WD

WRITER'S DIGEST
BOOKS

WritersDigest.com
Cincinnati, Ohio

For more resources for writers, visit www.writersdigest.com/books.

17 16 15 14 13 5 4 3 2 1

Distributed in Canada by Fraser Direct
100 Armstrong Avenue
Georgetown, Ontario, Canada L7G 5S4
Tel: (905) 877-4411

Distributed in the U.K. and Europe by F+W Media International
Brunel House, Newton Abbot, Devon, TQ12 4PU, England
Tel: (+44) 1626-323200, Fax: (+44) 1626-323319
E-mail: postmaster@davidandcharles.co.uk

Distributed in Australia by Capricorn Link
P.O. Box 704, Windsor, NSW 2756 Australia
Tel: (02) 4577-3555

Edited by Rachel Randall
Designed by Claudean Wheeler
Cover images by Maica/iStockphoto.com
    & alexfiodorov/Fotolia.com
Production coordinated by Debbie Thomas

# ACKNOWLEDGMENTS

**THE AUTHORS:**

Cat Adams (catadams.net), Stephen Almekinder, Darrell Bain (darrell bain.com), Dana Marie Bell (danamariebell.com), Meg Benjamin (meg benjamin.com), Charlotte Boyett~Compo (windlegends.org), Ora le Brocq, Carl Brookins (carlbrookins.com), Marilee Brothers (marilee brothers.com), P.A. Brown (pabrown.com), Luisa Buehler (luisabuehler. com), Margaret L. Carter (margaretlcarter.com), Diana Castilleja (dianacastilleja.blogspot.com), Rowena Cherry (rowenacherry.com), Anny Cook (annycook.com), Norm Cowie (normcowie.com), Mary Cunningham (marycunninghambooks.com), B.J. Daniels (bjdaniels.com), Dyanne Davis (dyannedavis.com), Denise Dietz (denisedietz.com), Carola Dunn (caroladunn. weebly.com), M. Flagg (mflagg-author.com), Jena' Galifany (jenagalifany. bravehost.com), Robert Goldsborough (robertgoldsborough.com), Joanne Hall (hierath.co.uk), Lorie Ham (musicstoryteller.wordpress.com), Kelley Heckart (kelleyheckart.com), J. M. Hochstetler (jmhochstetler.com), Mary Jean Kelso (authorsden.com/maryjeankelso), Michelle Levigne (mlevigne. com), Deborah MacGillivray (deborahmacgillivray.co.uk), Ann Tracy Marr (anntracymarr.com), Phoebe Matthews (phoebematthews.com), Fiona McGier (fionamcgier.com), Marilyn Meredith (fictionforyou.com), Nicole Morgan (nicole morgan1.webs.com), C.R. Moss (crmoss.net), Fran Orenstein (fran orenstein.com), Linda Varner Palmer (lvpalmer.com), Cindy Spencer Pape (cindyspencerpape.com), Christy Poff (cpoff.brave journal.com), Stella and Audra Price (stellaandaudra.com), Hank Phillippi Ryan (hankphillippiryan.com), Vijaya Schartz (vijayaschartz. com), Janet Elaine Smith (janetelainesmith.com), Annette Snyder (annettesnyder.atspace.com), Beth Solheim, Marissa St James (msjbookshelf.blogspot.com), Liz Strange (lizstrange.com), Regan Taylor (regantaylor.com), S.D. Tooley (sdtooley.com), Jane Toombs (janetoombs.com), Janet Lane Walters (bookswelove.net/walters.php), and N.J. Walters (njwalters.com).

**THE PUBLISHERS:**

J. Ellen Smith, Publisher, Champagne Books (champagnebooks.com); Kim Richards, Co-founder and CEO, Damnation Books and Eternal Press (dam nationbooks.com and eternalpress.biz); Alicia Condon, Editorial Director,

Kensington Brava (kensingtonbooks.com); Laura Baumbach, Owner/Publisher, MLR Press, LLC (mlrbooks.com); Miriam Pace, Owner, Parker Publishing, Inc. (parker-publishing.com); Christina M. Brashear, Publisher, Samhain Publishing (samhainpublishing.com); Joan M. Shoup, Publisher and Editorial Director, Sheaf House Publishers (sheafhouse.com); Debra Womack, Publisher, Whiskey Creek Press, LLC (whiskeycreekpress.com); and J.M. Smith, Owner, Wild Horse Press (the-wild-horse-press.com).

## ABOUT THE AUTHOR

Creating realistic, unforgettable characters one story at a time ...

Karen Wiesner is an accomplished author with 98 books published in the past 15 years, which have been nominated for and/or won 125 awards, and has 32 more titles under contract. Karen's books cover such genres as women's fiction, romance, mystery/police procedural/cozy/amateur sleuth, suspense, paranormal, futuristic, gothic, inspirational, thriller, horror, chick-lit, and action/adventure. She also writes children's books, poetry, and writing reference titles such as her bestsellers, *First Draft in 30 Days* and *From First Draft to Finished Novel: A Writer's Guide to Cohesive Story Building*, and her newest, *Writing the Fiction Series: The Complete Guide for Novels and Novellas*, available from Writer's Digest Books. Her previous writing reference titles focused on non-subsidy, royalty-paying electronic publishing, author promotion, and setting up a promotional group like her own, the award-winning Jewels of the Quill, which she founded in 2003. Jewels of the Quill produced two award-winning group anthologies per year published by Whiskey Creek Press from 2005-2011. All were edited by Karen and others. For more information about Karen's fiction and series, consult her official companion guide *The World of Author Karen Wiesner: A Compendium of Fiction*. Additionally, Karen is a member of Infinite Worlds of Fantasy Authors and World Romance Writers. Along with her writing, Karen enjoys designing websites, graphics, and cover art. She lives in Wisconsin with her husband and son.

For more information about Karen and her work, visit her websites at karenwiesner.com, firstdraftin30days.com, falconsbend.com, and jewelsofthequill.com. If you would like to receive Karen's free e-mail newsletter, Karen's Quill, and become eligible to win her monthly book giveaways, visit http://groups.yahoo.com/group/KarensQuill or send a blank e-mail to Karens-Quill-subscribe@yahoogroups.com.

# TABLE *of* CONTENTS

# THE APPEAL OF THE SERIES

*"The tiger springs in the new year. Us he devours."*

~T.S. ELIOT

Imagine you've spent a seemingly endless amount of time trying to figure out what it is you want in this world. You've been incredibly selfish and ignored the best thing that's ever happened to you, and now that person is walking out of your life with the words, "Frankly, my dear, I don't give a damn." Now it's all over. You can't forget it until tomorrow because it's gone with the wind ... or is it? What if you could go back to Tara? What if you could get Rhett Butler back?

While I'll keep my mouth shut on the wisdom of taking over someone else's story (especially a story whose author so adamantly did *not* want to continue it), the fact is that the sequel Alexandra Ripley wrote to *Gone With the Wind* spent many weeks on the bestseller list because fans of the original desperately wanted to return to Tara and see Scarlett get her happily-ever-after. They weren't satisfied to simply let the story go as it ended. To the point of obsession, they *had* to have more. That inability to let a story go without follow-up or further detail is the hallmark that leads to prequels, sequels, trilogies, and a full series.

Author Thomas Helm has said that the test of a good novel is dreading to read the last chapter. That goes for the author of the book as well as its fans. If you're dreading the last chapter, this may be the best reason your book should become a series. No one wants to let a fantastic book go and will avoid anything that looks like "the end." Paranormal author Dana Marie Bell says, "Speaking as a reader, I *love* series. I love revisiting characters, checking in on their happily-ever-afters." Mystery/paranormal author S.D. Tooley adds that readers of series get caught up in the history of characters who become like family, and because their stories are part of a series, fans know they'll get to see them again. This tempers the sense of loss a reader feels in finishing one story. There's more to hope for.

Writing a series is something that is near and dear to my heart. With five trilogies and twelve series (four of them spin-offs) under my belt or in the works—ranging from three to twelve (currently) books each—writing a stand-alone novel is unusual for me. One novel can spawn many more because my characters become so real, I sometimes feel like the secondaries are tugging on my sleeve while I'm immersed in the world they live in, demanding to know when I'm going to write their stories. As Abelard said to Heloise, "Against the disease of writing one must take special precautions, since it is a dangerous and contagious disease." Writing *series* feels very much like an obsession to me. Simply getting to know characters through the eyes of the main character in a single book has rarely been enough for me. I need to know who they are, what made them into the people they are inside and out, and what they're going to do now. My characters feel as real to me as the people who populate my reality. The worlds I create are places I want to return to again and again. My readers tell me the same, and so together we fulfill our mutual need for more of these characters, more of this world, more of this particular story line. You can't get quite the same satisfaction from a stand-alone novel because, with no continuation in store, that sadness always shows up at the end.

Authors who write series promise readers that the fun doesn't *have* to end, that there's more excitement to come, more adventures and worlds to explore, more of these lives to be lived. Books in a series are comfort reading because you know what you're getting yourself into. There's no risk. If the author is skillful, and you become invested in a way that takes over your mind and heart, you can allow yourself to leave the physical world and join in a quest with the friends you've made.

As a series author, you can also spend more time developing your characters over the course of the series. You enlarge your loyal readership with a series since these fans will put your books on their "auto-buy" lists. This can mean less work because you've probably done most of the research with the first book in the series, and all writers know that less research means more writing time.

J.M. Smith, the owner of Wild Horse Press, says, "A series is always intriguing to us because they sell better than most stand-alone titles. In a proposal, we like to hear what the author has planned for the series." When an editor contracts a series, he is looking for something compelling that will attract readers in droves. If you can get an editor obsessed and looking for future titles within your series, you'll probably be able to do the same with readers if your promotion is done well. If your readership builds, your publisher will also look upon you more favorably and will try to keep all of your books (in your series *as well* as any others you've written for the house) available for those fans who start in the middle and want to see what else you have to offer. Your publisher might suggest that you keep a series going because one book can sell many others. Nearly always, if a series is selling, the publisher will want more. Miriam Pace, the publisher at Parker Publishing, Inc., says, "For an established author whose sales are good, we'll almost always take a series over a single story because that author already has a reader base. Readers are loyal."

There's no denying that the series "tiger" has sprung and is devouring readers of every genre.

## WHO'S READING, WRITING, AND PUBLISHING THE SERIES?

A better question might be *who isn't* reading, writing, and publishing series? Ask anyone what the most popular books have been in the last couple years, and inevitably the answers will lead to books within a series: Harry Potter, Twilight, Stephanie Plum, Captain Underpants, Robert Langdon, A Series of Unfortunate Events, Star Wars, and basically anything, both series and non-series, by Nora Roberts. Authors are writing series, publishers are publishing them, and readers are buying them by the truckloads.

In the course of writing this book, I interviewed nearly one hundred authors and publishers of series. These interviews were simply fascinating to me, and you'll be reading a lot from them throughout this book. I'll also be putting the interviews in their entirety on my website for readers to enjoy. Visit me at karenwiesner.com, click on the "nonfiction" button, and look for *Writing the Fiction Series* to find these interviews.

Like most authors, children's, young adult, and historical romance writer Mary Jean Kelso's love affair with the series started in her childhood. "I write series because, as a young reader, I always wanted to know what happened to the characters after a book I read ended. It was like their lives weren't really over yet. I felt a loss that the story was over and wondered what they would do next."

Charlotte Boyett~Compo, multigenre speculative fiction author, concurs: "Even if one book in the series isn't as good as the others, most readers will buy the next one simply because they have become invested in the story and the characters. As an author, I don't like leaving [the characters] once I've put all that time, energy, and creativity into their conception. It's like abandoning your baby. I always discover something I wish I'd included or I wish I'd had the characters do after the book has been published. Doing another book with the same characters gives me a chance to finish what I started. It also might satisfy the suggestions from readers about where they'd like that character and story line to go next. I pay close attention to reader and reviewer feedback. That way I see what works and what doesn't."

Deborah MacGillivray is the award-winning author of Scottish medieval historical novels and contemporary paranormal romances. "Money is tight for everyone," she says. "People don't want to risk those hard-earned dollars on a book that doesn't please their tastes. A series extends that comfort zone. If you like other books by the author and enjoyed the series, you will be more prone to keep buying them. It's cash in the bank for the publisher since a series book is less risk for them. It's also easier to promote." Audiences can be built over the long haul, and doing so makes sense for authors and publishers. Fantasy author Joanne Hall's experience has told her the same thing: "I think publishers like trilogies and series because they're effectively getting a three-or-more-for-one deal. It gives them a chance to build interest in an author over a longer period of time and means that people who buy one book in the series are likely to buy the next two, or four, or twelve."

Anny Cook, author of fantasy and paranormal books, stresses that she prefers to write series: "I spend many hours creating the world and culture for my stories. It seems wasteful to discard the time spent by writing only one book in that setting. Also, I hate to give up my characters after only one book. Writing series allows me to spend more time with the men, women, and children I've grown to love while writing their stories."

Most of the authors I talked to mentioned how invested they become in their characters. Letting go can be something akin to physical pain. "I write series because I keep 'meeting' interesting characters that have their own stories to tell," says futuristic, western, and romantic suspense writer Regan Taylor. "Things happen in my life, dreams come to me, and between the two, a story unfolds. I don't like saying good-bye and knowing I'll never see someone again. With a series, even though the characters aren't real, they are parts of my psyche and parts I don't have to say good-bye to as long as there is another story to be told."

On a fellow writer's blog, R.G. Alexander, a multigenre author, speaks about why she writes series. She says she becomes obsessed with learning the story of the hero's brother, the heroine's best friend. She is compelled to know what happens with the other characters. She also writes series so the secondary characters can also have their stories told. What is it about the series, Alexander asks, that's so appealing? Is it the familiarity of the world? The fact that we get to delve deeply into the private lives of interesting people? The adventures we go on? That we, as fans of the series, can pick up on subtle nuances and inside jokes that outsiders can't? Our own nosiness? Or is it simply, as Alexander puts it, "the matchmaker in us that makes us want to see everyone from the villain to the waiter who was over-tipped have a happily-ever-after?"

When I asked Christina M. Brashear, the publisher at Samhain Publishing, why series are so popular and whether series books sell better than stand-alones, she said, "Readers love to revisit their favorite characters. My philosophy has been that new books sell old books."

The love affair writers, publishers, and readers have with series is one that won't go away anytime soon. In fact, it stands to reason that it will only grow in popularity.

## THE PURPOSE OF THIS BOOK AND WHAT YOU'LL FIND IN *WRITING THE FICTION SERIES*

One of the things I've noticed in all my years of writing series, and particularly while conducting interviews for this book, is that little, if any, information exists for writers on how to write a series. Writers want to know the common pitfalls in crafting a series and the best ways to get organized and plan for one. I was stunned at the number of times I found authors uncertain about what constitutes a series versus a trilogy or a serial. The confusion I noted about the very *definitions* of the various book groupings was a revelation for me, and I'm sure many readers of this book will appreciate clarification in this area as well. I was also surprised by authors who saw the connections that make up the books in a series as set in stone, and I was flat out amazed at the sheer diversity and creativity of these authors in handling so many aspects of writing their series. Though I have written many series in my career, even I have a lot to learn. I think authors the world over will find this topic as fascinating as I do, especially if you've never written a series but want to try your hand at one or if you've written a series or two and wish there were more help and guidelines to aid you in the process of writing a series.

Therefore, the purpose of *Writing the Fiction Series* is to cover all things series and provide a one-stop resource for the who, what, where, when, and why of this monumental endeavor. I will note up front that I believe a series name is part of its branding (see chapter five for more details about branding). Not only should the series title be included everywhere the name of a book is spoken or written about, but the word *series* or *trilogy* should be capitalized in order to further solidify the branding. In other words, I never refer to my series Family Heirlooms as simply that. Always, I refer to it as the "Family Heirlooms Series" because that's the full title and most effective way to brand it to my readers. That's why you'll see every series mentioned within this book with the word *series* or *trilogy* capitalized.

This book is divided into six chapters, followed by two appendices. Chapter one discusses the catalyst for the series—stumbling into one, setting out to write one, and having a publisher coordinate one. The chapter includes the definitions of the various book groupings, such as the ongoing book series, trilogies, and just about everything in between. The types of series ties are also explained. In other words, what connects the books in a series? There are four main types of ties, and I'll discuss them in depth.

Chapter two hones in on the importance of finding the focus of a series, including topics like story arcs versus series arcs, stand-alone stories versus cliff-hangers, single genre versus multiple genre, and novel versus novella series or a combination of both.

In chapter three I delve deeply into the two most crucial aspects of a series—characters and consistency—and I also include a section with series readers' and writers' tips covering other considerations when writing your series.

Chapters four and five lay out a variety of series organizational techniques that include worksheets and checklists you'll find useful as you work, along with the most important aspects of marketing a series—namely branding.

Chapter six delves into series endings: It helps you determine whether a book's ending is motivated by the author, publisher, or reader, and whether it is left open-ended or provides definitive closure. *Writing the Fiction Series* finishes up with some thoughts on how to make your series stand out in a sea of other series.

At the end of most of the chapters, I provide exercises to grow your series muscles. These exercises build on each other so that by the time you finish the final chapter you should have a good start for your series plan.

The two appendices reference all the supplemental materials you'll need to write your own series:

- **APPENDIX A** contains worksheets and checklists to aid you in your quest to write a consistent and well-developed series.
- **APPENDIX B** contains case study examples of popular series as well as an example of a popular series with all its series, story, and plant arcs broken down. The examples will come in handy as you plan for a set of stories that must contain vital connections from one book to the next.

Throughout this book, I'll provide off-the-bookshelf examples of various series. For the bookshelf examples, in nearly every section, the offerings include one listing from the following genres (in this order):

1. Young Adult/Children's
2. Romance
3. Horror/Paranormal
4. Mystery/Suspense/Thriller
5. Science Fiction/Fantasy/Futuristic
6. Historical/Western/Time Travel/Regency

Keep in mind, of course, that most genres overlap, so many of the examples could be listed in more than one genre. Listings of fewer than six were not chosen specifically for genre and, in some cases, were the *only* examples I could find.

## GETTING STARTED

While at first glance writing a series may seem easy—maybe even a no-brainer—the fact is that if a series isn't well planned, it won't be well read. *USA Today* Bestseller List romance author B.J. Daniels says, "Series are a lot of fun—and a lot of work. But once you get into it, they become easier because you know this place, these people. There is a comfort there. Just don't get too comfortable because the books need to be different enough that a reader won't read the back cover and wonder if she's already read it."

Deborah MacGillivray offers this wise approach to writing a series: "Always treat each book as a stand-alone. If you imbue your novel with that special life force that is all its own, your series will be strong from start to finish. If your readers don't love that first book, that second one will never be read." The same can be said for the third, fourth, or twenty-eighth book in a series. Each book must be at least as exciting as the last, and it must bring something new to the table. Don't we all get disappointed when a favorite author gets sloppy or stuck in a groove or begins to coast along in a series that no longer has vitality for anyone involved? Don't let that series be your own. This book can help you avoid that common pitfall.

Returning to the idea of treating each book in a series as a stand-alone, don't forget that the point of a series is that readers who follow it from one book to the next *will* get a richer, more complex, and more emotional experience than those who read only a single book in the series. Those readers will understand the subtle nuances one-time browsers won't pick up on. If you as the author don't include vital connections from one book to the next, readers will lose their desire to read your series. Each book in a series should come with your unbreakable promise to the reader that she'll get something extra, something more exciting and fulfilling, by following the series—something she wouldn't get with a book that simply stands alone (whether as part of a series or not). Each book in a series must fulfill the handshake contract the writer has silently made with the reader: *Stick with me, and I'll show you a world, characters, and adventures you'll never grow bored with.*

Break that promise and the series as a whole will suffer. In turn, it will reap other unwanted consequences because publishers decide the fate of a series and its author based on sales ... or lack thereof. Beware! Fulfill the handshake agreement, and you'll amass readers with the kind of fierce loyalty you and I both dreamed about while standing in line to purchase the last Harry Potter novel a few years ago. I think all authors can agree that those are the kinds of fans you never, ever want to disappoint.

So how do you get started? Well, first, you need a germ of an idea for a series. Maybe you've already finished a first book and know that you want to go further with it. Maybe you've had an entire series mapped out in your head for a while, but you haven't started because you're not sure how to develop it into a series. Or maybe your publisher has commissioned you and other authors to write a specific series. Whatever the case, have an idea and *grow* that idea. While most will advise you to write what you read or write what you know, I've often wondered if that isn't a questionable way to make a decision this important. I've read countless fantasy novels but so far have not felt compelled to actually write one. My favorite genres to *read* in aren't necessarily the ones I could imagine myself *writing* in. In the same vein, I've written novels about undercover spies, werewolves, and abuse victims, but I don't have individual experience with any of the three. Still, according to readers and reviewers, I wrote each with realistic, ultra-empathetic, and personal verve. As über-hot series author Janet Evanovich says, "If I wrote about what I knew best, my books would be about someone sitting in a room with a parrot squawking in the corner—typing away for hours on a computer. Bor-ing!" Instead of writing what you know, go with the idea that burns inside of you, the one that absolutely must be told *by you*. The rest will get done one way or another.

Once you have your idea for a series, you're ready to get started!

# CHAPTER ONE

# SERIES CATALYSTS, DEFINITIONS, AND TYPES

*"We shall not cease from exploration, and the end of all our exploring will be to arrive where we started and know the place for the first time."*

~T.S. ELIOT

How does a single title become a series? As cozy mystery author Luisa Buehler says, "It's not a series until after Book 3." Logically, a story that's larger than life and outgrows the confines of a stand-alone book could become a sequel, a trilogy, a tetralogy, and finally a series. In this chapter, we'll talk about what propels a stand-alone book into the realm of a series, the definitions of the various book groupings, and the connections that solidify a group of books into a series.

## THE CATALYST OF A SERIES

As we discussed in the introduction, there are three major ways a stand-alone book ends up as a series. The author may stumble into it, meaning she set out to write a single title but it turned into a series. The author may have planned from the very start to write a series (before any of the books were written). Or a publisher may have commissioned a series and then brought in authors to write the individual books. Let's discuss each of these catalysts for a series.

## STUMBLING INTO A SERIES

It happens quite naturally: You're writing a stand-alone book, and you get caught up in the characters' lives, their situations, and their worlds. In essence, you've fallen in love, and the idea of saying good-bye is the worst form of torture. Then a glimmer of realization hits you: You don't necessarily have to close this story with the words *The End*. What if this love affair could go on a little longer, for years, or maybe even indefinitely?

A lot of authors have gone through this situation exactly. Instead of letting go of a good thing, they turn it into a *fantastic* thing by making it into a trilogy, or in some cases, a series. These writers will do anything to avoid bidding a tearful farewell to their characters and worlds—anything to extend a hand to a reader who wants to get back aboard their particular train for another thrilling ride.

Futuristic romance author Rowena Cherry wrote the book of her heart and thought it was the only book she would ever write. But that one book led to another and another and another. "I'm a little bit in love with some of my heroes, so it suits me very well to throw a series of parties and invite them all back. ... As a reader, I love to revisit fictional characters who have enchanted me, just as I will return to a spectacular restaurant and order the same specialty of the house."

Author of multigenre romances Christy Poff is another writer who would rather not say good-bye to the characters she creates. "I need to feel satisfied that it's done, because if I don't, I have to figure out how to finish it so I will be."

I can personally relate. In one instance, a rare single-title gothic inspirational romance of mine, *The Bloodmoon Curse*, set in my fictional town of Bloodmoon Cove, was published in 2006. Six years later, I became seriously interested in ghost stories. It was then that I came up with a story I couldn't wait to write. In the process of preparing a proposal to submit to one of my publishers, I remembered that *The Bloodmoon Curse* had a ghost in it. I remembered how much I had loved writing that story and the town it was set in. Just like that, I stumbled into the idea of creating a series out of the location. I sold the first four books in my Bloodmoon Cove Spirits Series within seven minutes of submitting the proposal. Book 5 came shortly thereafter. After *The Bloodmoon Curse* is released from its contracted term, it'll become the second in the series offered by another publisher. This is one series I plan to continue for as long as possible.

Readers *do* become invested in characters' lives, situations, and worlds—a relationship is forged, but it's one that can't continue or progress if the book is a stand-alone. Suspense author P.A. Brown says, "I know when I read a book I love, I want it to go on. I want to know what happens with those people, so series fulfill that need." Janet Elaine Smith, cozy mystery and historical writer, concurs: "People come to identify with the characters, and they become like old friends. I have a lot of women tell me they want to sit down and have coffee in the morning with Grace Johnson (from the Patrick and Grace Mysteries). I write series because once I get to know my characters, they won't leave me alone." Vijaya Schartz has this to add: "When reading in the same series, the reader feels safe about his emotional expectations being met."

How do you know you have a series after writing a stand-alone? Along with many other authors of the same mind, Luisa Buehler rarely sees any confusion about whether a single title will become a series. You have a potential series on your hands "if, after the first book, the characters take you by the hand and show you what else they've gotten themselves into." Janet Elaine Smith also says that "with the Keith Trilogy, I intended to write just the first one, but a picture of Sir Walter Scott kept jumping out at me from the pages of an old *Encyclopedia Britannica* when I was checking research information, so I finally read it and discovered a mystery that had to be told that tied in perfectly with the first book. I had no choice."

But it's not only authors and readers who crave a series. Publishers and editors can fall in love with them, too. "It wasn't until my editor kept asking me about Jason's best friend, Michael, that I even considered a second book," Regan Taylor says of her Descendants of Earth stories. Cat Adams (co-writers C.T. Adams and Cathy Clamp, paranormal authors) didn't plan to write a series either. The initial book in the Tales of the Sazi Series was a stand-alone novel and, when it sold, the publisher offered a contract for that book, as well as a sequel. Author P.A. Brown says that "many times an agent or editor will be more open to new writers if they believe a submission will be the first of a series. It makes it less likely that the author will be a one-shot wonder." Laura Baumbach, owner and publisher of MLR Press, encouraged one author to write a series because "I knew readers would want more the minute they finished the first book." Stumbling into a series can be serendipitous for all involved.

## WRITING A SERIES ON PURPOSE

Alternately, authors find that some series present themselves before the first book is even written. For many authors, writing a series comes naturally to them in the course of brainstorming, interacting with their characters, and building a world.

I love all things series, so it's a very rare thing for me to write a single book that has no connection to others I've done. This has been the case with several of my series, including the Incognito Series (romantic suspense). Many years ago, I had an idea for a story that utterly captivated me. The first book in the series was born with that intriguing concept, and I quickly came up with eleven possible story lines for the series. When I was writing the fifth book, I became fascinated with a whole set of new characters I'd developed within the story, as well as the fictional town of Fever, Texas, I had created just for this particular book. None of the characters fit the current series, so I knew a spin-off was necessary, and I started brainstorming accordingly. The Cowboy Fever Series (contemporary romance) was spawned and, in the course of writing blurbs for each novella I planned in that series (more about blurbs in chapter four), I discovered that I wanted to do more than just five novellas. This new character would need more room for her story, so a full-length novel would follow. I also decided to do a spin-off trilogy of my Incognito Series, Shadow Missions, and as a bonus in the trilogy collection (coming December 2016), I'll include a "final mission" that completes the Incognito Series and Shadow Missions as a whole.

Unexpectedly, the same thing happened to me with my Woodcutter's Grim Series (romantic paranormal/horror). I'd visited the fairy tale horror town of Woodcutter's Grim only in novellas: first in a four-novella collection (which actually included the final book in the series), then in a second novella collection containing a miniseries within the overall series that deals with the Shaussegeny family curse. I wanted to do novels set in this town, so I deliberately included characters in the second set of novellas in order to build interest for them for the upcoming novel I plan to write. As it stands, I have a beginning and end to the series, along with many books in between. I plan to continue writing middle-of-series novels and novellas indefinitely for this one.

Going into a series, even one that's planned, can be intimidating. Multigenre author Janet Lane Walters says, "Series are tricky. *Writing* series is not for the faint of heart."

Joanne Hall adds, "Problems can occur if you let your dominant mind-set become one of 'I'm writing a trilogy or series,' rather than 'I'm writing a *story*.'" Also, it's intimidating to think of what's required to finish one book, let alone a whole series. As Janet Lane Walters said earlier, writing a series is not for the faint of heart.

Nevertheless, there are excellent reasons for writing a series, not the least of which is Luisa Buehler's testimonial that she always intended to write a series and had the second book almost completed when she sold the first. Because she had the second one in hand, she ended up signing a two-book contract instead of one. What could be better?

Because the point of this reference is, of course, to enter the process of writing a series in a prepared way, in a later chapter I'll address why it's so important to be thinking about a series *before* you begin writing one, if possible, and how advance planning and organization can turn a good series into a brilliant one.

## THE PUBLISHER-GENERATED SERIES

The evidence that series are popular with the masses is proven by the fact that so many publishers decide to commission their own series, usually one based around a very specific theme. In almost all cases, these series fall in the romance, paranormal, or fantasy-oriented genres and are written by a variety of authors who are handpicked by the editor. The publisher-generated series can be one of the trickiest for an author to participate in, depending on how the series is coordinated. For the most part, when a publisher decides to commission a series, the editors heading the project will come up with plots and assign each book in the series to a different author. The editor will produce a "bible" for the authors, so background, backstory, key characters, series arcs, and threads are broken down book by book.

During her career with Silhouette (Harlequin Enterprises Limited), Linda Varner Palmer participated in a couple of "events" (as she called them) that involved other writers. For instance, she participated in an astrology series. "I wrote the Gemini book. I didn't interact with any of the authors or have a specific guideline other than the hero had to be a Gemini. Another series involving a theme was one that incorporated the 'something old, something new, something borrowed, something blue' wedding idea. I had 'something borrowed' as my assignment, but, again, I didn't interact with other writers."

Cindy Spencer Pape, romance author, participated in the Wayback Texas Series from Wild Rose Press. "The editor maintained some pretty detailed databases and did extensive continuity checks." Cindy has also done two trilogies with authors Regina Carlysle and Desiree Holt. In these, the authors check and double-check themselves. They brainstorm together and each sets up the information for her particular hero and heroine, which the others incorporate into their stories. At that point, the first book is written and sent to the other two authors, who make corrections, then the second book is written, and each of the participating authors corrects it as needed, and so on.

Multigenre author Jane Toombs was "the caboose" of The Orphan Train Series from Champagne Books. *The Outcast* was the sixth and last story, in which all the girls who rode the orphan train in the beginning of the series meet back in Boston at the end of Jane's book, to show that all have survived their tribulations along the way and come out winners. Jane says, "I finished [all but the last chapter of] the book late, only to find the two books before mine weren't in yet. My publisher saw to it that I could read these books as soon as she had them, which helped a lot in writing the end of my own story. Plus all the first chapters in each book had to agree as well … which I had a few problems with, but no one else seemed to. And it turned out okay. I'm not sure I'd want to be the last book if I ever did this again though." Jane's publisher, J. Ellen Smith, said of the process, "Our Orphan Train Series is a series of six books, each by a different author. They started out with a prologue that was given to them to work with, which starts the basis for the series. Each book had the same prologue (or a very similar one), and the author took it from there to show the life of her heroine and how she evolved. It took a lot of coordination between the authors to keep things consistent, which they accomplished via synopsis sharing, loop chats, and e-mails."

N.J. Walters, another multigenre author, was part of the Ellora's Cave's Hearts of Fire Series with three other authors, and says of the process, "It's a huge challenge to work on a series with other authors. You have to know you can work well together. This series is a paranormal one, so we worked out the mythology before we started writing. It took a lot of planning and talking, give and take. But, in the end, it was worth it. Each individual book is unique, yet they all advance the major story arc. We also came up with a common prologue but tailored it for each of our main characters. The final book in the series we wrote together. It's not short stories in one book but one book written by four authors. There was a lot of passing back and forth on that one to ensure character continuity. Each author made certain that what she'd done with her characters in her individual book was reflected in the final book. It was hard work but extremely rewarding. Compromise is the key to a project like this. That, and respect for the other authors' ideas and writing process."

With the publisher-generated series she participated in, Vijaya Schartz was given a blurb for each book and a "bible" to describe the time period, the political climate, the different organizations involved, and so on. "I had to provide a detailed synopsis and three chapters of the novel before signing the contract. It is a challenge. Not all the authors involved have the same vision, and it takes close collaboration to make the series homogeneous. I usually volunteered to write the first books in the series, so I would set the standard and wouldn't have to deal with all the strange things implemented by other authors over the course of the series. Once a new detail about the world created is implemented in one book, all the other authors have to acknowledge and respect its existence. One of the other authors in the series was a friend, so we exchanged chapters as we wrote. We also read online chapters from the other writers."

Paranormal author C.R. Moss says that participating in a publisher-generated series is an interesting process. "There's a lot of brainstorming in the beginning. A point of contact then creates the bible and sends it to all members who are participating. The bible contains the characterizations, setting, and miscellaneous information that everyone can refer to as they're writing their story. During the first round of critiques, consistency and continuity between stories is checked and fixed. It requires lots of give and take, keeping the lines of communication open, and being open to ideas."

The idea of participating in a publisher-generated series isn't one a lot of authors are thrilled about—because of the fear of inconsistencies, squabbles, lack of control concerning the story and characters, and simply because, as Joanne Hall puts it so eloquently, "I like playing in my own sandpit!"

On the topic of keeping the lines of communication open between authors, Vijaya Schartz spoke of a publisher who'd commissioned a series that she participated in and then went belly up. Another publisher wanted to rerelease the series years later, at which time Vijaya suggested it could be the start of an original, single-author series. Her new publisher loved the idea and sent her a three-book contract with the understanding that the company wanted many more books to follow.

## OFF-THE-BOOKSHELF EXAMPLES OF PUBLISHER-GENERATED SERIES

**HOPE CHEST SERIES** with Pam McCutcheon, Paula Gill, Karen Fox, Laura Hayden, and Maura McKenzie

**IMMORTALS SERIES** with Jennifer Ashley, Robin T. Popp, and Joy Nash

**CRIMSON CITY SERIES** with Liz Maverick, Marjorie M. Liu, Patti O'Shea, Carolyn Jewel, and Jade Lee

**THE ORPHAN TRAIN SERIES** with Rebecca Goings, Angela Ashton, Kim Leady, Ciara Gold, Lee Ann Ward, and Jane Toombs
**WAYBACK TEXAS SERIES** with Linda Carroll-Bradd, Amber Leigh Williams, Crystal-Rain Love, Autumn Jordan, P.A. Borel, Celia Yeary, M.J. Fredrick, Anne Carrole, Abbey MacInnis, Marguerite Arotin, Cindy Spencer Pape, Sylvie Kaye, Mallory Mitchell, Lynda J. Coker, Judith Rochelle, and Rita Thedford

## DEFINITIONS OF BOOK GROUPINGS

In the introduction of this book, I mentioned how stunned I was to frequently find authors and publishers who were uncertain about what constitutes a series versus, say, a miniseries or a serial. The confusion I noted about the very *definitions* of the various book groupings was quite a revelation for me, and I'm sure many readers of this book will appreciate the clarification I provide in this area.

So what are the rules in book grouping? Are there any rules? In his book *Writing a Novel*, Nigel Watts says, "There are only three rules to writing a successful novel. Unfortunately, nobody knows what the three rules are." I would have to say it stands to reason that this rule or nonrule applies to most everything writing-related, but especially to such convoluted things as book groupings.

While I'm sure this stems from a lot of different problem areas, there does seem to be a lot of uncertainty about the definition of a series versus a trilogy versus a serial, and so on. One of the mystery authors I interviewed for this book said (as if it were written in stone) that a trilogy plot carries over from book to book, whereas a series carries over only the same characters "with a new case to solve;" some reference may be made about a previous plot but not too much.

However, in my research, I discovered that there were few rules about what constitutes any specific type of book grouping. You might find dozens of instances where a trilogy continues one long-term story arc (more about arcs in chapter two) throughout all three books. You'd be just as likely to find a trilogy in which each story stands alone with a much looser connection, as well as a longer series in which one continuous story arc runs through all of the books in the series (or not necessarily).

The only place you might see rules about this type of thing is within individual genres. For instance, perhaps when writing a mystery trilogy, it's an unspoken rule that all of the books must have a long-term story arc that is introduced in the first book and resolved in the last. (Mind you, I don't know if such a rule actually exists, but I tend to override existing rules with impunity.) However, publishers do have their own rules. You'll never find a playbook that's definitive enough to squash an author's spirit of creativity in bending or breaking rules if her story demands it.

Let's go over common fiction book groupings. Please be aware that other types of media (e.g., television) use these terms as well (and that's probably why there's so much confusion about them in the literary world), but their interpretations won't be anything like those associated with writing fiction. To aid in creating a more standardized usage of these terms, I offer what seems to fit each group best, based on what the term is usually used to refer to in the world of fiction writing. Ultimately, the only true rules for each grouping are the ones you enforce on yourself or are compelled to adhere to because your publisher says so.

## BOOK SERIES

The word *series* has many connotations when it comes to fiction writing, but, in the most basic sense, an ongoing book series is any continuous or interconnected set of stories. Each book in this set of stories has common characteristics that identify it as part of a related group and generally is written by the same author, though that isn't always the case. For the purpose of this reference, we're including in this category those books that have to be read sequentially (e.g., Harry Potter Series) as well as those that can be read in any order (Nancy Drew Series). A series must have a tie or a touchstone of some sort, such as a recurring character, a group of central characters, a shared premise (commonly called a theme) or plot, or a specific setting. I'll talk more about each of these later. An ongoing series can have anywhere from four books to infinity. Off the top of most readers' heads, notable series are Sherlock Holmes, The Wizard of Oz, Cherry Ames, Discworld, The Baby-Sitters Club, James Bond, and many more.

These are the kinds of series I'm going to talk about. Every genre of fiction has at least one series published.

---

## OFF-THE-BOOKSHELF EXAMPLES

**YOUNG ADULT/CHILDREN'S:** Andy and the Albino Horse Series by Mary Jean Kelso

**ROMANCE:** Whitehorse, Montana by B.J. Daniels

**HORROR/PARANORMAL:** The Vanishing Breed Vampire Series by Margaret L. Carter

**MYSTERY/SUSPENSE/THRILLER:** Grace Marsden Mysteries by Luisa Buehler

**SCIENCE FICTION/FANTASY/FUTURISTIC:** Dragons of Challon by Deborah MacGillivray

**HISTORICAL/WESTERN/TIME-TRAVEL/REGENCY:** The American Patriot Series by J.M. Hochstetler

---

## SERIAL

The terms *serial* and *series* are often used interchangeably in novel writing—mistakenly so. Unlike a series, a serial, episode, or periodical includes consecutively released installments of *a single body of work.* This was a popular form of writing in the nineteenth century, when many writers earned a living by writing stories in serial form for popular magazines. Serials are simply parts of a whole. For example, Stephen King's novel *The Green Mile* was published originally in serial format (and was later put together in one volume) but, of course, didn't go on to become a series. The same goes for *The Lord of the Rings,* which wasn't a trilogy or a series but more of a single work so large that it was published in three volumes. I won't focus on serials in this reference.

Something very similar to a serial is a miniseries—another frequently misused term. Many use *miniseries* to mean exactly the same thing as a series, or, in the case of category romance publishers, each continuity line is referred to as a *series imprint* and any true "series" within the series imprint are considered *miniseries*. For instance, Silhouette Romantic Suspense (one of their series imprints) publishes Ingrid Weaver's Eagle Squadron: Countdown miniseries within that imprint.

In actuality, a miniseries most accurately refers to a finite, usually planned number of stories told *within* an existing series. For instance, my Woodcutter's Grim Series (romantic paranormal/horror) is an ongoing set of stories, a series. Books 4 through 7 are all set in Woodcutter's Grim, but these four stories deal with the curse on the Shaussegeny family (who were mentioned in the previous three books as well as the final book in the series). This miniseries within the overall series deals with a central group of characters and an overarching plot that starts in Book 4 of the overall series and concludes in Book 7. This is the kind of series I'll talk about in this reference, since writing a miniseries is no different than writing a book series.

---

### OFF-THE-BOOKSHELF EXAMPLES

**YOUNG ADULT/CHILDREN'S:** The Darling Buds by Johnny Dale

**ROMANCE:** A Happily Ever After of Her Own by Nadia Lee

**HORROR/PARANORMAL:** Selene, A Saint City Novel by Lilith Saintcrow

**MYSTERY/SUSPENSE/THRILLER:** The Moonstone by Wilkie Collins

**SCIENCE FICTION/FANTASY/FUTURISTIC:** The Archangel Chronicles by C.E. Grayson

**HISTORICAL/WESTERN/TIME-TRAVEL/REGENCY:** A World So Wide by Margaret Donsbach

---

## PREQUELS, SEQUELS, AND INTERQUELS

A prequel is a story portraying something that precedes the original work; i.e., the story happens before the original. One very popular example is in

C.S. Lewis's *The Chronicles of Narnia*. *The Magician's Nephew* was a prequel to his hugely popular *The Lion, the Witch and the Wardrobe*, which was written first.

A sequel is a follow-up story to an original story, which often contains the same setting and/or characters but which happens after the original. Homer's *The Odyssey* is often considered a sequel to *The Iliad* because it expands on the plot and characters established in the first story.

An interquel is a story that happens between two or more works and acts as a bridge between them. An example is *The Godfather Returns* (1955 to 1962), which takes place between *The Godfather* (covering the years 1945 to 1955) and *The Godfather's Revenge* (years 1963 to 1964). Incidentally, the original author, Mario Puzo, didn't write the interquel or the sequel. He passed away and author Mark Winegardner took over—a popular thing to do these days[1].

Almost always, prequels, sequels, and interquels are written after the original book. Many other similar terms exist, such as *midquel, parallel, sidequel, quartet,* and *companion piece,* but they won't add much more to the conversation in this section. Only when any of these can lead to a series will we deal with them in this reference.

---

## OFF-THE-BOOKSHELF EXAMPLES

**PREQUELS:** *First King of Shannara* by Terry Brooks; *Hannibal Rising* by Thomas Harris

**INTERQUELS:** *Comanche Moon* by Larry McMurtry; *Ender's Shadow* by Orson Scott Card

**SEQUELS:** *The Lost Word* by Michael Crichton; *Through the Looking Glass* by Lewis Carroll

---

[1] I have to admit I would literally roll over in my grave if anyone took over writing my books or series, and I agree with author S.D. Tooley who says her personal pet peeve about series is "when dead people are writing them." She goes on to explain: "When the writer of a popular series dies, publishers find someone else to write it and use the dead author's name. I don't believe anyone knows the author's characters better than the creating author, and to pass a series to someone like a baton in a relay race just doesn't seem right."

## TRILOGY

A trilogy is a set of three interconnected stories. (Incidentally, a tetralogy is a set of four interconnected stories and doesn't really need its own section because everything mentioned here concerning a trilogy applies to a tetralogy.) Almost always, these involve the same character(s) and/or setting and are tied together by a recurring theme. Sometimes the trilogy (or tetralogy) becomes a series and, in that sense—and in the sense that the process of writing each is similar—the same principles of writing can be applied to this kind of book grouping. For the purpose of *Writing the Fiction Series*, the only difference between a trilogy/tetralogy and a series is that a series has more books. So, yes, this book grouping is addressed throughout this reference.

---

### OFF-THE-BOOKSHELF EXAMPLES

**YOUNG ADULT/CHILDREN'S:** The Eddie Dickens Trilogy by Philip Ardagh

**ROMANCE:** The Circle Trilogy by Nora Roberts

**HORROR/PARANORMAL:** The City Trilogy by Darren Shan

**MYSTERY/SUSPENSE/THRILLER:** The Osgoode Trilogy by Mary Martin

**SCIENCE FICTION/FANTASY/FUTURISTIC:** Old Kingdom Trilogy by Garth Nix

**HISTORICAL/WESTERN/TIME-TRAVEL/REGENCY:** Heaven Tree Trilogy by Edith Pargeter

---

## SPIN-OFF

A spin-off refers to when a series' viewpoint, plot, or theme from the previous story line shifts to a new subseries. Generally, the new protagonist (or set of characters) first appeared in a minor or supporting role within the original series, or the setting or premise/plot is carried over with all new characters, frequently generationally. The previous protagonists might have cameo roles in the spin-off series to give it a jumping-off point. *The Lord of the Rings* can certainly be considered a spin-off of *The Hobbit*. While there are some common characters, for the most part the next generation takes off in *The Lord of the Rings*. Spin-offs can easily become a series, so authors can use the same principles for writing them as a series.

## OFF-THE-BOOKSHELF EXAMPLES

**YOUNG ADULT/CHILDREN'S:** Beyond the Spiderwick Chronicles by Holly Black and Tony DiTerlizzi

**ROMANCE:** Conard County: The Next Generation by Rachel Lee

**HORROR/PARANORMAL:** *The Short Second Life of Bree Tanner* by Stephenie Meyer

**MYSTERY/SUSPENSE/THRILLER:** The Diogenes Trilogy by Douglas Preston and Lincoln Child

**SCIENCE FICTION/FANTASY/FUTURISTIC:** The Empire Series by Isaac Asimov

**HISTORICAL/WESTERN/TIME-TRAVEL/REGENCY:** The Lord John Grey Series by Diana Gabaldon

Now that you know the common catalysts of a series and definitions of book groupings, we can move on to what connects the books in a series.

## TYPES OF SERIES TIES

If each book in a series doesn't somehow tie together or have a touchstone that helps the reader figure out how they're connected, you could hardly call these books a series. I like how Mary Jean Kelso, author of the romantic historical Homesteader Series, puts it: "There needs to always be a firm stake to tie the story to. You can wander off into other places and introduce new characters but, in some way, the main element will always be in the back of the reader's mind. For instance, even though my characters go to other places and get involved in different scenarios, they always come back to the homestead. It is that drive to return 'home' that seems to hold the series together." When you're considering what the touchstone of your series is, ask yourself what "home" you'll be returning to in each story.

What follows are the four distinct types of series, but keep in mind that authors frequently combine one or more of these in a single series. In fact, you'll see the overlap between series ties in the variety of examples I'll give in each section. There are so many different combinations you can use to make your series stand out as unique in a sea of competition.

## RECURRING CHARACTER

In a recurring character series, a single character (sometimes called a continuity or continuing character) is the touchstone of the series and comes back in each story. Sometimes a recurring character story actually has two characters who make appearances in each book and are both the main characters of the series. For instance, Tommy and Tuppence Beresford are a sleuthing duo created by Agatha Christie. For the most part, both make appearances in every book, and the stories shift between their individual points of view. For the sake of simplicity, I'll be referring to a recurring character (regardless of whether it's a duo) as a single character throughout the rest of the book, but remember that you can have more than one recurring character who makes an appearance in every book in a series.

The reader follows the recurring character from one journey—something that must be personal and emotional and provide growth for the character—to the next. Almost always in a series of this type, there's a large cast of secondary characters, and these are brought forward or dropped back, depending on the particular book. Ongoing casts of this sort keep the recurring character fresh for the reader. This type of series is very popular in mystery/suspense stories, as well in the fantasy, science fiction, and paranormal genres.

For example, Agatha Christie had her popular Hercule Poirot and Jane Marple series. Bella Swan was the primary character in Stephenie Meyer's Twilight Saga. James Bond chases espionage and action and adventure everywhere he goes, from one book to another. Ben Holiday was the main character in Terry Brooks's unforgettable Magic Kingdom For Sale—Sold! Series, set in the magical kingdom of Landover. Brooks did a spin-off of the five-book series in 2009 with the High Lord of Landover's daughter Mistaya, which takes place five years after the events in *Witch's Brew*.

Dan Brown has sent his recurring character, Robert Langdon, through fast-paced treasure hunts in three Robert Langdon novels to date. Brown has stated that he has ideas for approximately twelve books featuring this character. Lorie Ham, author of the Alexandra Walters mystery series, writes about a gospel-singing single mom who lives in a small town in California. The books show people behind the scenes of the gospel music world.

Diana Gabaldon's megapopular Outlander Series defies categorization but currently includes eight huge novels that center around a time-traveling nurse in the twentieth century and her eighteenth-century Scottish husband. The Lord John Grey Series was a branch-off of the original series, including a secondary character who was part of the main series. On her website, the author states, "The Lord John Grey novels are in fact part of the series, rather than being a spin-off—but these novels are constructed differently and are focused on Lord John as a central character. Also, while they do include Jamie Fraser as an important character, they don't include Claire, as they (so far) take place during a stretch of time where Claire wasn't physically present. This subseries can be read either independently of the main series, or as part of it." Diana plans to eventually end her Outlander Series on a happy note but has also contracted for a prequel to the series.

---

## OFF-THE-BOOKSHELF EXAMPLES

**YOUNG ADULT/CHILDREN'S:** Twilight Saga by Stephenie Meyer

**ROMANCE:** Tales of an Urban Werewolf Series by Karen MacInerney

**HORROR/PARANORMAL:** Sookie Stackhouse Series by Charlaine Harris

**MYSTERY/SUSPENSE/THRILLER:** Snap Malek Novels by Robert Goldsborough

**SCIENCE FICTION/FANTASY/FUTURISTIC:** Blood and Ashes Series by Michele Acker

**HISTORICAL/WESTERN/TIME-TRAVEL/REGENCY:** The Sharpe Books by Bernard Cornwell

## CENTRAL GROUP OF CHARACTERS

Another series features a central or core group of characters who have either a loose or specific connection that ties them together, and one or two of these characters are featured in each subsequent book. Generally, the first book in the series sets up the central characters and their ties to one another. The series stories are usually stand-alone books that have roots in the first book. Rowena Cherry explains, "Instead of everyone having one adventure all at the same time, they take turns." Popular groups for this type of story are family/relatives, friends, co-workers, or members of an organization. Generally, romance novels, women's fiction, paranormal, science fiction, and fantasy are popular candidates for this type of series. The only mystery series I found that came close to having a cast of characters was Joe Gore's DKA File Novels.

However, perhaps the Falcon's Bend Series I write with German author Chris Spindler can be included. In Books 1 and 2 and our first novella collection, the recurring characters were detectives Pete Shasta and Danny Vincent. In Books 3 and 4, patrol officers Amber Carfi and Warren Jensen became the recurring characters. In the second novella collection, all four of the recurring characters were featured in the stories, and another character in the series, Lisa Shasta, Pete's wife, became an amateur sleuth in several stories. She'll be the recurring character in the fifth book in the series. In this way, a cast of characters are featured in this mystery series.

Having a recurring character is almost exclusively the way to go in mystery novels. (If anyone has heard of or writes a cast of character mystery series, I would love to hear about it. Contact me from my website at karen wiesner.com.)

Justine Davis's Redstone, Incorporated Series is published by Silhouette Books and is romantic suspense that features a group of people employed by Redstone, Incorporated. My romantic suspense Incognito Series focuses on the operatives who work or worked for a covert government organization called the Network. The Kaleidoscope Series includes seven stories with co-workers all employed in the Kaleidoscope Office Building.

Kate Jacobs's The Friday Night Knitting Club Series, as you would expect, focuses on a group of knitters. Debbie Macomber features a similar senario in her Blossom Street Series.

My six-book, romantic inspirational Family Heirlooms Series focuses on the Samuels family siblings. In the first book, *Baby, Baby*, all six brothers and sisters are introduced, but the eldest daughter, Tamara, is the focus of the story. The middle brother, Joshua, leads the next story, *Shadow Boxing*. In the third, *Foolish Games*, the eldest brother (and Tamara's twin), Peter, gets his book. The youngest sister, Samantha, comes next in *Glass Angels*. The final two stories include *Shards of Ashley* (youngest brother Jay) and *Worlds Collide*, with second-oldest brother, Marcus. Popular author Nora Roberts has several series with family as the connecting tie, including the MacGregors and the O'Hurleys among many others. In Linda Varner Palmer's Three Weddings and a Family Series, the hero of the first book discovers he has adult half-siblings (twins). Each twin then has a book.

Terry Brooks's long-running fantasy series, Shannara, includes members of the Ohmsford clan throughout numerous generations. Terry also has another series, The Word & Void, in which he portrays an urban, postapocalyptic world where an invisible war is waged in contemporary America and all over the world while Knights of the Word battle the Void's demons. In a seriously cool move, Terry combined his Shannara and Word and the Void Series in his Genesis of Shannara Series.

In nearly all series with a core group, all the characters are introduced in the first book in smaller and larger degrees and will continue to make cameos throughout the rest of the books in the series. You, the author, will need to connect these characters in a way that you can bring them back together naturally in later books (more about how to do this later in this chapter). Additionally, in real life we tend to hang around with people who like us, but in fiction, stories must have a variety of contrasting characters—some who are likable and others who aren't. It's your job as a series author to create a believable connection between very different characters.

---

## OFF-THE-BOOKSHELF EXAMPLES

................................................................

**YOUNG ADULT/CHILDREN'S:** Redwall Series by Brian Jacques

**ROMANCE:** Konigsburg Series by Meg Benjamin

**HORROR/PARANORMAL:** The Brotherhood of the Blood Series by Kathryn Smith

**MYSTERY/SUSPENSE/THRILLER:** DKA File Novels by Joe Gores

**SCIENCE FICTION/FANTASY/FUTURISTIC:** Bainevah Series by Michelle L. Levigne

**HISTORICAL/WESTERN/TIME-TRAVEL/REGENCY:** Love Comes Softly Series by Janette Oke

---

## PREMISE/PLOT SERIES

While characters are nearly always the most important part of any story, many series use a premise or plot as the basic theme that connects each of the books. This could be just about anything: a shared theme, object, or even a timeline. I'll talk more about arcs—which have a lot to do with premise and plot—in chapter two. Action/adventures, suspense and thriller, inspirational, and paranormal, horror, science fiction, and fantasy genres are usually premise- or plot-based series.

Inspirational romantic suspense author Hannah Alexander's Hideaway Series focuses on medical mysteries. The long-running Rogue Angel Series, written by many authors, features archaeologist and heir to Joan of Arc's mystic sword, Annja Creed. In each novel, an adventure based on history, mythology, or heavy fantasy has Annja looking for lost cities, mysterious codes, and puzzles. Christy Poff writes a torrid romance series called Internet Bonds in which all the stories have a connection to the Internet. In my Family Heirloom Series, each story passes down a nugget (or heirloom) of faith, including accepting God's will (Book 1), building love (Book 2), healing (Book 3), forgiving (Book 4), learning trust (Book 5), and persevering in adversity (Book 6).

The premise of each of Tom Clancy's Net Force Series is a special division of the FBI that is set up to combat Internet crime. Linda Varner Palmer's Silhouette romance series, Home for the Holidays, revolves around the holidays. In Janet Elaine Smith's Women of the Week Series, the common thread is that each of the main women in the books is named for the day of the week she was born (the first one is Monday Knight). Each of their lives revolves around the old poem that begins, "Monday's child is fair of face...". Carl Brookins's crime series, Sailing, is about a couple who sail in and out of venues of murderous trouble.

Charlotte Boyett~Compo is best known for her signature Reaper creations. "They appear in each and every one of my series. Hybrid were/vamp shape-shifters, they have dark hair, amber eyes, wear all black, and are very strong Alpha males with tragic pasts. Readers love that conception. The first Reaper came out in 1998 in *BloodWind* and that book has sold more than any of my other eighty novels. Someone is turning it into a screenplay as well. The Reapers have earned me many fans over the years and the latest series, The Western Wind Series, has been accumulating new readers consistently for the last several years. I have readers tell me they love the Reapers."

In the first four books in Jane Toombs's Dangerous Darkness Series, the heroes were once in a Special Ops group together, but the paranormal element in each book is different. In the last four books in the series, all the heroines and the one hero are in the same witch family, and each faces a different paranormal element. Incidentally, that also makes this series a central group of characters type.

---

## OFF-THE-BOOKSHELF EXAMPLES

**YOUNG ADULT/CHILDREN'S:** Unbidden Magic Series by Marilee Brothers

**ROMANCE:** Blossom Street Series by Debbie Macomber

**HORROR/PARANORMAL:** Novels of the Final Prophecy by Jessica Andersen

**MYSTERY/SUSPENSE/THRILLER:** Diet Club Series by Denise Dietz

**SCIENCE FICTION/FANTASY/FUTURISTIC:** The Willard Series by Darrell Bain

---

HISTORICAL/WESTERN/TIME-TRAVEL/REGENCY: Knights Templar Series by Michael Jecks

---

## SETTING SERIES

The setting series is almost as popular as the character series, although, of course, if you don't have wonderful characters to fill these settings, your stories won't be as magical. When setting serves as the tie-in for each book in the series, you're free to create a colorful world that your readers will enjoy visiting time and time again. Setting series can have characters that change, but the place is always the same, or a recurring character will return to the same series setting in each book. For instance, Harry Potter goes to Hogwarts in each book in the series. Nearly every genre of series uses this kind of touchstone.

In my contemporary romance Cowboy Fever Series, I created the fictional place of Fever, Texas, where all the neighboring ranches in the series are located and visited during the course of the series. My police procedural, the Falcon's Bend Series, written with Chris Spindler, is set in the fictional town of Falcon's Bend, and my paranormal/horror romances are set in the magical horror children's story place of Woodcutter's Grim. I've also created a spooky little town called Bloodmoon Cove for my Bloodmoon Cove Spirits Series. Additionally, I created the small town of Peaceful, Wisconsin, for my Family Heirlooms Series, and I carried it over into the spin-off Friendship Heirlooms Series, and even into two non-series books, *Home* and *Destiny*.

Mystery author Marilyn Meredith's Deputy Tempe Crabtree Series is set in a small mountain community near an Indian reservation. In most of these books, an Indian legend or mystical aspect plays a major part. In addition, much conflict occurs between Tempe and her preacher husband when she dabbles in the supernatural.

In Vijaya Schartz's sci-fi/fantasy romance series Chronicles of Kassouk, a science spaceship made by humans and named Noah's Ark crash-lands on an unknown frozen planet renamed New Earth. The survivors, while fighting the elements, eventually lose their technology, but the animals are released and many species survive. Civilization starts from scratch on a small scale. When the series picks up again several centuries later, a medieval civilization has formed and thrives until spacefaring races intervene. Sometimes the series stories are many years apart. The society struggles, grows, and matures from crisis to crisis and learns from various outside influences, not all beneficial.

Janet Elaine Smith, who writes a cozy mystery series called Patrick and Grace Mysteries, sets her odd-numbered books in New York City, where Patrick and Grace live. The even-numbered books take place all over the country. The author's readers often ask her, "When are Patrick and Grace coming to my town?"

---

### OFF-THE-BOOKSHELF EXAMPLES

**YOUNG ADULT/CHILDREN'S:** Lynne Garrett Series by Mary Jean Kelso

**ROMANCE:** Visitation Series by Lori Foster

**HORROR/PARANORMAL:** Castle of Dark Dreams Series by Nina Bangs

**MYSTERY/SUSPENSE/THRILLER:** Sofie Metropolis, P.I. Series by Tori Carrington

**SCIENCE FICTION/FANTASY/FUTURISTIC:** Winterhold Series by Stephen Almekinder

**HISTORICAL/WESTERN/TIME-TRAVEL/REGENCY:** Highland Heroes by Veronica Wolff

---

What ties your series together is extremely important. It's the thing that will bring readers back for more. While some overlap is bound to occur between ties, defining your ties will help you establish the pattern from one book to the next, and doing so will make the connections for each story in the series stronger.

## BUILD YOUR SERIES MUSCLES EXERCISE

Go through your favorite series books and try to identify what book grouping they fit into and what series tie(s) are evident in them. Once you have a firm grasp of what makes a series a series and what connects series books together, your understanding of how you want to work your own series will be much stronger.

Now that you know the catalysts that drive a series, the definitions of the various book groupings, and the types of series ties out there, I'll show you how to find the focus of your series.

# CHAPTER TWO

# FINDING THE FOCUS
# OF A SERIES

*"Every experience is a paradox in that it means to be absolute, and yet is relative; in that it somehow always goes beyond itself and yet never escapes itself."*

~T.S. Eliot

After you make the decision to write a series, you have a lot of questions to ask yourself. While a lot of authors may handle these questions on the fly or by the seat of their pants, huge opportunities are unfortunately missed using this method of "organization." J.K. Rowling spent five years writing *Harry Potter and the Sorcerer's Stone*, and during that time she planned the next six books in the series. If she hadn't done so, I often wonder if the books would have been so incredibly well set up. Rowling is the queen of series plants (which I'll discuss in detail later in this chapter). She introduced so many aspects of her series long before they became truly important, and in the process built in believability and authenticity. If she had just thrown in a detail when it was needed in a particular book, that detail would have come across as contrived and convenient. In Appendix B, I present something invaluable that demonstrates the importance of planning a series in advance of writing each book.

Though I believe planning is crucial to the success of a series, I've discovered in my experience that there are few set-in-stone rules. Should each story in a series have an overall series arc that runs through each book and ties up only in the final one? Or is it adequate if each story has a loose connection to the others and each individual book has its own story arc that ties up fairly neatly at the end? Should all the stories be stand-alone versus having a cliff-hanger? Should each story in the series be a single genre, or can individual stories cross into multiple genres? Should all the series stories be novels, or can some be novellas? For every dozen books you can find that do one or more of these things, you can find just as many that don't.

In *Writing a Novel,* Nigel Watts goes further in his position on rigidly following every regulation: "THERE ARE NO RULES. A novel is not a wind-up machine which either works or it doesn't—it is a social convention which is constantly changing. ... Slavishly following a convention is not only misguided, it can be unhelpful: A good novel is a strange thing—you can break every 'rule' in the book and still write a wonderful bestseller."

I'll try to answer some of the questions I posed above, but be aware that there are few rules for this process except the ones you make for yourself—or the ones your publisher requires you to abide by.

## STORY ARCS VERSUS SERIES ARCS

Am I the only writer confused by this whole "story arc" concept? It's been presented to me in multiple ways, and none of the explanations quite fit my own perceptions in terms of story building. In this section I'll define the story arc, discuss what others have said about it, and present my own version of the concept. (I feel this discussion is necessary, as an author must make sense of the craft in his own way—and hopefully some who are as confused as I've been over the years will discover a definitive answer.) After I've set down the basics of what an arc is, I'll discuss *story* arcs as opposed to *series* arcs.

## STORY ARCS

In its simplest form, the story arc is an extended or continued story line. That's fairly easy to grasp, right? But when it comes to what this definition actually entails and how it serves its purpose in the course of a novel, well, that's where things get murkier. In a story, an arc is supposed to move the character or situation from one place to another. Essentially, we're talking about change here—the quest, the causality of narrative, the domino-effect transformations. In a story, this follows a pattern that can be described as ordinary life in balance: The character is brought to a low point and the structures he has depended upon are removed. Therefore the character is motivated and/or forced to find new strength or situations without these structures, and he faces his demons and triumphs. Resolution ensues, and balance is restored.

Now, as I said, the story arc is discussed often in writing circles, and it can come in several different forms and have more or fewer steps toward completion. These steps can be nicely graphed into a visual that can help you see how the story arc works behind the scenes.

The most generally presented arc pattern I've seen is this one:

1. Equilibrium
2. Inciting incident
3. Progressive complications or plot points
4. The black moment
5. Crisis
6. Resolution

Nigel Watts presents the pattern as follows:

1. Stasis
2. Trigger
3. Quest
4. Surprise
5. Critical choice
6. Climax
7. Reversal
8. Resolution

In his book *Plot & Structure*, James Scott Bell's presentation is different because it isn't locked specifically into story arc steps (something I appreciate, since writing is a craft without absolutes), but it essentially follows this pattern:

1. Beginning point
2. Disturbance
3. Two doorways/transitions
4. Impacting incidents
5. Deepening disturbance
6. Moment of change/epiphany
7. Aftermath

Finally, most writers have heard of the "hero's journey":

1. Introduction to hero's world
2. Call to adventure
3. Choices
4. Crossing the threshold
5. The mentor or teacher arrives
6. Encounters with the forces of darkness
7. Internal dark moment that must be overcome in order for the hero to proceed
8. A symbol or talisman aids in battle
9. The final battle is fought
10. Hero returns to his world

I think you can see why story arcs can get very confusing. Several of the examples I've cited have steps that seem redundant, and I'm uncertain as to whether all of these steps are truly necessary for every story. But I do think most of these story arc steps add up to about the same thing, and my goal is to simplify the steps as much as possible. As I said, I am sorry to introduce yet another story arc pattern into the world, though mine is one derived from what I think are the most likely and basic steps from each of the previous lists. I think what you'll see coming up is based on the bare essentials and allows the writer a lot of freedom to tell her story in the way that seems right to her. Here are the steps (in one-word bites, for simplicity) followed by a graph that should visually simplify the mechanics of the arc that will run through your story. This will be summed up with explanations for each step.

1. Introduction
2. Change
3. Conflicts
4. Choices
5. Crisis
6. Resolutions

Essentially, life as well as fiction is balanced with states of emotion over time. In fiction, the emotion is generally more extreme. It has to be, because what is fiction except a portrayal of life that skips over all the dull moments? On the graph on the following page, you'll see this balance of happiness and misery along the left side, rising vertically. The passage of time is illustrated as the horizontal line that runs beneath the foundation of the story. Within this line I've included what are commonly considered the three acts of every story: beginning, middle, and end. You'll see where each of these steps falls (or straddles, most likely) within that timeline.

You can also think of the story arc as an equation that your story will move through from beginning to end. Where you see the arrows, insert the words *leads to.*

Introduction → Change → Conflicts →
Choices → Crisis → Resolutions

## STORY ARC STEP 1: INTRODUCTION TO THE CHARACTER'S LIFE

The first step is to introduce the character's ordinary life, in which she may or may not be content. She's achieved some sense of balance. So what you see in opening scenes is the core character—the product of years and experiences—in her normal daily situations. As James Scott Bell says, the character will protect this core self because most people resist change violently.

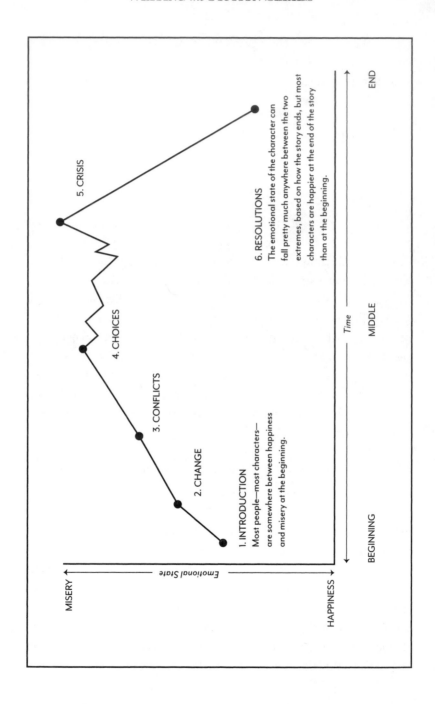

MISERY

Emotional State

HAPPINESS

5. CRISIS

6. RESOLUTIONS
The emotional state of the character can fall pretty much anywhere between the two extremes, based on how the story ends, but most characters are happier at the end of the story than at the beginning.

4. CHOICES

3. CONFLICTS

2. CHANGE

1. INTRODUCTION
Most people—most characters— are somewhere between happiness and misery at the beginning.

*Time*

BEGINNING

MIDDLE

END

In general, writing experts advise that you make this introduction very quickly (don't think of this as your last chance to introduce the character) and move on to the next step in the arc.

## STORY ARC STEP 2:
## CHANGE IN THE CHARACTER'S LIFE

Change ... it's a form of conflict, and it's what turns the character's life upside down and completely disrupts it—sometimes beyond recognition. The structures the character has depended on in his life have now been removed because of this change.

Change should be internal—it's essentially the alteration of life and needs to affect the character deeply—but this change will also manifest itself externally. Whatever change you present must be logical to the character and his situation, and must impact him in a way that he can't ignore or turn away from, no matter how much he might want to. In chapter three I'll talk more about character. For now, realize that this is *his* story, *his* conflicts, *his* hard choices. While he most certainly will consider walking away, it's never truly an option—if it were, you wouldn't have a story.

## STORY ARC STEP 3:
## CONFLICTS IN THE CHARACTER'S LIFE

Conflict is essentially the progressive complications the character faces as a result of the disruption of his equilibrium. Conflict is what motivates and forces the character to act—to start on the quest that will make up the bulk of your story.

It's important for you to understand the difference between plot conflicts and character conflicts. Plot (external) conflict is the central (tangible or intangible) outer problem standing squarely in the character's way. Said character must face and solve this problem. She wants to restore the stability that was taken from her, and this produces her desire to act. However, the character's internal conflicts will create an agonizing tug-of-war with the plot conflicts. She has to make tough choices about whether or not she should face, act on, or solve the problem (more about this in chapter three). You can also think of plot the way Janet Evanovich does: The characters in your story are like train cars, and the plot is the engine that pulls them down the track from one place to another.

Plot conflicts must be urgent enough to require immediate attention. The audience must be able to identify with both the internal and external conflicts the character faces in order to be involved enough to care about the outcome of the story. Plot conflicts work hand in glove with character conflicts. You can't have one without the other, and they must become more intense and focused the longer the character struggles. The stakes are raised, choices are limited, and failure and loss are inevitable. In *Novelist's Essential Guide to Creating Plot*, J. Madison Davis defines plot "like a cone that characters are moving through from the wide end to the narrow. It closes in the farther along they go." In other words, once the conflict rears its ugly head, the only direction left to go is forward—the other options disappear behind the characters. They can't go back the same way they came, even if they want to.

Character and conflicts develop in accordance with the character's choices, goals, and motivations (in other words, causality in motion).

## STORY ARC STEP 4:
## CHOICES IN THE CHARACTER'S LIFE

In order for a character to make a choice, his goals and motivations must be clarified from the very beginning of your story. Goals are those things the character wants, needs, or desires above all else. Motivation is what gives him drive and purpose to achieve those goals. Goals must be urgent enough that the character is willing to undergo the hardship and self-sacrifice inevitable in pursuing them. Multiple goals collide and impact the characters, forcing difficult decisions. Focused on the goal, the character is pushed toward it by believable, emotional, and compelling motivations that won't let him quit. Because he cares deeply about the outcome, his anxiety is doubled. The intensity of his anxiety pressures him to make choices and changes, thereby creating worry and awe in the reader.

Goals and motivations are constantly evolving (not *changing* necessarily, but growing and refining in depth, intensity, and scope) to fit character and plot conflicts. Your character's goals and motivations will certainly evolve from the beginning, through the middle, and to the end of your story, since he's modifying or reshaping his actions based on the course his conflicts are dictating.

## STORY ARC STEP 5:
## CRISIS IN THE CHARACTER'S LIFE

At the crisis point (also called "downtime"[1]) in the story, the character is faced with his most vicious demons. This is the bleakest portion of the story, when all hope is seemingly lost. The obstacles standing in the way are too numerous, too monumental, too impossible. The character believes she's lost everything and that danger's on its way. She's convinced there's no stopping the worst from occurring. The ultimate dread is produced because few people can relax when they know everything they ever wanted is about to go down the toilet. The main character is forced to reflect on what's happened and what could have been, and she seems to give up the fight. The character has had a glimpse of the happily-ever-after she's convinced has slipped through her fingers. That naturally produces restlessness, recklessness, and intense edginess.

Following this crisis point, tension has to be built back up quickly to avoid losing the reader. The black moment, climax, or showdown comes. It's at this place in the story that the character has an epiphany—one that must be completely organic to your story and everything that's led up to this point. It has to be utterly logical within the scheme of the structure you've set up, and it has to stem from the character—not from any other source. In other words, she absolutely must solve her own problems. She must find her strength and act in the hope of triumphing and bringing about resolution. This epiphany provides the momentum for the final clash.

## STORY ARC STEP 6:
## RESOLUTIONS IN THE CHARACTER'S LIFE

The character wins, resolution ensues, and balance is restored. Enough said? Actually, no. If it were, "the end" would come with the end of the

---

[1] In my book *First Draft in 30 Days*, I define downtime as a point when the character steps back from the tension and reflects. This usually happens just before the black moment in the story.

showdown. The fact is, the character can't be the same person she was when she started the story. She can't settle back into the same life she had, though she may settle in the same place she started. She's changed—her core self has altered in a way that changes her perceptions. What the character has gone through has produced a life-changing effect, and the way she views the world has been radically altered. The character again finds contentment and/or balance in her life. Most readers hope the change will lead to happily-ever-after, but it doesn't have to. Something just shy of that may fit better.

Remember that this change can't be evidenced by word of mouth alone—the reader must be able to see the change in the character through his actions. If you want a bold example of this, think of Ebenezer Scrooge. He doesn't simply contemplate how different he feels the morning after his encounters with the ghosts. When he realizes he has a second chance to be a good person, he doesn't merely dance around his frigidly cold bedroom. He buys the prized turkey for Bob Cratchit, raises Bob's salary, and assists him in caring for his family, ultimately becoming a second father to Bob's son, Tiny Tim. Scrooge donates to the poor. He builds a relationship with his nephew. The changed man joyfully leaps off the last pages of the story, and the reader doesn't doubt for a second that the new Ebenezer's change of heart will stick.

Not all stories need such a dramatic moment of change, of course. The end of your story can be much more subtle, but allow the reader to at least see a glimpse of this change. How your story ends is essentially a reward to your reader for taking the journey with you. James Scott Bell says, "You want to leave your readers with a last page that makes the ending more than satisfying. You want it to be memorable, to stay with readers after the book is closed. … Your audience will judge your book largely by the feeling that they have felt most recently, namely, *the end*. Leave a lasting impression and you will build a readership."

Story arcs are specific to each particular book. They're introduced, developed, and concluded within that particular story. Each story will contain scenes and subplots that advance the story arc. These are interspersed with the individual story arcs, commonly called plots or subplots (also called threads). A subplot (or parallel plot) is a subsidiary story line that exists with the main plotline (the arc). One or more of these follow the same forward path as the main arc and are developed alongside or, more specifically, woven *within* the arc.

A subplot needs to do much more than simply fill pages and bulk up the story. A subplot must add complexity and substance (three-dimensionality) to the story, and it must relate to the arc thematically without overwhelming the main arc. A subplot shouldn't be given equal value to the main arc, as this would produce a very confusing novel in the same way a secondary character suddenly overthrowing the hero would. A subplot must mesh with and enhance the arc in a way that makes the two inseparable. It's a symbiotic relationship. A subplot also helps you control the pacing of the story arc. In other words, you want something that places obstacles in the hero's path and prevents the climax from coming too soon.

In a series story, a story arc is short term because it will be neatly tied up in a single book within the series. That might sound strange, but this will make more sense when you realize that the *series* arc is the long-term thread that runs its course through *every book* until the series concludes.

## SERIES ARCS

Okay, it's been established: Every story must have a story arc. Now I want to talk about the quintessential focus of this book: *series*. Most series have an overall *series* arc, along with the individual story arcs specific to each individual book. An overall series arc is a plot thread that's introduced in the first book in the series, is alluded to in some way in every subsequent book, but is only fully resolved in the final book of the series. The series arc plays out separately from the individual story arcs, but both arcs are crucial and must fit together seamlessly. The individual book's story arc is, as we've said, short term. It's introduced, developed, and concluded within the individual book. The series arcs are long term. They're introduced in the first book, developed over the course of the series, and resolved in the final book in the series. As an example, in *Harry Potter and the Chamber of Secrets,* the story arc is the chamber of secrets plotline. The overall series arc, in the most simplified terms, is "good (Harry) overcomes evil

(Voldemort)"—and that's true for every book in that series. The series arc runs beneath the individual story arcs in each book. I'll get very specific about these things in Appendix B, where I'll go through the entire Harry Potter Series, mapping out a good number of the series arcs, the individual story arcs, and the series plants, which I'll explain soon.

There is an exception to every rule, and that's the case here: Certain types of series don't need series arcs because they're open-ended. In other words, no clear end is in sight, and therefore there is less need for a tightly delineated series arc that must resolve in the final book. In an open-ended series (such as some sleuth mysteries that have a single recurring character—e.g., Hercule Poirot), each book in the series is a stand-alone. I will talk in more detail about that later in this chapter. In this case there's little need to come up with a series arc because the author isn't planning to run a plot thread through the entire series that will conclude in the final story. Though the Hercule Poirot Series eventually did end, a series arc didn't run through each of the stories. Even Poirot's final case was a stand-alone (though this case connected to details of the very first mystery he solved). In an open-ended series that has an infinite number of books, the resolution the author has promised and the reader expects won't come in a final series book but at the end of *each book* in the series. Those resolutions are the ones that fans are looking for and must be given in order to feel satisfied.

In any case, keep this in mind if you're writing an open-ended series: While you're not required to have a series arc in this one instance, it wouldn't hurt to have one. You can include one even in an open-ended series. If you choose not to, you'll work with story arcs for each stand-alone book in your series.

All series that aren't open-ended *do* need an overall series arc—whether it's clearly defined or done subtly. This notion is the crux of the confusion authors have with the series arc concept. Like series ties or touchstones, series arcs can be extremely loose, even ethereal. They can be simple themes, such as "good overcomes evil," or "happiness and love are discovered." Even a loose series arc needs to build ties to and connect all of the stories. Each book in the series will contain scenes and subplots that advance the series arc. These are interspersed with individual story arcs, and most of the time the writer switches back and forth between series and story arcs throughout the course of each book (you'll see this clearly demonstrated in the case study example in Appendix B). In the final book in the series, series and story arcs will merge in the way you've led your readers to expect. All of this is essential to gaining reader favor and satisfaction.

The easiest way to discover your overall series arc is to determine the type of series tie that will connect all of the books. Your series tie almost always indicates what your series arc should be. In a romance series, for instance, a series arc may be something as simplified as the one I had for my Kaleidoscope Series: "All the co-workers at Kaleidoscope Office Building find true love." The defining qualities of each story in this contemporary romance series are obvious. The series arc ran steadily through each story in the series, perfectly paralleling the individual story arcs in the seven individual books. In this way the series tie helps to define the series arc and make sure it runs its proper course through each book in the series. For the Kaleidoscope Series, I wrote a final scene in which the main characters celebrate their good fortune in finding true love. It was emotionally satisfying to come to that scene, and it was exactly what my readers were looking for.

When you're reading Appendix B (the series, story, and plant arc breakdown example), you can compare and contrast series and story arcs to see just how interconnected they are, how well they mesh, and how crucial they are to the developing story lines in each book in the series. But before you go there, I'll tell you a little bit more about arcs.

## CLEARLY DEFINED ARCS

This is another aspect of the series that seems to elicit a lot of confusion or strong opinions amongst writers. Some of the authors I interviewed for this book believe that a clearly delineated series arc is crucial—and I agree that for some series, it *is* crucial, especially if the writer has introduced a mystery or quest that isn't solved by the end of the first story. In that situation your arc must be clearly defined from the get-go, and it must develop exponentially throughout the course of the series until its resolution in the last book. The clearly defined series arc seems to be extremely popular in any speculative fiction genre, as well as in action, suspense, and thriller genres. This is true because most of these genres require definitive closure, and therefore the series arc must also have definitive closure.

If the series arc is left out of even one book in a series with a clear-cut arc, readers might wonder where the author is going with the series, and they might even believe that the overall quest is too weak to sustain the life of the series. Needless to say, that can get incredibly frustrating, boring, and ultimately disappointing. This long-term thread can't be left hanging indefinitely. The author must keep it alive in each book as it runs along the back edge of the foundation of every story in the series. If it doesn't, you might want to reconsider writing a series and instead write the story as a single book. Or you might try to make your series arc much looser.

---

## OFF-THE-BOOKSHELF EXAMPLES OF CLEARLY DEFINED SERIES ARCS

**YOUNG ADULT/CHILDREN'S:** Deltora Quest Series by Emily Rodda

**ROMANCE:** Blood Brothers Series by Nora Roberts

**HORROR/PARANORMAL:** Mortal Instruments Series by Cassandra Clare

**MYSTERY/SUSPENSE/THRILLER:** Hideaway Series by Hannah Alexander

**SCIENCE FICTION/FANTASY/FUTURISTIC:** The Heritage of Shannara Series by Terry Brooks

**HISTORICAL/WESTERN/TIME-TRAVEL/REGENCY:** Regency Jewel Series by Helen Ashfield

---

## LOOSELY DEFINED ARCS

I've established that all series that aren't left open-ended need to have a basic, overall series arc, even if it's subtle. If your series will have an ending, you need to define your series arc. Your series arc conclusion will come in the final book, and that resolution must satisfy the expectations of your readers.

In the course of writing this book, I thought long and hard about the viability of the popular belief that some series (the ones that are intended to have an end) don't need overall series arcs. Then I received back-to-back reviews for the fourth and sixth books in my Wounded Warriors Series (from the same reviewer, Dark Divas Reviews), and these showed me how I'd inadvertently included a series arc from book to book that I never even realized I'd designed while I was writing each story. I'm going to include portions of a few reviews here because they illustrate the looseness of the *series* arc but also the cohesiveness and pleasure derived from that long-running thread within the *story* arcs.

For *Wayward Angels*, Book 4:

> "Gregg's story ... at last! One of the things that impresses me the most about Karen Wiesner's writing is that each story has its own direction, its own flavor, and each of them are supremely well matched with the characters. We met Gregg in the first book in the series—*Reluctant Hearts*—and he's been present in each subsequent story. That's another thing that I'm enjoying about the series—that we never lose touch completely with any of the characters. Yes, they've all got their own story, but because of the closeness of the group, no story takes place in a vacuum. Wendy and Paul, from *Reluctant Hearts*, continue to be a part of the lives of the rest of the group. Just as Steve and Kristina from *Waiting for an Eclipse* and Gwen and Dylan from *Mirror Mirror* are still around. I like that continuing connection. We are, after all, following a core group of friends: Tommie, Steve, Paul, Mitch, Wendy, Jessie, Brenda, and Gwen have known each other for most of their lives, while Gregg became a part of their 'clan' at a later date."

For *White Rainbow*, Book 6:

> "I was quite surprised to find that Jessie had a story of her own! After all her hijinks, her manipulations, and her out-and-out disdain for anyone at all, I was hard put to think that she could be redeemed. Truly though, without the group, Jessie would not have survived—the continuing support from everyone is

what made the difference. In *White Rainbow*, Karen Wiesner has come up with a powerful conclusion to her Wounded Warriors Series, one that will keep fresh the impact that the characters and books have had. I thank Karen Wiesner for the chance to connect with Wendy and Paul, Steve and Kristina, Gwen and Dylan, Gregg and Stormie, Jessie and Flint, and Tommie … always Tommie in the background."

The individual story arcs for all six books in this series were, loosely, journeys that the hero and heroine both went on, individually and together, in their romance. The series arc was the core group of characters finding happiness and love. That sounds pretty general, doesn't it? But these reviews (among dozens of similar reviews for both books) prove that the loosely defined series arc worked extremely well with the individual story arcs. My readers were satisfied with not only the individual books but the series as a whole.

If your series will come to definitive closure, you need an overall series arc, regardless of how loosely or clearly defined it is. Spell out your series arc for yourself so you can work from that premise from start to finish. If you know early on that you'll be writing a series that requires closure and you can work with some sort of blueprint or outline for your individual stories, use the worksheet in Appendix A to map out your series, story, and plant arcs. In chapter three I'll talk more about developing series and story blurbs that are based on your arcs.

## OFF-THE-BOOKSHELF EXAMPLES OF LOOSELY DEFINED SERIES ARCS

**YOUNG ADULT/CHILDREN'S:** Mrs. Piggle-Wiggle Series by Betty MacDonald

**ROMANCE:** Long Tall Texans Series by Diana Palmer

**HORROR/PARANORMAL:** North of Nonesuch Series by Jane Toombs

**MYSTERY/SUSPENSE/THRILLER:** Uncommon Heroes Series by Dee Henderson

> **SCIENCE FICTION/FANTASY/FUTURISTIC:** Culture Series
> by Iain M. Banks
> **HISTORICAL/WESTERN/TIME-TRAVEL/REGENCY:** The Ryland Brothers
> Series by Kathryn Smith

## PLANT ARCS

When planning series and story arcs in a series that will have a definitive ending, you will also utilize *plants*, which are aspects of the story that set up something yet to come. When first mentioned, these aspects hardly seem important but become crucial later. They could be a character, a setting, an object, a premise or plot of some kind, or even an event that is "planted" within a story. In a fantasy, science fiction, suspense, or adventure series, a plant is often an object with great power that the character needs to find and then use for good or evil. A plant can be anything. The only rule is that a plant arc should emerge naturally from the story.

In a series a plant frequently grows in meaning either in the book where it's mentioned, in another book in the series, or over many books in the same series. As I mentioned before, the earlier you set up these things, the more believable they are when they're needed. If the plant is produced at the precise moment it's needed, without having roots much earlier to set it up realistically, it'll come off as contrived or simply convenient to the plot.

Before we go much further, I need to add the same disclaimer I mentioned for series arcs. An open-ended series may not need plant arcs, though you can certainly use them in your individual series stories if they work. Their importance in terms of series arcs will be limited since there won't be a series end in sight.

It's interesting to note that the literary foreshadowing technique of planting originally dates back to *One Thousand and One Nights (Arabian Nights)* and was called "repetitive designation"—in other words, repeated references to a character or element that originally appears insignificant but reappears later and becomes important. In 1889 the basic premise for this became known as "Chekhov's gun," whereby an element was introduced early in the story, but the significance of it wasn't clear until a later time. The term derived from Russian dramatist Anton Chekhov's statement that you couldn't put a rifle on stage if no one was thinking of firing it.

This technique is considered a plot device, which is an object, element, or character in a story with the sole purpose of advancing or overcoming some difficulty in the plot. I love the way author Nick Lowe describes it: "In normal usage, when people talk of a plot device they mean something in the story that's just a little bit too obviously functional to be taken seriously. All these FTL drives, instant translators, oxygen pills, and so forth: contrivances so basic to getting interplanetary stories off the ground that we no longer worry about their implausibility." Clearly, you want your plot device (plant) to be believable, and your goal in setting one up is to allow your audience to suspend their disbelief and accept the device without another thought.

As an example, a plant could be something like Dumbledore (in the first Harry Potter book) using his Put-outer (later referred to as the Deluminator) to extinguish all the streetlamps on Privet Drive. This object is used frequently throughout the series, and the reader accepts it each time because the setup was there early enough to make it believable. By the time Book 7 comes, the fact that Ron uses this object to find his way back to Harry and Hermione requires no contrivance whatsoever. The reader accepts it easily. If you've read the series, you know exactly why this little innocuous device is so crucial—and how it would have made little sense in the series to introduce it in the final book instead of in the first. Though the most crucial purpose of this device isn't revealed until the final book in the series, the early plant was vital to reader acceptance. Without plants like this, the series would have suffered greatly. As I said earlier, J.K. Rowling excels brilliantly at loading her series with countless plant arcs that initially seem like throwaway details but become crucial later.

If a series that will have a finite life isn't set up and planned early enough, many of these plants will never see the light of day—and the series will suffer in ways you may not realize until it's too late. Plants must be set up so they aren't viewed as arbitrary contrivances or conveniences. As multigenre author Denise Dietz says so colorfully, "If your character is afraid of snakes, don't have her suddenly overcome that fear because your plot needs a 'snake scene.'" Readers can easily become confused and annoyed enough to roll their eyes when presented with plants that seem thrown in or that don't fit with the rest of the story.

Now that you know enough about series, story, and plant arcs, feel free to skip to Appendix B to see how they work together throughout the course of a series.

Now I'll answer some basic questions authors have about writing a series.

## STAND-ALONES VERSUS CLIFF-HANGERS

First, some definitions: A stand-alone story can refer to a work of fiction that has no relationship with any other piece of fiction and doesn't fit into any of the book groupings I've covered (series, sequels, trilogy, and so on). In other words, a stand-alone story *stands alone* without ties to other books. But a stand-alone story can also mean that you don't have to read the other books in the series in order to understand and follow the individual books in that series. So a stand-alone is one that has all the story threads tied up logically at the end and the reader isn't left hanging on any major story arc points. That definition of the word *stand-alone* is the one I'm referring to here.

Keep at the forefront of your mind, however, that the point of a series is to build on a story premise and keep readers following along from one book to the next. Even if a series book stands alone, readers want all the goodies that go along with a series book: world familiarity, deep explorations of the characters' lives, old and new adventures, and all the subtle nuances, insider jokes, and crucial intimacy experienced and shared by avid followers. If these elements aren't present, the reader sees no advantage in reading a series book over a stand-alone. Your goal as the writer should be to offer stand-alone books in your series *as well as* to make sure that each series offering enhances the previous one(s) and makes the reader eager for those coming up. The experience of reading a series book should be incalculably richer for those readers who are following along closely. If you don't provide that depth, fans will lose interest quickly.

In clear contrast, a cliff-hanger is basically a method in which the main character is in a precarious situation at the end of a story and the outcome of that situation is in doubt when the story closes. In other words, the story ends with the climax scene and there is no resolution to follow. Think of *A Christmas Carol*. If the author had wanted to leave that story on a cliff-hanger, we would never have seen the ways in which Scrooge became a changed man. We would have been left with a giant "To Be Continued!" banner after the final ghost visited Scrooge. The purpose of this method, naturally, is to leave the reader dying to know what happens next.

I was actually fascinated to learn that the term *cliff-hanger* may have originated with Thomas Hardy's serialized novel *A Pair of Blue Eyes*, in which Hardy left one of the main characters literally hanging off the edge of a cliff. This led to the archetypal cliff-hanger in Victorian prose, and all serial writers began to use it—in many cases, even if they didn't quite agree with the theory. One such writer in that time period rightly disapproved since the use of this suspense violated "all proper confidence between the author and his reader."

I'm pairing the stand-alone story with the cliff-hanger story in this section because they are both hotly debated subjects. Yes, a cliff-hanger is the epitome of a page-turner, but the greatest suspense comes at the end of the novel and thereby denies the reader resolution. Using this technique can build anticipation and even profit for a sequel. However, nearly all of the series-writing authors I interviewed cast a disapproving eye on reading stories with cliff-hanger endings or using a cliff-hanger in their own work. They focused almost exclusively on the frustration and unfairness of a cliff-hanger—well-justified arguments. As the Victorian-era writer Anthony Trollope said, a cliff-hanger forces the reader to wait—possibly indefinitely—for all threads in the story to effectively be tied up.

All writers know that publishing is in a constant state of flux. Is it fair to make readers wait for a sequel that will give them closure, knowing that the publisher might close up shop, postpone the release of a book in a series, or grow bored or disillusioned with continuing the series, the author, or the genre? "No reader wants to wait a year or more to find out the conclusion of a book," publisher Laura Baumbach wisely says. Her colleague Miriam Pace adds, "I personally do not like unfinished stories, my reason being that by the time the next one has come out, I've probably forgotten what happened in the original story and, if the time lag is a long one, I may no longer even have that book to refer back to."

What if something happens to the *author* and the story is never concluded properly? "Each story should be a stand-alone and have an ending in case the publisher decides to pull the plug because the series isn't working or the author cannot finish it for some reason," says Christy Poff. "A book needs to resolve certain points in order to be complete." Also consider that a cliff-hanger might, and frequently does, present a situation in which the reader is so desperately anticipating the sequel, the delivery can't possibly live up to what it was built up to be.

Charlotte Boyette~Compo is another author who believes series stories should stand alone. "The reason is simple: Not everyone will start a series. Some people simply don't like the notion of reading one. Each book should tell its own story. I learned that from the WindLegends Saga Series. It is one long, continuous story, and some readers just don't want to invest the time. It also has cliff-hanger endings in each book that seem to annoy some readers. While the series has many diehard fans, it doesn't sell as well as the series that have stand-alone books."

Paranormal author Dyanne Davis said that she ends each of her books with a cliff-hanger, which she knows a lot of readers hate. She never viewed it as unfair. "Considering that I'm also a reader, I don't mind. I will scream, curse the author … and wait hungrily for the next book."

This author is rare in her patience. Obviously, the writer who leaves her story on a cliff-hanger hopes readers will eagerly come back for the next installment, which promises to resolve the situation the previous story was left in. However, very few authors believe a cliff-hanger can be justified, *ever*. Speculative fiction author Margaret L. Carter says, "I feel upset, sometimes to the point of outrage, when a novel in a series ends on a cliff-hanger. With the long time span that usually intervenes between the publications of successive books, that trick doesn't seem fair to the reader. Sometimes, of course, this happens because of the publisher's choice, and the author has no control. I think it's important that each book come to some sort of satisfactory conclusion, a logical resting place for characters and readers, even if the overall series arc continues with unresolved problems and mysteries." N.J. Walters points out the true danger in using cliff-hanger endings: "Give closure at the end of each book. Otherwise the satisfaction is missing and you run the risk of losing a reader for future books."

Regan Taylor says she never wanted to read a series book and realize at any point that "someone knows something you don't." P.A. Brown speaks of coming upon authors on their third or sixth book in a series: "If I'd had to read the previous books to understand what was going on, and they weren't available ... I'd probably be annoyed and enjoy the book less."

That certainly is a viable reason for avoiding cliff-hangers completely. But there's a catch-22: What happens if readers pick up one of the middle books in a series and find out that they have to read the first books in order to make sense of this one? Writing a stand-alone book for each in a series is important, but is it advisable to write a stand-alone so well there's no need to read the previous stories to make sense of a middle one?

No! Authors want to leave an intriguing piece dangling in beginning and middle stories in a series—something that will compel readers to go out and find the other books. Additionally, you want readers to continue reading through the rest of the series—and that means leaving something to look forward to. In that mildest of senses, something like a cliff-hanger is needed that will pick relentlessly at the reader until the next book in the series is released. Remember what I told you earlier: Even while each book in a series must stand alone, it must also provide valid connections and intimacy from one book to the next. Otherwise, there's little purpose in even writing a series.

A stand-alone story resolves all or most of the issues specific to that work. Earlier I spoke about story arcs (short-term) versus series arcs (long-term). In a series, the series arc must continue to grow and develop throughout each book, and in that way, these threads remain unresolved until the final book. This is acceptable because the *story* arc in each individual book has been resolved completely, and the reader can leave the story with a sense of closure, satisfaction, and certainly anticipation for the next book in the series, especially if you've given them something to think about in the meantime. Mary Jean Kelso believes "there can be a sense of mystery coming in the next book without leaving readers hanging and wondering *Who shot JR?* I like to tie everything up in a neat bow and yet introduce something or someone that makes the reader wonder what will happen in the next book." Joanne Hall adds, "In terms of reader fairness, it's perfectly fair to string them along until they're tearing their hair out and begging on their knees to know what happens at the end of the last book. It's *not* fair to let them down with a feeble ending, or to leave important issues completely unresolved. It is okay to leave them a little sad, and to leave a few things hanging, especially if you're planning future books."

So it's not only fair but necessary to end each book in a series (except the last, unless the series is open-ended or ceases abruptly—sooner than expected) in a way that creates an immense amount of excitement for the next book in the series. C.R. Moss says, "To keep the series moving along, there should be a 'What about...?' question that makes the reader want to pick up the next book." Science fiction/fantasy author Stephen Almekinder agrees that a book should be able to stand alone, but also "have enough connections to the book that comes before it or follows it to keep a reader interested in finishing the series. Certain aspects of the plot can be wrapped up in a single book, but the general movement must be toward the ultimate end of the series." Janet Elaine Smith adds, "It is good to have a teaser at the end of each book, but that doesn't mean the story for that particular book leaves you disappointed because you feel you were cheated of satisfactory resolutions."

Closure can build suspense for what's to come in a more gratifying way than a cliff-hanger ever could. Luisa Buehler writes that a story arc resides within each book, and each book resides within a series arc. "Think of an umbrella covering characters who are each holding their own umbrella. For me, it's important that each book's story can stand alone because that's how the story from the *first* book can still live in the *last* book."

I've found that writing a stand-alone book is essential for the reader to feel happy when he finishes the book—as long as the experience of reading any series book is inestimably deeper than reading a true standalone book. If I'm writing a series with a central group of characters as the touchstone and the series arc is loosely defined, setting up the main character(s) that will be featured in the *next* book in the series at the end of the *current* book builds anticipation for that upcoming release. Always leave hints about what's to come to impact readers in a positive way and prevent them from running into the arms of another series.

---

## OFF-THE-BOOKSHELF EXAMPLES OF SERIES WITH CLIFF-HANGER ENDINGS

**YOUNG ADULT/CHILDREN'S:** The Animorphs Series by various authors

**ROMANCE:** Katie Chandler Series by Shanna Swendson

**HORROR/PARANORMAL:** Midnighters Trilogy by Scott Westerfeld

**MYSTERY/SUSPENSE/THRILLER:** Forensic Mystery Series by Alane Ferguson

**SCIENCE FICTION/FANTASY/FUTURISTIC:** The Dark Tower Series by Stephen King

**HISTORICAL/WESTERN/TIME-TRAVEL/REGENCY:** Inferno Club Series by Gaelen Foley

---

## OFF-THE-BOOKSHELF EXAMPLES WITH STAND-ALONE SERIES BOOKS

**YOUNG ADULT/CHILDREN'S:** Fablehaven Series by Brandon Mull

**ROMANCE:** Code Name Series by Christina Skye

**HORROR/PARANORMAL:** Unbound Series by Lori Devoti

**MYSTERY/SUSPENSE/THRILLER:** In Death Series by J.D. Robb

SCIENCE FICTION/FANTASY/FUTURISTIC: Celta's HeartMates Series by Robin D. Owens

HISTORICAL/WESTERN/TIME-TRAVEL/REGENCY: American Chronicle Series by Gore Vidal

## SINGLE GENRE VERSUS MULTIPLE GENRES

When multiple genres make an appearance in a series and even in a single book, it's called "straddling the fence," and it's becoming more and more common these days. Not only common, but in some ways irreverent and possibly even over-the-top, especially when you consider Seth Grahame-Smith's *Pride and Prejudice and Zombies*. Quirk Books, the publisher of these hybrid novels that combine classic novels with mania and pop culture horror, also publishes Ben H. Winters *Sense and Sensibility and Sea Monsters* and others like it.

In most cases, however, the combination of genres in a novel or series isn't so strange. After all, what goes together better than romance and suspense? These are two distinct genres, and yet they make perfect sense when paired either in a single book or separately in a series. It's also not much of a stretch to combine historical and time-travel fiction in a series. But what happens when a series that starts out as contemporary fiction suddenly dives into the pools of the supernatural or historical? Can that work? Or will you lose readers who expected one thing and got quite another? Among the authors and publishers I interviewed, the responses were about as varied as genres can sometimes be.

Some authors weighed in *against* changing genres from one book to the next in a series. Luisa Buehler says, "Readers expect a series that starts as one basic genre to stay that way. It's unfair to set them up for a traditional mystery with no graphic violence, sex, or language, then shift to a serial killer who kills brutally in great description." N.J. Walters goes further: "You have to always keep your readers in mind. They're expecting something particular when they read a series. If all the books in the series are contemporary, for example, it would be strange to throw a paranormal in there. Your readers who don't like the paranormal will be disappointed. In my opinion, a writer owes it to the readers not to change midstream. If you want to write a book in a different genre, then write one. Make it a stand-alone, or start a new series."

Vijaya Schartz agrees, "I discovered that, at least within a series, you want to remain in the same genre. Readers are funny that way. They expect the same atmosphere, the same type of story, and if you switch gears on them, they'll not only notice, they might resent you for it. I write in various genres (contemporary romantic suspense, paranormal romance, sci-fi, and fantasy romance, to name a few) and I noticed that my readers do not always cross over from one genre to another. They know what they like, and that's all they want to read." Publisher Laura Baumbach adds, "Readers have expectations once they start a series, and I believe in giving them what they want. The series needs to stay on track and stick to one genre."

Consider that librarians and bookstore owners won't know how to shelve books that lump too many genres into one. While no one wants to be pigeonholed, it's what often happens in the distributor setting of selling books.

Despite the arguments against writing in multigenres within one series, many of the authors and publishers I interviewed saw no problem with crossing genres within the books in a series. Fantasy and mystery author Fran Orenstein says, "Overlap adds depth and interest. Why can't fantasy have romance, or mystery have comedy?" Luisa Buehler may be against taking major leaps but advocates "stretching the basic genre." Cat Adams believes that "readers today are, for the most part, willing to ignore bookstore shelving requirements to expand their vision." Publisher Miriam Pace refuses to pigeonhole her authors. "I want them to show me how versatile they are. I feel the more stories they can write in different genres, the wider their readership." Fellow publisher J.M. Smith takes a practical approach to this: "It's okay to mix genres as long as you have one that continues throughout. For instance, Wild Horse Press publishes the Ashton Grove Werewolves Series, which is predominantly paranormal, but there are a few books in the series that have fantasy and science fiction thrown in as well, with fairies, sorcerers, psychics, etc."

We've stressed that there are no rules, right? Charlotte Boyett~ Compo puts this sentiment into perspective when she says, "While I appreciate my readers' opinions, I'm not writing the books with that in mind."

Authors of series do have to write a story the way it needs to be written, even if it ends up leaving the domain of the genre they started the series in. One way to handle this is to plan the series carefully. When I was writing my Wounded Warriors Series, I knew that one of the characters was psychic. I set up this detail in the first two books before I got to her story, and when this contemporary women's fiction/romance series reached the third book, *Mirror Mirror,* I think readers were prepared for a journey into the supernatural because I'd already established it in advance. I don't believe it *would* have worked if I hadn't planted that arc right away. Incidentally, while I didn't return to the supernatural in the next three books, I also didn't hide from the fact that this middle story contained it. How well executed something like this is in a series story is always determined by how well you set it up in advance.

I did the same thing in the tenth book in my Incognito Series, which is made up of action-adventure/romantic suspense novels. In *Hypnotized* I introduced the concept of mind reading within the background of using such technology for terrorism. The reviews and reader feedback I've received have convinced me this worked for *Hypnotized* regardless of how unlikely it was to find a book with a somewhat supernatural plot thread near the end of the long series. I also think this genre straddling worked in part due to the fact that, within an author's note that preceded the story, I included actual reports of the United States military attempting to develop a technique for mind reading. This grounded the supernatural premise in fact, and the story mirrored the chilling reality. The supernatural element was reality based and therefore fit the series premise naturally.

In any case, I believe it's true that some genres simply lend themselves to straddling extremely well. Romantic fiction can fit well with most, if not all, other genres. Mysteries have also proved to be easily stretched in this regard. One example is Carrie Bebris's respectfully rendered and amazingly executed Mr. & Mrs. Darcy Mystery Series, which remains true to Jane Austen's romance novels but presents a mystery to unravel that occasionally has a believable paranormal twist.

If genre straddling was a complete no-no, it would make no sense that historical mysteries are so popular these days. Time-traveling elements are also being effectively woven into any and every genre convincingly, including romance, historical, suspense, speculative fiction, and countless young adult series.

I think we can conclude that authors don't need to follow too many rules when it comes to straddling genres, but they must keep readers in mind when doing anything off-the-wall. If you lose more readers than you gain, what's the benefit?

---

## OFF-THE-BOOKSHELF EXAMPLES OF
## SERIES THAT STRADDLE GENRES

**YOUNG ADULT/CHILDREN'S:** Percy Jackson and the Olympians Series by Rick Riordan

**ROMANCE:** Sisters of Colford Hall Series by Deborah MacGillivray

**HORROR/PARANORMAL:** Dark-Hunter Series by Sherrilyn Kenyon

**MYSTERY/SUSPENSE/THRILLER:** Sadie Witt Mysteries by Beth Solheim

**SCIENCE FICTION/FANTASY/FUTURISTIC:** The god-Princes of Tigron Books by Rowena Cherry

**HISTORICAL/WESTERN/TIME-TRAVEL/REGENCY:** Gaslight Mysteries by Victoria Thompson

---

## NOVEL SERIES VERSUS
## NOVELLA SERIES

Here again, we face the validity of rules. Should it be a rule that all the books in a series appear as novels or novellas, or can the size of a book be mixed up according to the dictates of the story, the author, the publisher, or reader preferences? Let's say you have begun writing a series in which all the stories have been released as novels. Can you then release a novella? Many readers are choosy in this regard, sticking to one or the other as a matter of taste or habit. Some readers don't find novellas as satisfying or as deep as novels, while other readers don't have the time or attention span for anything *but* novellas.

Authors rarely have control of this sort of thing in the traditional publishing industry since most mass-market publishers don't publish novellas except in anthology format, and most publishers put together their own novella collections with the authors of their choosing. If you're an author who has a publisher of this sort, the decision of whether to stick to novels might already be decided for you. Small-press publishers rarely have the same rules, and authors are free to submit either novels or novellas with an equal chance for publication. Small-press authors may even submit their own anthology collections with or without other authors. I think it was proven that most readers don't care about size when a spin-off novella in Stephenie Meyer's Twilight Saga was released. Readers didn't want the series to end, so they grabbed *The Short Life of Bree Tanner*.

A few years ago, I started something that I believe is pretty unheard of in the publishing industry, in the form of literary "greatest hits" compilations. Back in 2003, I formed Jewels of the Quill, which is a group of published authors that band together to promote. In 2005 we decided to put together group anthologies, including an annual volume of *Tales from the Treasure Trove* along with holiday anthologies released near Christmas, Valentine's Day, and Halloween each year. Many of the authors in these anthologies, including myself, were writing novellas that were part of an original series developed specifically for the anthologies. Some of my fans asked why they couldn't buy these series novellas in a separate collection that included only my own stories, prompting me to pitch an idea to our anthology publisher. With their go-ahead, we started putting together what I called "Dame collections," which were like "greatest hits" packages with bonus material. These included collections of non-series stories by individual authors as well as series stories by those individual authors who were originally published in the group anthologies. In each case, it made sense that a never-before-published story or two would be included to make readers more eager to purchase these 100,000-word (more or less) collections.

To date, I've had five of these collections published myself, including the *Dame Amethyst Treasures* collection, which included three of my non-series stories that had been previously published in various Jewels of the Quill anthologies. I added a bonus, never-before-published story to the collection to make it a worthwhile purchase for my fans. To the two series stories published in different Jewels of the Quill anthologies, I added two bonus stories in my *Adventures in Amethyst Series* collection. My *Kaleidoscope Series* collection includes five of my stories published in Jewels of the Quill anthologies with two bonus series stories. My first *Woodcutter's Grim Series* collection includes, again, two published stories and two bonus stories. The second *Woodcutter's Grim Series* collection includes one story published in a Jewels of the Quill anthology and three new stories. Also published is the *Cowboy Fever Series* collection, which includes one novella in the series previously published in a group anthology and four bonus novellas.

The twist with both the Woodcutter's Grim and Cowboy Fever Series is that I knew before I ever started writing either of them that I wanted to write a *novel* for each of these previously all-novella series. The first novel in the Woodcutter's Grim Series, *The Deep* (October 2013), will actually be the eighth book in the series and will be released about a year after the *Woodcutter's Grim Series, Volume II* collection (September 2012). I do plan many more novels for this series in the future. The first novel in the Cowboy Fever Series, *Drifter's Heart* (December 2013), will be the sixth book in the series and, again, it will come out about a year and a half after the *Cowboy Fever Series* collection is published in May 2013.

In this situation, I don't believe there are rules. I write for small-press publishers, and my fans seem to read whatever I offer, regardless of the size and genre. I also expect that my *Dame* collection readers will be utterly thrilled to find out that I'm planning to write at least one novel for the series. While I've seen a novel series turn out a novella occasionally, it's rare that a novella series will offer a novel.

Unless your publisher prohibits this sort of thing or your readers are adamant about staying within their reading size requirements, how can you lose?

---

## OFF-THE-BOOKSHELF EXAMPLES OF SERIES THAT INCLUDE BOTH NOVELS AND NOVELLAS

**YOUNG ADULT/CHILDREN'S:** Malazan Book of the Fallen Series by Steven Erikson

**ROMANCE:** Cedar Cove Series by Debbie Macomber

**HORROR/PARANORMAL:** Twilight Series by Maggie Shayne

**MYSTERY/SUSPENSE/THRILLER:** Hercule Poirot Mysteries by Agatha Christie

**SCIENCE FICTION/FANTASY/FUTURISTIC:** A Song of Ice and Fire Series by George R.R. Martin

**HISTORICAL/WESTERN/TIME-TRAVEL/REGENCY:** Sackett Series by Louis L'Amour

---

In this chapter I've established that while a lot of authors handle the questions that crop up in writing a series on the fly, huge opportunities can be missed when one does so. As soon as you know you're writing a series, sit down and work out the details, including series, story, and plant arcs. Also try to answer the basic questions I've put forth: Should your series arcs be loosely or clearly defined? Should the series stories be stand-alone or cliff-hangers? What genres will your series stories encompass? And finally, should the individual stories be novels or novellas?

## BUILD YOUR SERIES MUSCLES EXERCISE

What is your series tie(s)?

> Recurring Character Series
>
> Central Group of Characters Series

Premise/Plot Series

Setting Series

Combination of These (list)

In developing your series blurb, your tie(s) will frequently help you figure out what the blurb should include. In one or two sentences, try to define your series arc. At this point it's fine to write something as simple as "Cast of characters will find soul mates" or "College professor follows the trail to an ancient artifact that could save the world or destroy it." You will build on whatever you come up with in later chapters. In chapter four I'll take this beginning and put it into the actual series arc equation to come up with a series arc. By the time you finish reading this book, you should have a good setup for your series.

Now that you know how to find the focus of your series with series, story, and plant arcs, and I've answered some basic questions about the dos and don'ts in writing a series, let's talk about the top two requirements in approaching a series, characters and consistency, along with some important considerations you'll face in the process of establishing your own series plan.

# CHAPTER THREE

# TWO CRUCIAL Cs FOR YOUR SERIES: CHARACTERS AND CONSISTENCY

*"If you start with a bang, you won't end with a whimper."*

~T.S. ELIOT

All the authors and publishers I interviewed for this book mentioned two things that are absolutely necessary when it comes to creating a satisfying series: awesome characters and unflagging consistency. Without these two elements, it's likely your series will never become firmly established and therefore will never take off. Both of these "Crucial Cs" must be established at the beginning of a series and build steadily, believably, infallibly throughout each book. In this chapter, I will break down both of these concepts and explore them fully. I'll round things off with some other aspects of good novel and novella writing that you might also consider for your series.

## CHARACTERS

Characters are the number one reason readers love series. This is not to say that readers don't also love setting and plot, but without characters who strike a chord with readers, no setting or plot can save a story. Characters rule. An intriguing, lifelike character is one who can make any story or setting work.

That said, characters, plot, and setting are *all* crucial to amazing stories. I often hear authors say, "I'm a character-driven writer" or "I write action stories." Others are fascinated by world creation. It's as if these writers feel they can focus on one area and safely ignore the other two.

When authors tell me they write plot-driven stories, I immediately scoff because plot is only a third of what's necessary for a story. Are they telling me they use only a portion of what's vital in their work? I have the same reaction when writers say their work is character driven or setting dominated. Again, each of these is only a third of the whole. I'm not denying that there are action-driven stories with weak internal conflicts or one-dimensional characterization, or stories that are so focused on setting that the characters are lost in them. You can also find stories that are inundated with major characters, but readers don't get to know any of them well enough to care one way or another. Unfortunately, plenty of examples exist in each category, and most of them don't satisfy readers.

I firmly believe you must address all three components—plot, setting, *and* character—in each story to make it cohesive[1], so when I talk about characters in this section, I'll also expound on plot and setting. Since the three go hand-in-hand-in-hand, authors should really reconsider the wisdom of lumping themselves into specific designations. Is this a radical idea or just good writing sense? You decide at the end of the next section.

## CHARACTER DRIVEN, PLOT LOADED, OR SETTING DOMINATED?

As James Scott Bell says in *Plot & Structure*, "Plots need characters, and characters need plots." I would add that both plots and characters need settings, too. The fact is, whether or not you should write a character-driven, plot-driven, or setting-dominated set of stories isn't a fair question. There's no "versus" about any of this. Let me tell you why.

I believe that the author has only so much control over choosing the kind of story she writes, and that our muse does exert a certain influ-

---

[1] Read my book *From First Draft to Finished Novel: A Writer's Guide to Cohesive Story Building* to see how obsessed I am with the concept of story cohesion.

ence over us concerning this choice. Additionally, the idea itself usually comes with its own agenda. When a spark of an idea initially forms, who can know if we conceive of it ourselves, or if it's given to us as a gift? In any case, the spark will generally present the groundwork for your novel, whether it's in the form of the plot, characters, or setting. Ideally, it will be a combination of all three. You as the writer choose whether to move forward with the spark as it's given to you, and you choose how you're going to develop and mold this creation so it becomes as real and tangible to others as it is to you.

When I first started writing, my characters were so overwhelmingly lifelike to me that "action" plot elements outside of a basic theme, character development, conflict, and a romance were a nuisance. Being with my characters, watching them live their lives and have intensely consuming, complex relationships, was nothing short of a miracle to me. This is not to say that the books I wrote didn't *have* plot. Yes, plot is conflict in any form you can think of, internal as well as external, but plot isn't necessarily fistfights, life-threatening danger, chasing mysteries, or even blood-spewing action. Plot can be as simple as answering the questions: *How did I get into this situation? And how do I get out?* In other words, it can be as simple as confronting the past, both actively and passively or actively facing the present and future, over the course of the novel or novella. If a story fulfills the audience's three-tiered need for entertainment, escape, and understanding, you've created something enduring that will be read over and over again.

Every book I've written since the beginning has been character driven and developed in a rich setting that includes conflicts from start to finish. Something to keep in mind is that in fiction, conflict must always manifest itself both internally and externally. In the beginning the development of characters overwhelmed me, and, for me it was a wondrous process in which I eventually learned how to introduce plot and setting in a way that formed an amalgamation. In order to develop character, both plot and setting must also focus on and match the specific character. I'll start with plot.

E.M. Forster defines plot as "a narrative of causality which results in a completed process of significant change, giving the reader emotional satisfaction." In simplified terms, this means that change happens to a character, inside and outside, and one change results in another change. We as readers follow this character on her journey of domino changes, and our hearts and heads are satisfied with whatever resolutions the character experiences at the end of the road.

Now let's relate plot to character: A character's internal conflicts are emotional problems that make her reluctant to achieve a goal. They're brought about by *external* conflicts, and they keep her from learning a life lesson and making the choice to act. The character can't reach her goal until she faces the conflict. In order to care about the outcome, the audience must be able to identify with both the internal and external conflicts the character faces. Character growth throughout the story is key to a satisfactory resolution.

The initial story spark you receive from your muse will usually suggest the character's conflicts, and these conflicts are almost always based on someone or something that is threatening what the character cares about most passionately. In some instances, a loved one is in jeopardy, or something the character desperately wants, needs, or desires is at risk of being lost. It's your job as the writer to give the character incentives to persevere until his goals are achieved and he's attained what he's been fighting for.

Internal conflicts are different from external ones, but they're related causally. In other words, you can't have one without the other. Internal and external conflicts depend on each other, and therefore they need to be cohesive. Internal conflicts are all about characters, and external conflicts are all about plot. But keep in mind that both internal and external conflicts belong to the main character. After all, if both didn't affect her in some profound way, they wouldn't be *her* conflicts and therefore wouldn't even be a part of her story.

Think of it this way: Everyone has a passionate hot button: cruelty to animals, breast cancer, child abuse. You know your own. But not everyone has the strength of passion for your particular hot button that you do. We're all individuals and we usually put our passion into something that has touched us deeply in our lives. If your mother died of breast cancer, you'll want to see that particular disease cured. It's your hot button. This doesn't mean you don't sympathize and care deeply about other causes, even if you're not quite as passionate about them. What it does mean is that if something critical happens in the area of your passion, you're probably going to step up and fight for what you believe in. Now, because you're telling a story about your particular character, and she has hot buttons, too, her hot buttons will naturally be her conflicts. All of these conflicts must parallel, intersect, and collide for a story to be truly cohesive. Even though external plot conflicts may stem from an outside force or situation, they nevertheless belong to the main character as much as her internal problems do. Like I said, if she didn't care deeply about the external plot, it wouldn't be her story.

In the Harry Potter Series young wizard Harry constantly battles his internal conflict. His parents are dead and he's been forced to live with his detestable and magic-hating aunt, uncle, and cousin. In the external plot conflict, Harry must come to terms with his accidental relationship to Voldemort, who killed his parents. His contact with this Dark wizard affects him inside and out. You can see how the internal and external conflicts differ—one's outside, one's inside—how they parallel, intersect, and collide, and how you can't really have one without the other.

Also keep in mind that if your conflicts travel in a straight line, if your character solves her problems without creating further complications or failures, your reader will grow bored with the story and less intrigued by the character. Let's say your character's motivation is to get into the office and procure what she needs without being seen. If she goes in, gets it, and the world goes on a-spinnin'—done deal, no problem—that's boring. But if she's almost caught before she even ducks in, if the antagonist actually enters the room while she's there and she has to dive under the desk, and if the antagonist drops a pen and bends down near her to retrieve it—*that's* exciting. These examples are offshoots that greatly complicate her goal. Though it isn't easy and she's sweating bullets by the time she gets what she needs, the reader will appreciate her struggle and root for her even more. You'll rouse more emotion and interest in the reader if the intensity of conflicts continues to rise on a causal course. As a story and a series progress, you'll revisit each main character's internal conflicts, as well as the character's goals, motivations, and plot conflicts, in order to show the growth and development of character and plot.

Ultimately, the difference between plot (external) and character (internal) conflicts is that plot is the central (whether tangible or intangible) outer problem that the character must face and solve. The character wants to restore the stability that was taken from her by the external conflict, and this produces her desire to act. However, a character's internal conflicts will create an agonizing tug-of-war with the plot conflicts. She has to make tough choices that come down to whether or not she should face, act on, and solve the problem. Plot conflicts must be so urgent as to require immediate attention. Plot conflicts work hand in glove with character conflicts. You can't have one without the other, and they become more intense and focused the longer the characters struggle.

In terms of setting, characters must blend naturally with the surroundings you've placed them in, just as plot must become an organic part of your character and setting. If a story doesn't work, it could very well be because your character, setting, and plot elements aren't blending naturally. Your setting is a basis for building your story—it enhances the characters, conflict, and suspense, and provides a backdrop for all three to flourish. If your setting doesn't work with the other elements, it will be more difficult to create cohesive characters and plots.

The importance of creating a setting that's cohesive with character and plot can be illustrated by imagining different settings for classic novels. What if *Moby-Dick,* instead of being set at sea, had been set in, say, a lighthouse? Captain Ahab (a man who's never been on anything bigger than a sailboat) boasts around town about how he'll get the whale. Much of *Moby-Dick*'s appeal would be lost if it'd been set on land instead of the sea. If *The Amityville Horror* had taken place in, say, a department store, the horror would have fizzled. If Harry Potter had gone to a local public school (or St. Brutus's Secure Center for Incurably Criminal Boys, as Aunt Marge had suggested) instead of the magical boarding school Hogwarts, the series would have been radically different.

You may have noticed that Agatha Christie often set her novels in places where the cast of characters can't escape, while also limiting the number of characters who could have committed the crime. This greatly increases tension and also focuses the plot on these particular characters, allowing the reader to participate in unraveling the mystery in a closed setting, where the surprises will be highly logical ones that stem from the trinity of characters, setting, and plot.

While many stories have settings that suit the character and plot, I'm sure you can come up with dozens of books with settings that are simply adequate. That is, the author could have spent more time making the setting extraordinary—so the reader actually wants to visit it again in another book. My advice is to make a setting that does more than simply fit your characters and plot. Make that setting come *alive* in readers' minds. Make them want to visit and revisit it when they're reading your series, and even when they're not.

Pieces of the character and plot details should be woven into setting. Good setting descriptions *should* convey character and plot elements—otherwise these descriptions serve as general information without a strong, cohesive purpose. Describe the setting in a way that not only fits your characters and plot, but also supercharges your story. What does the setting reveal about the character's personality? What in the setting means the most to him? How will this setting build the stage for conflict and suspense? How can you make it so real that your reader will believe the place actually exists?

In the beginning of my writing career, I did write a lot of character studies, but I eventually moved into the action-heavy genre of mysteries (amateur sleuth, private investigators, and police procedurals), horror, paranormal, action/adventure/spy, and suspense. In all of these works, I married the concepts of character, plot, and setting so each balanced with and brought out the best in the others.

The one thing I've never done is to write an action-driven story that lacks strong internal conflicts or characters that grow and develop throughout the course of the story or series, and to do so in a compelling setting. To me, that's not even a choice, nor do I believe any author can afford to consider it in the course of her writing career. The stories and series will suffer if she does.

The best part of a story and series with solid, cohesive characters, plot, and settings is that your readers will invest themselves mentally, emotionally, and possibly even physically (if you can make them cry or bite their nails, you've got them hook, line, and sinker!). In this scenario, you've created a net the readers won't want to disentangle themselves from until they know everything, and they'll feel like they're leaving a piece of themselves behind each time they reluctantly set a series book down—especially that last time when they read "The End."

Perhaps, then, it's more accurate to say that your *approach* to a story is character, plot, or setting driven. In her book *Story Structure Architect*, Victoria Lynn Schmidt, Ph.D. speaks about a plot- or character-driven approach using the example of a tornado story line. When you approach the story line from a plot-driven point of view, if a tornado suddenly descends upon the town, the characters have no means to stop it. They brace themselves and react to what's happening. As Victoria says, "They don't cause the tornado—the tornado causes them to react to it." When you approach a story in a character-driven manner, even if a tornado comes through the town, characters are given the time to decide what to do. The focus of the story is on the characters' decisions, and that's what moves the story in different directions. The characters have options and they make choices that affect the outcome in a character-driven story. In a setting-dominated story, the focus is almost always on the place as seen through the eyes of the people who populate it. The focus is on the town—the setting—devastated by the tornado.

When I think of the setting-driven approach, I think of *Avatar*. The film is focused on the setting—the world of Pandora—and everything, including characters and plot, was approached from that point of view. In the movie *Twister* it was the twister (the plot) that took control, and the setting and characters worked within that approach. In *Steel Magnolias* setting and plot were predominantly approached from the angle of character development.

While there are no rules in writing, all stories must be a symbiotic triangle of character, plot, and setting. How you *approach* your story will be character, plot, or setting driven. In this way, diverse readers will always be satisfied.

## INTRODUCING AND REVISITING CHARACTERS, PREMISE/PLOT, AND SETTINGS

Regardless of whether you have one recurring character or a central group of characters who differ from one book to the next, whatever your premise/plot and setting, you'll be introducing and revisiting your series tie(s) throughout your series. The initial introduction of a character or characters, premise/plot, or setting is as important as how you revisit each of these in later books. Backstory is necessary in all books in a series, but in varying degrees.

Earlier I talked about how, if a reader starts reading in the middle of your series, you want to give her glimpses of previous books in the series that will intrigue her enough to pick up those earlier books. You don't want to give her everything so she feels no need to read about what happened before. In many cases very little is required to give the reader a basic grasp of what's going on. Too little, however, can be confusing and can even cause the reader to stop reading.

Bob Rich posted a hilarious article for his Bobbing Around column called, "How NOT to Continue a Series." In the article, he referred to picking up a bestseller that was part of a twenty-five-book series. The book started with a two-page editorial from the author, sketching out the premise of the book. This was followed by the beginning of the book, which had not one, not two, but three separate characters musing about events from the past—the author was providing necessary information from prior installments to set up this particular story in the series. These musings continued for thirty-five pages. Nothing else happened beyond a ship setting sail. As you can imagine, Bob never got through chapter two because he was bored, and he wondered if fans of the series skipped the rehash. In which case, what was the point of including it? Familiar readers didn't need the endless orientation, and new ones never made it past the soliloquies. (One wonders how this best-selling author got to be best selling in the first place with this kind of sloppy writing.) As the title of this article stated, this is certainly how *not* to continue a series.

While lurking behind the scenes on various automatic mailing list servers (hereafter referred to as listservs), I "heard" readers talking about the importance of the author writing a series book that was "immediately accessible." Brilliant! But what does it mean? Essentially, this means that while some nuances from previous books in the series escape the reader, that's okay—as long as nothing takes him out of the current story for too long. A reader should be able to follow the current story without having to read any of the other books. One reader said that jumping into a story without enough information is like having to start reading a book on page seventy-two or to stop reading it fifty pages before the end. However, others mentioned how annoying it is to hear every detail of a previous book in the series—so much so that they didn't care to read books that include extensive backstory.

The following three passages contain brilliantly executed hints about the last book in the series that don't overwhelm the current story.

From *Harry Potter and the Prisoner of Azkaban* (third in the Harry Potter series) by J.K. Rowling:

> Hagrid wasn't a fully qualified wizard; he had been expelled from Hogwarts in his third year for a crime he had not committed. It had been Harry, Ron, and Hermione who had cleared Hagrid's name last year.

In this example you're given just enough insight to provoke your curiosity to find out more about the situation that cleared Hagrid's name in the previous book. No more is warranted or necessary in this particular story.

From *Waiting Games* (second in an unofficial trilogy about teenager Jessie's first-ever romance with her eighteen-year-old guitar instructor, Michael) by Bruce and Carole Hart:

> A love song.
> It started playing about half an hour ago in the practice room at The Eddie Nova Guitar Institute in Hackensack, where Michael teaches and I take lessons.

> It started when Michael forgave me for lying to him about
> my age and telling him I was sixteen, when I was really thirteen.
> Which happened just before Michael opened his arms and
> took me in and kissed me.

Again, nothing else needs to be said to establish what happened in the last book and what's about to happen in the current one.

From *Eclipse*, Book 3 of the Twilight Saga by Stephenie Meyer:

> Ever since my former best friend (and werewolf), Jacob Black,
> had informed me about the motorcycle I'd been riding on the
> sly—a betrayal he had devised in order to get me grounded so
> that I couldn't spend time with my boyfriend (and vampire), Ed-
> ward Cullen—Edward had been allowed to see me only from sev-
> en till nine-thirty p.m., always inside the confines of my home
> and under the supervision of my dad's unfailingly crabby glare.
> This was an escalation from the previous, slightly less strin-
> gent grounding that I'd earned for an unexplained three-day
> disappearance and one episode of cliff diving.

You not only know what happened before, but you know what's going on now with this simple, to-the-point summary.

You have good reason to resist overloading a story with too much information and too many resolutions from previous books in the series: You can easily negate the very reason readers should read those books. Nobody will tell you it's easy, but writers of series need to become masters at reestablishing three-dimensional characters, settings, and the premise/plot in a mere paragraph or two.

I thought it would be interesting to illuminate the succinct ways an author can get back into the series after the first book. Here I'll look at Terry Brooks's six-book[2] Magic Kingdom of Landover Series for examples of how he reestablishes the premise of the first book in the series. I include the page number these summaries appeared on to give you an idea

---

[2] As of the writing of this book, the count is six, but there has been talk of another book in the future.

of how soon or how late such a summary can appear without confusing the reader about the series premise.

From *The Black Unicorn*, Book 2 (page 5 of the paperback):

> It had been more than a year since he had passed into the mists of the fairy world somewhere deep in the forests of the Blue Ridge Mountains twenty miles southwest of Waynesboro, Virginia, and entered the kingdom of Landover. He had paid a million dollars for the privilege, answering an advertisement in a department store catalogue, acting more out of desperation than out of reason. He had come into Landover as King, but his acceptance as such by the land's inhabitants had not come easily. Attacks on his claim to the throne had come from every quarter. Creatures whose very existence he had once believed impossible had nearly destroyed him. Magic, the power that governed everything in this strangely compelling world, was the two-edged sword he had been forced to master in order to survive. Reality had been redefined for him since he had made his decision to enter the mists, and the life he had known as a trial lawyer in Chicago, Illinois, seemed far removed from his present existence. Still, that old life was not completely forgotten, and he thought now and then of going back.

I'm beyond impressed with this one-paragraph sum-up. It perfectly describes what happened in the first book in the series, compelling the reader to go back and read it. However, it gives enough information that it's not actually *necessary* to read the first book in order to enjoy the next one.

From *Wizard At Large*, Book 3 (page 3 of the paperback):

> When he had purchased the Kingdom of Landover from Rosen's Department Store Christmas Wishbook and come into the valley—almost two years ago now—Fillip and Sot, on behalf of all the G'home Gnomes, had been the first to pledge their loyalty. They had aided him in his efforts to establish his kingship. They had helped him again when Meeks, the former Court Wizard, had slipped back into Landover and stolen his identity and his

throne. They had been his friends when there were precious few friends to be had.

Again, a very nice look back to the previous book (and the first one) all while staying firmly focused on the current story. Let's keep going.

From *The Tangle Box*, Book 4 (page 21 of the hardcover; incidentally this came much later than the previous examples because of a prologue from the point of view of the villain in this story):

> It was a little more than two years since he had come to Landover, a journey between worlds, between lives, between fates. He had come in desperation, unhappy with the past, anxious for a different future. He had left his high-rise in Chicago for a castle called Sterling Silver. He had given up his law practice to become a King. He had buried the ghosts of his dead wife and unborn child and found Willow. He had bought a magic kingdom out of a Christmas catalog when he knew full well that such a thing could not possibly exist, taking a chance nevertheless that perhaps it might, and the gamble had paid off. None of it had come easy, of course. A transition of worlds and lives and fates never does. But Ben Holiday had fought the battles his journey required of him and won them all, so now he was entitled to stay, to lay claim to his new life and world and fate, and to be King of a place that he had believed once upon a time to be only a dream.
>
> To be Willow's husband, lover, and best friend, he added, when he had given up on the possibility that he could ever be any of those things to a woman again.

This passage is a little longer, but much more is packed into it, and it's still little more than a paragraph. The past three books sound very interesting, and the current one is getting fleshed out nicely.

From *Witches' Brew*, Book 5 (page 5 of the paperback):

> Ben Holiday had come into Landover when his hopes and dreams for a life in his old world had dried to dust and reason had given way to desperation. Purchase a magic kingdom and find a new life, the ad in Rosen's Christmas catalogue had promised. Make

yourself King of a land where the stories of childhood are real. The idea was unbelievable and at the same time irresistible. It called for a supreme act of faith, and Ben had heeded that call in the manner of a drowning man reaching for a lifeline. He had made the purchase and crossed into the unknown. He had come to the place that couldn't possibly exist and had found that it did. Landover had been everything and nothing like he had expected. It had challenged him as he had not thought anything could. But ultimately it had given him what he needed: a new beginning, a new chance, a new life. It had captured his imagination. It had transformed him completely.

It continued to baffle him, though. He was still trying to understand the nuances. Like this business of time's passage. It was different here from his old world; he knew that from having crossed back and forth on more than one occasion and found seasons out of synch. He knew it, too, from the effect it had on him—or the lack thereof. Something had been different in the way he aged over here. It was not a progressive process, a steady rate of change, minute by minute, hour by hour, and so forth. It was difficult to believe, but sometimes he did not age at all. He had only suspected that before, but he was certain of it now. This was a deduction arrived at not from observing his own rate of growth, which was not easily measured because he lacked objectivity and distance.

No, it was from observing Mistaya.

Something I found very interesting in this rather longer foundation passage was how Brooks combines the past with the present. You surely recognized many of these details from the previous summaries, and yet he tailors this one specifically to fit the new story. It's the most obvious way of incorporating backstory, and this example is well done.

Now, one more time, read on to revisit the premise of this series in a book that takes place long years after the last book, in which Ben Holiday's daughter, Mistaya, is the focus:

From *A Princess of Landover*, Book 6 (page 11 of the hardcover):

> Well, that was hard to explain, and Mistaya knew she better not even try if she wanted to keep the truth about herself a private matter. Princess of Landover, born of a human come from this world and a sylph who occasionally turned into a tree—how could she explain that? Telling them the truth about her father was out of the question. Telling them about her mother might give some credence to her commitment to saving trees, but it wouldn't do much for her overall credibility. Telling them about her real life, which was not in Landover, Maryland, as they thought, but in the Kingdom of Landover, which was another world entirely, would only lead to them locking her up for evaluation. There just wasn't much she could say.

This, quite simply, puts the reader back on track with what has happened in the previous five books. More details are sprinkled in later, but this is all that is needed to firmly establish the series premise.

Let's face it, the first book in a series is generally the easiest to write. The author doesn't have to find creative ways to reintroduce anything. The process is organic in a first book. It's new to you and therefore new to readers. But in subsequent books in a series, the information is no longer new, and so it has to be recycled in a way that doesn't result in those nasty information dumps associated with second and subsequent books in a series. But how do you cleverly remind readers how this new book connects to the previous ones in the series? Additionally, if you're revisiting a recurring setting, character, or cast of characters in a series, should they be portrayed in exactly the same way as they were in the previous books? If not, how much should change?

Below, I address two potentially problematic areas you'll need to address when writing a series.

## AVOIDING INFORMATION DUMPS

I'm a huge fan of Phil Farrand's Nitpicker's Guides for *Star Trek* and *The X-Files*. I'll talk more about these in the next section of this chapter because they contain something vital that series authors need to watch out for. For now, I want to focus on a term Phil uses in his books to describe a problem that runs rampant in most series: *cabbagehead-isms*. A fellow nitpicker of Phil's observed that, in some shows, a primary character doesn't have the necessary information to complete the job. This results in *cabbage-isms*: awkward, ponderous explanations used to convey information. In other words, the television show creators decide that viewers need to know certain facts in order to understand what is going on in the episode or that they need a way to turn technical explanations into layman's terms. The easiest way to do this is to make some of the characters look like baffled fools by asking questions about things they don't know. Phil Farrand expanded this term to *cabbagehead* as it applies to the character who performs this act of cabbage-ism.

A way to describe this same concept in terms of writing is *information dump*. Especially in a series, readers need to have certain information to understand the story line. Characters have to be revisited, and their roles need to be explained in previous books and reestablished in the current one. The same is true for the premise/plot and settings of a series. In some way—hopefully a creative, organic way that feels completely natural rather than overwhelming—an author must convey necessary information to readers. Keep in mind that some books in a series have a long lag time between the publication of one story and the next, and that readers may forget big or small details. Refreshing the readers' memories is vital, but, as I've established, there's nothing worse than having a dozen or more solid pages of information front-loaded into a book to convey facts the reader needs to know to fully understand the story you're about to tell. Resist the urge to catch the readers up comprehensively with what has happened in the previous story. With each progressive book in the series, it may become increasingly difficult to avoid an information dump.

You can use several methods to impart necessary information creatively, and I'll go over these in a moment. Keep in mind that a dense "So far in the series …" synopsis will put off any reader unless you can convey the information in an imaginative, organic way that fans won't skip over or grow bored reading. However, it has been done, and a couple of examples can be found in two fantasy novels: a classic and a modern bestseller. In *The Lord of the Rings* Tolkien included a more or less (depending on what edition you have) thirteen-page synopsis of what had happened in *The Hobbit*, a precursor to *The Lord of the Rings*. It contains great details about historical events and specific personal journeys, and the reader is finally brought into the current story with the words: "Of Bilbo's later adventures little more need be said here."

I'd venture a guess that little more needed to be said of Bilbo's *earlier* adventures, either. The other example is Christopher Paolini's Inheritance Cycle. Books 2 through 4 include various-size synopses of what has happened so far in the series. These synopses naturally grow in size as the series progresses. Was I put off by either of these prologue synopses? Honestly, no. I'm a fan of these particular authors, and I appreciated the chance to get caught up since the last time I read something from them. Additionally, fantasy novels do seem to get away with this practice. However, I will add that I think newer fans might clutch their chests a little in panic at seeing such intense introductions to these works.

A short prologue (no more than a page or two) is another popular means to convey vital details a reader needs to know. This prologue describes the main points of the previous books, allowing the reader to get up to speed. While prologues have fallen into disfavor these days, using one may very well be the best, most concise way of getting the information across from one series book to the next. Try to be creative in how you handle your prologues. You want to put a fresh spin on them each time so they don't feel like recycled information. In the miniseries I'm doing within my Woodcutter's Grim Series dealing with the Shaussegeny family curse, I started the first story with a full-blown scene showing exactly what happened when the curse was brought down on the family. In each of the next three books in the miniseries, I included small sections of that scene that pertained to the particular main character in that story, since each of the cast of characters affected by the curse dealt with a different aspect of the curse. I revised these smaller sections slightly to give them the slant needed for that story, and I kept them very brief—just enough information to set up the curse, give the reader a taste of the previous stories, and segue into the new story.

I've never been one to avoid what everyone else in the writing community proclaims wrong or bad. Personally, I've used prologues whenever they seemed the wisest way to handle a lot of information that didn't take place at the same time as the rest of the story. Using prologues to impart information can be an extremely viable option if done skillfully.

Remember, when your story opens, the reader will always be more focused on what's happening *now* versus what happened *in the past*. Give the reader time to *want* to know what occurred before. First chapters are for hints and allusions. You can start folding in the important backstory after that point, in small doses. That's, in fact, how most authors handle the imparting of necessary information: giving pieces a little at a time throughout the course of the beginning chapters of a story. Give only enough so readers won't be hopelessly lost, and remember that a touch of lingering mystery will motivate the reader to keep reading as long as she's not confused.

In much the same way as a prologue, a newspaper article, a diary, an old letter, or some other form of communication can creatively present necessary information. A brief, decisive flashback early in the story can also convey crucial details without hitting readers over the head. A scene of dialogue between two characters is also a popular method of conveyance and may be all you need to give your readers the information they require—as long as it's fascinating, necessary, and not at all obvious. Keep dialogue short to prevent yourself from falling into long speeches that won't sound natural to readers. Also, if you decide to distribute information in a narrative, always give it from the point of view of the character most affected by the explanation. You'll get more impact. I highly recommend reading these informational sections of your story out loud. Does any of it sound overwhelming or unnatural, like you're trying to make one of the characters in the scene the cabbagehead? On the other hand, put yourself in the place of a person who's never read any of the books in your series before. Do you hear the voices of readers saying "Huh?" a lot while you're reading these informational scenes out loud?

In Books 2 through 4 of The Amber Chronicles (published consecutively in *Tales from the Treasure Trove, Volumes IV-VII, Jewels of the Quill* anthologies), Janet Lane Walters introduced brief fairy-tale beginnings to set the premise of the series—just enough so as not to overwhelm followers while still providing the new readers with what went on before and what to expect in upcoming pages.

In Book 3, *The Amber Dragon*, she didn't beat around the bush at all. The introductory line simply stated: "A tale from the days of the onset of the curse on the Riva family and the entrance of the first prince into the world of the amber globe ..." Short, simple, but very effective in establishing what happened in the two previous series books. From there, she went straight into the current story.

In the first book of my Incognito Series, I introduced a covert government agency called the Network along with many of the key players in that organization. Admittedly, it was a complex series with a lot of characters to keep track of in the first book, many who would be crucial to subsequent books. Although each book after the first focused on two main characters (hero and heroine), I couldn't avoid the necessity of including the other members of the organization that made up the Network in each book. I also had to reestablish the premise of the Network with each new book—an organization that requires the life and loyalty of each of its operatives, who have no choice but to "love in the shadows." The first book was easy to establish. Everything was brand new and exciting—and, like I said, most authors *will* find the first book a breeze to get through without any awkward cabbage-isms.

Once the first book was done, I thought long and hard about how I was going to introduce this complex organization, the operatives within that place, and the premise of the series in each book that followed. A prologue wouldn't work for this particular series, nor would little bits of necessary information, since the reader needed to know certain information from the very start. Introducing small pieces of information gradually would only confuse instead of enlighten. Upon the advice of my agent, I finally decided to include what I called a "Network Hierarchy" at the beginning of each book. This hierarchy was a straight-to-the-point reference that included all the names, ranks, and roles of each major player in the series. At the beginning of this hierarchy, I included a short paragraph (four sentences) that established the organization and premise. The actual hierarchy was updated with each new book in the series, but it appeared in the same format in Books 2–12 and never ran longer than three pages. Although most new readers probably read only the establishing premise paragraph, and those who had followed the series from the start most likely didn't need it, it provided a very handy reference if the reader needed to jump back at any point to read the particulars of a character appearing in the story.

This hierarchy freed me up in so many ways. In addition to the establishing premise paragraph that appeared in the hierarchy, I needed only to include one simple paragraph within the actual story that went into a bit more detail. Plus, I never needed to give too much information about the key players in the series, as all the vital information usually appeared in the hierarchy. I didn't feel compelled to inundate the reader with a description or detail that didn't fit naturally in the narrative. Any other information was minimal and gave only the bare necessities for understanding that particular story.

I also made sure the hierarchy included a list of the previous books in the series in relation to which hero and heroine were featured in each one so readers could easily go back and find out more about secondary characters from book to book. I almost never gave much information about what had happened previously in the series—unless that information was necessary to the current story. If the reader wanted to know more, she'd have to go back and read a previous book to find out. My hierarchy pages (I'm including the one for the twelfth book in the series) basically look like this:

---

## THE NETWORK

The Network is the world's most covert organization with underground headquarters in Chicago beneath a front technology company called ETI. Having unchallenged authority and skill to disable and destroy criminals, the Network takes over where regular law enforcement leaves off in the mission for absolute justice. The price for

---

that justice is high, requiring the life of every man and woman who serves. For them, there is no life and no love, only duty.

## ORGANIZATIONAL HIERARCHY

**Oversight Committee:**
#1 (1st in Command): Captain Shannon McKee, Head in Washington, D.C. †
Chase Giovanni, Committee member§§
Jocelyn Dominica, Oversight Psychiatrist§§

**Level 1 Operatives:**
#2 (2nd in Command): Angelo Pluzetti, Liaison between Oversight and the Network†††
#3 (3rd in Command): Captain Ron Blair, Head of Operations†
#4 (4th in Command): Hunter Savage, Master Strategist^^^
#5 (5th in Command): Kirsten Ulrick, Head Team Leader/Mission Coordinator**
#6 (6th in Command): Roan Emory, Head Team Leader/Mission Coordinator (KIA)^

**Level 2 Lead Operatives:**
Sheena Logan, Psychiatrist
Rockwell "Vlad" Vlademar, Weapons Master
Cara "Inspector Gadget" Ross, Technology
Justine Fielding, Comm & Systems Analyst^^
Dr. Celine Savage, Medical†††

**Level 3 Operatives:**
Lona Reznik, Head of Analysis
Susana Ortega, Analysis Team^^^

**Level 3 Field Operatives:**

*Alpha Team:*

Ashton Barnett, Leader**
Dez Luttino, 1st Position††
Natalie Francis, 2nd Position***

*Beta Team:*
Noah Harlow, Leader§
Rhiannon Murray, 1st Position§
Matt "Shep" Shepherd, 2nd Position
Victor Leventhal, 3rd Position§§§
Lucy Carlton, 4th Position§§§

**Level 4 Field Operatives:**
Kyle Vincent, Red Team Leader (MIA)*
Nova Granger, Red Team Leader††
Reb Porter, Green Team Leader***


*\*No Ordinary Love*, Book 1
*\*\*Until Death Do Us Part*, Book 2
*\*\*\*Bounty on the Rebel's Heart*, Book 3
*^Dead Drop*, Book 4
*^^Under the Spell*, Book 5
*^^^Renegade's Rose*, Book 6
*†Undercover Angel*, Book 7
*††Hard to Handle*, Book 8
*†††Dance in Shadows*, Book 9
*§Hypnotized*, Book 10
*§§Mind Games*, Book 11
*§§§Dark Approach*, Book 12

In his A Series of Unfortunate Events (in which all the books do stand alone but, of course, build on each other and are better if read back to back), Lemony Snicket includes an amazingly focused, concise introduction to the series that opens each new book and creatively imparts a summary of what's happened to the Baudelaire children before. I love how, in the process of conveying just enough information to get the reader up to speed, he spends those first few moments advising said reader to choose another book if she wants something comfortable or happy to read. He also includes "letter to the editor" teasers in the back of every book to get the reader pumped up for the next offering.

You can find out if you've left out too much information or inadvertently created an information dump in the second or subsequent books of the series by simply asking someone who's never read your series before to read the most current book. If she asks questions about the characters or plot, or if she feels like she's missed something, you haven't done your job effectively. Alternately, if she feels hit over the head with too much information about previous books or mentions the "overwhelming" backstory, you need to do more work. Either way, you'll be spurred to find other, more effective ways of getting vital information across.

Other authors have found creative ways, which I'll include below, to handle information dumps. These may encourage you to find equally imaginative means to convey your information.

**ROWENA CHERRY:** "When we were allowed 120,000 words for a novel, we had the luxury of repeating vital information two or three times. With a contract for only 90,000 words, it's tough. I try to make the best possible use of back cover blurb, front matter, and the strategic placement of the family tree as backup. There are always going to be readers who skip pages. If they do that with my series books, they are very likely going to be confused. My solution is a "Greek Chorus" character who is a commentator. He—Grievous—repeats back instructions, verbally checks in quite a snarky manner whether he has understood what seems to be going on, and exclaims when one of the principal or secondary characters makes a passing reference to something or someone from a previous book in the series. It's not perceived as an information dump if it is hilarious. Of course, if my reader does not share my sense of humor, I am sunk."

**JANET ELAINE SMITH:** "In the Keith Trilogy, I interwove the patriarch of the clan telling stories to his youngest son, making them exciting (and giving the little guy nightmares!), thus weaving in the tales of the past in a fun way. Sort of like telling stories around a campfire."

**CRIME FICTION AUTHOR CARL BROOKINS:** "I assume my readers are intelligent people and, if they are following a character, they don't need much in the way of reminders. Some information is injected into the fabric of the stories as reminders. For example, my detective is only 5'2". So from time to time the problem is referred to obliquely, as in when a woman looks down into his eyes, or he wants to look through a window but it's too high up. My PR firm owner, Michael Tanner, may comment on a bad advertisment just in passing to remind readers he owns an important PR/advertising firm in Seattle."

**CINDY SPENCER PAPE:** "The introductions tend to come slowly, but I try to make sure there are scenes that give the information without feeling too dumpish. For example, *Motor City Witch* opens at the wedding of the characters from *Motor City Fae*. That way, readers see the bigger group, but it's not in a boring backstory context."

**LUISA BUEHLER:** "As for introducing reoccurring characters, I do it as you would in life. If Jan walks into Grace's home when her dad is visiting, the conversation may go something like this:

> "Jan, do you remember my dad, Mike Morelli? You met at Depot Days last year."
> "Of course I do. After the police left and the crowds dispersed, we had a coffee and a conversation about you." Jan winked. "Nice to see you again, Mike."

Hopefully that brief tag to how they met does two things: Readers who have read *The Station Master* immediately remember Jan. Readers who haven't read the book are curious about the "police and crowds" comment and may pick up the book. The point of introductions is to keep them realistically short and to inject tidbits throughout the time that the character is on the pages. Don't explain everything about the person—you wouldn't in real life. The characters become involved in a new mystery, but they bring their history/baggage with them."

**JOANNE HALL:** "One of the major characters in *Art of Forgetting* is a character from a previous book who is now dead but remains a presence in the story through memory and hearsay. [This approach] gives insights into all sides of his troubled personality."

**ROMANTIC SUSPENSE AUTHOR JENA' GALIFANY:** "In *Trials On Tour*, Book 2 of my series, I brought in a journalist to write a bio of the band. Valerie interviewed each of the band members while they traveled on the tour. Ty's adventures from Book 1 were discussed or commented on by the rest of the band to bring a new reader up to speed. The interviews also served to introduce the characters and tell more about them without the information dump approach."

There are so many ways you can handle the imparting of necessary information to readers in creative, organic ways that don't result in frontloading a story or dumping in paragraphs or even pages upon pages of descriptions and explanations. If you can't come up with something interesting, the best way to revisit characters, their roles within the overall story lines, the premise/plot, and the setting is to let your readers meet each of them as they would in real life: as they actually appear and in the most natural way possible. After all, readers don't want to be hit over the head, nor would they want to hear a person's entire life story or situation in one sitting. Dole it out in small pieces wherever it fits most naturally. If you can't insert it without using a jackhammer, it might not be necessary.

## BRINGING SOMETHING NEW

We've established that it's never a good idea to dump a large amount of information on a reader in any story. But something else is vitally important when you revisit characters, premise/plot, and setting in subsequent books in your series: It's vital to bring something new each time. Every series author and publisher I interviewed spoke of the necessity of introducing fresh developments not only to subsequent stories but to each of the main characters as well. These are the ingredients that bring readers back for more. No one wants to read the same story over and over, hashed around in a way that's supposed to make it new but really doesn't. Your premise/plot for each story must evolve in meaningful ways that expand the series as a whole. Similarly, main characters have to grow, change (or maybe a better, more accurate word is *evolve*), and develop while staying familiar and consistent to readers. Finally, settings have to be fleshed out in new and exciting ways.

In a series with a central group of characters, alternating between these characters is the most obvious means of keeping things fresh. You most likely introduced all (or most of) the main players in the first book, but in subsequent books you will be fully fleshing them out as you write their stories. Your setting may be the same but will appear slightly altered because different characters are viewing it with new eyes. Your premise/plot will probably evolve or be completely new.

In my Woodcutter's Grim Series, I establish a fairy-tale horror/paranormal town in which children's stories (and mythology, too) come to life in terrifying ways. Each story after the first reestablishes one or two characters who were previously introduced in the series and hadn't been given main character status yet. The setting of each story also evolves because I knew from the start that I wanted to provide closure for the series. In other words, I wanted the good guys to ultimately win over the evil. So in the first Woodcutter's Grim Series collection, I included the first three stories in the series along with "The Final Chapter." Technically *The Amethyst Tower* is the last book in the series, though I continued to write new books for a second collection that takes place while evil still holds sway in the town. Book 8, *The Deep* (available October 2013), the first novel in the "middle" series, will also be released before the evil is vanquished. The second novel, *Hunter's Blues* (coming October 2017), takes place just before *The Amethyst Tower*: "The Final Chapter." I hope to get a lot of mileage out of the "middle" stories in the series because I have so much to work with and so many directions I can go in. However, characters, setting, and the premises/plots constantly evolve, change, and grow with each new story. They're not simply a rehash of the story that came before. If I couldn't bring something new to the series, I would stop writing "middle" stories for it. Without something new, there's no point in continuing a series. You'll give your readers nothing to hope for.

Unfortunately, being a writer of series can include a catch-22. Sometimes a series drags on long past the point of author interest. Other times a series ends far too soon. That was the case for me with the Family Heirlooms Series. I fell in love with so many of the secondary characters in this series that I came up with book ideas for two of those characters, sold them as non-series novels, but then realized I had many more tales to tell that connected with but didn't really fit in as part of the Family Heirlooms Series. Thus, the Friendship Heirlooms Series was born, continuing the theme of nuggets of faith passed down as heirlooms from friend to friend, heart to heart, soul mate to soul mate.

Bringing something new gets a bit tougher when you have a recurring character. In truth, readers tend to fall in love with characters and they don't want them to change too drastically because they've come to expect this character to basically be who she is from the first book to the last. Nevertheless, if this character doesn't evolve at all, she'll quickly become boring. To be lifelike, recurring characters can't remain static from one book to the next. They'll learn something from the previous book in the series and evolve in subtle but slightly altered ways.

However, these changes must make sense. A character can't be a complete idiot who barely graduated high school in one book and a professor of advanced college mathematics in the next. Nor would it make sense for a recurring character to be a waiter in one book and a doctor in the next—unless you believably explain how he arrived there. (I once critiqued a series in which a main series character had a drastic career change from one book to the next, with no explanation for the development. It simply didn't work.) Characters can't be inconsistent in smaller ways either: Your character can't pointedly avoid going out after dark in the first five books in the series and suddenly start hanging around an unsafe neighborhood at all hours of the night in the sixth. All changes to a character's personality must be logical and consistent with what you've previously set up.

I apologize in advance for slipping into television mode when I'm talking about books, but the following example is universal, extremely visual, and makes the point very well. The character of Elaine in the sitcom *Seinfeld* began the series as a person who stood up for the causes she felt strongly about. She could be considered the most moral (if such a word can truly be applied to any of the *Seinfeld* characters) of the group early on. Who can forget her stand on wearing real fur in "The Stranded" episode in Season 3? But Elaine begins to compromise her principles repeatedly over the next several seasons. In one of the final shows, when someone mentions her previous stand on wearing real fur, she says, "Eh, who's got the energy anymore?" and the viewer believes it. We've seen her "de-evolution" coming for a long time, so by this point we're convinced she doesn't have the same opinions as she once did. We've actually seen her grow out of them. The changes work for this particular character because she never remains static, and the change is gradual and believable.

The series authors I interviewed had a lot of insight into bringing something new with each book, which I'll share with you now.

> **P.A. BROWN:** "Make the changes believable based on the character, not something thrust at him for plot purposes. It should be a change that *means* something to the character. It should either make him better or introduce some problem he needs to overcome, not just a change picked out of a hat and thrown at him just for change's sake. My characters grow, and while they don't change enough to become totally different people, they aren't the same at the end of the series as they were at the beginning."

> **TIME-TRAVEL ROMANCE AUTHOR MARISSA ST JAMES:** "Characters are like real people. Their lives are influenced by the changes they face. Some changes are good, some aren't, but the character should be learning from them, changing and growing because of them."

> **CAT ADAMS:** "Life and crisis alter a person's perspective. That's also true for a series character. As people learn, they discover new information. In one book, that new information usually solves the crime or averts the world crisis. In the next book, the person is armed with the new information, so they don't make the same mistake. Of course, as authors,

that makes us raise the bar even higher—to present a new crisis where the hero/ine is forced once again into the position of reacting."

**JOANNE HALL:** "I believe telling the story of a character across a series leaves much more room for growth and change than might be found in a single volume. I don't think it's vital that a character have a personality transplant between books, but it's important that their experiences affect them, and that the reader can see the change between the beginning of the first book and the end of the final one, even though some of this change will occur offscreen, in the gaps between books."

**MULTIGENRE AUTHOR MICHELLE LEVIGNE:** "Characters need to remember what they learned in their last adventure. Once, while I was doing edits, my editor said, 'Too-stupid-to-live moment. Please make this more logical.' The hero goes up the mountainside, facing one more difficult task after another, getting stronger and picking up new tools along the way. Going backward or staying in the same spot is death for the hero and for the reader. I would be bored *reading* that, so I'm not going to *write* that."

I've established the importance of marrying character, plot, and setting in all the books in the series, being creative in the ways writers revisit characters, premise/plot, and setting in a series by avoiding or handling imaginatively the requisite conveyance of important information, and always bringing something new to each story in the series. Now I'll talk about the other crucial *C* in writing a series: *consistency*.

## CONSISTENCY

Before this book was even a gleam in my eye, I hadn't yet stopped to think about what *consistency* was in the writing sense. In truth, I wasn't sure of the difference between consistency and continuity, if one even existed. As you can imagine, I've done a lot of research in the course of writing this book, and I think some definitions are in order. Consistency has a wide variety of meanings, and I'll include the most relevant ones here:

- Agreement or logical coherence among things or parts
- Correspondence among related aspects; compatibility
- Reliability or uniformity of successive results or events
- Agreement or accordance with facts, form, or characteristics previously shown or stated. Agreement or harmony between parts of something complex
- The state or quality of holding or sticking together and retaining shape
- Conformity with previous attitudes, behavior, and practice

All of these make sense in writing, especially when it comes to a series. All your facts must match what you've established before. Everything has to fit together and retain the shape you've set for it earlier on. Readers have to rely on the establishment and conformity of facts from start to finish.

What about continuity? Some of the definitions I found are:

- The state or quality of being continuous
- An uninterrupted succession or flow; a coherent whole
- Logical sequence, cohesion, or connection
- Smooth, without break
- A continuous or connected whole
- The property of a continuous and connected period of time

A lot comes to mind for these definitions as well, certainly in the perspective of writing a series. I've already established some of these definitions in chapter one, when I discussed the types of series ties you can use. With the definition of continuity, you follow the same theme of coherency, logic, and sequence that continues over a connected period of time. However, I don't want to confuse the issue by using the same word for two different purposes in this book. We used the word *continuity* in chapter one to describe a recurring character. We'll use the word *consistency* when referring to sticking with the established, logical facts in a series from start to finish.

In *Pride and Prejudice* Elizabeth Bennet says, "The more I see of the world, the more I am dissatisfied with it; and every day confirms my belief of the inconsistency of all human characters … ." That's very true, but in a work of fiction, consistency is a post all writers have to hitch their wagons to if they want their readers to be happy.

Large or small, many or few, consistency errors have the effect of undermining the work in ways that can be annoying, baffling, and even embarrassing. For instance, in a mystery, the minutest, most seemingly inconsequential detail can sometimes be the most vital in the piece. But what if the author falls off the consistency wagon and that hint or clue is never mentioned again? Or, in the same vein, what if the vital detail wasn't established beforehand and fizzles at the crucial moment? Remembering details and using them at the right time is one of the most important jobs of the series author.

While readers may miss consistency errors, large problems will confuse and possibly alienate them to the point where they never finish the book and/or never read anything else by that author. Also remember that a small section of readers seem intent on pulling loose threads and "showing up" writers at the slightest hint of unprofessionalism. That section of the population doesn't need more fodder. With that warning in mind, let's discuss the importance of maintaining consistency in a series. In this section we're going to emphasize how crucial it is to be consistent in a series, but we won't deal with specific ways of being consistent (and organized) until chapter four.

From the beginning, my Wounded Warriors, Kaleidoscope, Angelfire Trilogies (I and II), Gypsy Road, Cowboy Fever, and Family Heirlooms (and the spin-off Friendship Heirlooms) Series centered on groups of friends, co-workers, and families, and I always knew exactly how many books I would need to complete each series. I can't stress enough how much planning in advance for these series really helped the consistency and intrigue in each, and allowed for a sense of foreshadowing and intense characterization that built momentum for upcoming stories.

Also, I try to write at least a year ahead of my releases—and consistency is one of the reasons for this. If I've completed Book 1 in a series a year earlier, and I'm currently working on Book 2 or 3, or even a later one, and I discover I've made a mistake in an earlier book or realize something new needs to be added sooner to help set up the viability of another detail in a later book, I know I can make these changes to earlier books *before* they're published.

I'd finished writing all seven books in my Kaleidoscope Series and was going over the proofing copy before publication when I realized I'd made a mistake in Book 3: I had established that two of the background characters who were involved were living together. I was planning to feature that couple in Book 5, a story in which they *weren't* living together and absolutely never could, since the situation the heroine was dealing with forbade it. In a minor boo-boo, I also initially described one of the characters as being 6'5" tall. In two of the later stories, he was only 6'4". Where did the other inch go? Some readers might have wondered. But I was able to fix these problems before the book was released in December 2010. Working so far ahead of my releases provided me with the time to fix the problems I found before the book was released.

Joanne Hall works ahead as well. She says, "I outline the entire trilogy, very roughly, then break it down into its component parts and outline those individually, making sure I know how each book begins and ends, while still leaving room for surprises!" Doing so before the books are published is particularly helpful. The last thing an author wants to do is paint herself into a corner. When that happens, she somehow has to work her way out logically and believably. This can happen if some of her books are published before she writes one that needs more room for growth or tweaking of previous stories. If an author has stumbled into the series after the first or second books are published, he might find himself adjusting things in ways he never imagined. Linda Varner Palmer agrees: "It can be tricky and limiting if I don't have a good idea of where I'm heading and something I said in the first book isn't working in the last book."

Sometimes an author doesn't get a chance to fix inconsistencies or difficult situations that crop up once one or more books in the series have already been published. Says Cindy Spencer Pape: "I found Book 3 of my Crazy H Series hard to write because I'd given the hero a nine-month-old son and some pretty serious injuries. Since both of those were laid out in earlier books, I couldn't take them out." Needless to say, once a book is published, it can be very costly or even impossible to change anything, so planning a series in advance is the best way to prevent problems.

Charlotte Boyett~Compo believes one of the most difficult things about writing a long-running series is staying consistent. "If you make a mistake, you *will* be called on it by some observant reader, if not your diligent editor. Mistakes happen even to A-list authors. In one of Stuart Woods's Stone Barrington Series books, Stone and his girlfriend have a child. That child's sex changed in the next book. I'm sure Mr. Woods's editor got swatted for that one." Says Luisa Buehler, "Sometimes errors get in the book. All you can do is hope to change them in a subsequent printing." Some of Luisa's early books in her Grace Marsden Mysteries are being reissued, and she's very happy to be "able to go back to the first book and tweak it based on my perch from six books later."

Michelle Levigne admitted to having problems to work around in her series. "With the Tabor Heights books, events overlap, people visit from book to book, and I have a calendar system I set up to make sure that Max isn't in Tabor in one book, but in another book, on the same day, I say she's in Hollywood! Sometimes I've had to totally revise large sections of books because of a change I made in one book that creates a ripple effect through the others."

Writer of paranormal romance Ann Tracy Marr says, "I have not come across any major inconsistencies, but the more books in the series, the worse it will get. I doubt my publisher would allow me to alter a published book, so I had better not goof."

Speaking of publishers, J.M. Smith of Wild Horse Press told me she's pleased when authors have "more than one book ready to turn in at a time—that way we can catch things as we go." Champagne Books publisher J. Ellen Smith adds, "A reader will spot errors in a heartbeat. To avoid any, we keep author and editor together so that both are familiar with previous works and can spot the issues before they are problematic." Miriam Pace at Parker Publishing, Inc., goes a bit further: "There is little we can do to change an error once the book goes to print, but we've discovered that if we put the digital version out first, we can make the corrections before the books go to print. We also give the author one last chance to fix errors with the typeset manuscript. Errors will still get through and cause some embarrassment, but we do try to correct them if we can."

Kim Richards, co-founder and CEO of Damnation Books and Eternal Press, didn't mince words about the effect inconsistency can ultimately have on an author's career: "Inconsistencies should be dealt with in the editing stages. Honestly, though, if there are too many, we will ask for revisions before contracting, or we won't want to do the subsequent book." Scary! Advanced planning and stringent organization are needed to keep a series on track, and, as I said, I'll talk about ways to do that in chapter four.

When writing a series, consistency problems fall into five main categories. I mentioned earlier that I love Phil Farrand's Nitpicker Guides to *Star Trek* and *The X-Files*. These guides have a Nitpicker's Prime Directive, which is that "All nits picked shall derive from sources the creators consider canonical." (In other words, the television episodes and movies—and not the novels—are the only sources considered authoritative.) All authors should have a prime directive, or series bible, which you'll learn about in the next chapter. In the directive, you'll record things that are canonical and cannot be changed, altered, or manipulated unless you have an absolutely critical reason (and effective method) for doing so.

In each of his hilarious, thought-provoking nitpicking guides, Phil covers every episode of most of the seasons with a brief summary of the episode, ruminations, and great moments, followed by the nits he and other Nitpicker Guild members have come up with for it, each of which falls into one of four major categories: Plot Oversights, Changed Premises, Equipment Oddities, and Continuity and Production Issues. In terms of severity, these first two are major problems and you can only hope to catch the problems in preproduction so they aren't set in stone. The last two are minor. They're usually just embarrassing rather than series killing.

In *The Nitpicker's Guide for X-Philes*, Phil introduces a new category, Unanswered Questions, which could be major, depending on which question is left unanswered. I'll explore each of these inconsistency categories, molding them slightly to fit the needs of a series author.

## OVERSIGHTS

Oversights are a catchall category for anything in a plotline, character, or setting that concerns illogical, unexplainable, or unrealistic courses of action and plot holes, including coincidence contrivance (writer needs it to work and so creates the groundwork on the spot to patch up a means to force it to work) and convenience justifications (it was the only way to make A fit with B, so I had to do it, didn't I?).

A *deus ex machina* situation is one in which an improbable event or element is introduced into a story to resolve all the problematic situations and bring the story to a close. In a conventional Greek tragedy the producers actually lowered an actor playing a god onto the stage at the end of the play and he resolved all the conflicts. Talk about unsatisfying for the audience! Any author worth his salt needs to create plausible backstory and motivation for every action, and she has to make characters heroic enough to solve their own problems. That's why Oversights are so major in series consistency.

If your character does something that makes no sense in the course of the action or in terms of their internal conflicts and motivations, or if you include a plot point merely for convenience sake, you've got yourself a nasty oversight. If, in one book, your character is so scarred by the death of a spouse that he doesn't believe he can ever move on or fall in love again, and in the next book he has already become involved with someone new and never thinks about how he's a widower, you've made a huge oversight that readers probably won't tolerate, let alone accept. In other words, you go from one situation to the next without any explanation for the radical change. Remember the discussion on plants in chapter two: If you want something to be believable, you need to set it up logically and you need to set it up early enough so it will be readily accepted by the reader. That absolutely requires advance planning.

## CHANGED PREMISE

This category includes information given in one episode that directly contradicts information in another. In a series this can be fatal. Somehow *Star Trek* and *The X-Files* flourished despite the countless occurrences of these

Changed Premises, but both shows lose a little bit of respect each time a viewer recognizes one of these errors.

If your book series has a Changed Premise from one book to the next, readers will lose respect as well. If anything concerning character, plot, or setting conflicts with something that was previously established, it would fit under the Changed Premise heading. If you alter the structure or foundational facts that were previously set up in the series, even if you do it for a very good reason, you've changed the premise for the story, and readers will notice. If you can't find a way to make something believable within the entire scope of the series, you'll lose readers, perhaps for the remainder of the series. As an example, if your vampire can't see his own reflection in the first two books in the series, but in the third he desperately needs to be able to see his reflection in order for your plot to work, you've changed an established premise. You'll have to come up with a solid bit of plausibility to get readers to accept the change. If you create a world in which no outsiders are tolerated in the first three books, yet in the fourth one a stranger shows up and is ushered into the heart of the community with open arms, you've changed the premise of your series.

I've read the Harry Potter Series countless times (twice a year in its entirety, in fact), but something that bothers me every time I read it is the fact that in Books 2 through 4, the author states quite clearly that the carriages that take students from the Hogsmeade train station to Hogwarts are "horseless." In Book 5 we learn that they're not horseless at all but are pulled by thestrals, which are invisible to anyone except those who have seen death. Harry's mother was murdered right in front of Harry, and he spends most of the series remembering that event a piece at a time. If anyone could see those thestrals right from the beginning of the series, when the "horseless" carriages were first introduced in Book 2, it would have been Harry. Did Rowling not realize she needed to do something with these horseless carriages until Book 5, when thestrals become crucial to the plot, or did Hogwarts only just start using the thestrals to pull them, in which case, I wonder what pulled them before—simple magic? Why did school officials suddenly feel the need to have actual animals, albeit invisible ones, pulling them in Book 5?

In an interview Rowling stated that Harry couldn't see them before this point because Cedric Diggory's death hadn't happened until after Book 4. Um ... huh? I'm not sure I buy that, given the reasons I already stated about Harry's mother, but that's not a serious faux pas, all things considered. The author also added that the person viewing the thestrals must accept the death they've seen. Because Harry was too young and didn't remember fully his mother's death, he hadn't accepted it until this time. Again, this seems like a stretched explanation to me. Given Rowling's absolute brilliance in setting up countless plants that become important in later series stories, I think I would have preferred the author owning up to this Changed Premise rather than providing an unsatisfactory explanation. Yes, all writers make many mistakes, large or small. If they can be corrected plausibly or worked in so readers accept them, great. If they can't, the best we can do is admit our mistake and move on.

### TECHNICAL PROBLEMS

While problems with equipment and technical oddities were often an issue in the *Star Trek* and *X-Files* series, (and may be in your series, too, if you include a lot of technology that must be realistic), this kind of inconsistency can also deal with inadvertently or indiscriminately jumping into alternate viewpoints or changing descriptions of characters or settings because what was previously mentioned has been forgotten. If your character always speaks in a certain dialect and suddenly stops in a subsequent book, that's a technical problem. Names and jobs can also accidentally change through the course of a series. If your character's hair color or eye color changes, or if he was 6'5" in the first two books in the series but drops an inch in later stories, you have what may be considered technical problems.

For instance, in *The X-Files* both main characters used cell phones throughout most of the series, but the phones were used inconsistently, in ways that forced the viewers to question the logic. In one episode, Mulder was trapped underground in the middle of a desert called Nowhere—was there actually a cell phone tower nearby that allowed him to get good reception? In other cases Mulder and Scully didn't use the phones when they should have, and in each of these cases, it was convenient to the plot *and* for the writers/creators that they didn't use their phones to call the other to their rescue because it would have solved the plot of that particular episode too quickly.

These are probably minor and simply annoying issues at most, and you probably won't lose any readers with such blunders, but dotting all your *I*s and crossing all your *T*s will make fans appreciate you that much more.

## CONTINUITY AND PRODUCTION ISSUES

Again, in these television shows errors often crept up as a direct result of someone on staff not checking the manual or previous episodes before going ahead with the episode. How often was a setting shot reused and only slightly altered in *Star Trek* because coming up with something new would have been expensive or time-consuming? In a classic *Star Trek* episode, the creators decided to establish that the Romulans had stolen the design of Klingon ships—so they could use a Klingon ship they'd already created. Not only that, but the Romulans also used Klingon weapons. Cheaper for the creators, yes, but viewers can't help but groan at these production issues. If you're doing anything "halfway" with your series simply because it would be a hassle to find a better, more creative way of handling it, you're making your own production problems. Readers will feel your impatience and probably wonder why you skimped.

There are other issues to consider. For instance, timelines can become uncertain or erroneous or even overlap in the course of a series. This happened quite a bit in *The X-Files*, which gave dates for nearly every episode— dates that conflict with other episodes and create a conundrum that can't be repaired with any amount of reasoning. How could Mulder have been here, nearly losing his life, in this episode when it was established in a previous one that he was elsewhere doing something totally different? He can't be in two places at the same time.

If you give a character two birthdays or have him get younger instead of older as a series progresses, these are less crucial issues but nevertheless *problems*. I call issues like these minor because, unless you have fans who are ravenous and must know and understand every facet of your series, many won't sit down and figure out timelines or even see a problem. It's only authors who write a series that warrants a compendium (or two in Diana Gabaldon's case, with her Outlandish Companion volumes) who will have readers checking up on them constantly. That said, as an author, I've had a timeline problem only once or twice, but I cringe to no end whenever someone mentions those one or two mistakes (infrequently, but still...). An editor might resist making a change, however minor, before the release date of a book, but I've always been adamant and immovable about such things. No self-respecting author allows this kind of error to go unchecked if there's a way to fix it. Keep everything straight from the start and you'll never have to face the humiliation of being called on your goof.

## UNANSWERED QUESTIONS

Here Phil Farrand expresses his belief that the creators of the show intentionally left certain issues unsolved (namely, the overall series arc) to be resolved in later episodes or at the series conclusion. I bring this one up in the scheme of writing a series because I've always felt that the creators of *The X-Files* intentionally left the overall series arc dangling with so many frustrating unanswered questions in order to continue the show with movies. I also suspect they did this because they simply *wanted* to leave the resolution of the series arc mysterious and unanswered. They either didn't have a good resolution planned or they wanted to contain the mystery indefinitely.

If the author is never going to answer a nagging question, why invest anything, especially time and passion, in the series? Leaving a series arc dangling isn't something an author can do in a book series unless she sets up the series from the first as an open-ended one that probably won't have definitive closure. While each book in the series must have satisfactory individual story arc resolutions, all series arc questions must be answered in the final book of the series or readers will be furious, perhaps enough to ban you as an author for life. They'll feel cheated and rightly so. Don't underestimate the damage a vengeful reader can do to your career. (Have you read Stephen King's *Dolores*

*Claiborne*? Do it now and take heed!) To write a series is to promise the closure and/or resolution of unanswered series arc questions. Think of it this way: With the first book in your series, you've presented a question and asked your readers to be patient as you string out the development of this theme through several books. You've promised that an answer will be delivered in the last book. If you don't deliver it, you've stolen time, money, and even reader emotions, all with a careless shrug of purposeful neglect.

In the last chapter I told you how some open-ended series (no closure in sight) probably don't need series arcs and therefore don't require series arc resolutions. While my writing partner, Chris Spindler, and I didn't have a clear series arc for our Falcon's Bend Series, neither of us expected it to end as abruptly as it did. It was supposed to be an open-ended series that we would come back to as often as we wanted for many, many years. Our first publisher released Book 1 in hardcover, but then spent the next year hemming and hawing about publishing Book 2, though it was edited and ready to go. Chris and I recognized the sinking ship we were on. The publisher was having a private crisis and it affected the entire publishing company. We bailed, got another publisher interested, and Books 1 and 2 and the first novella collection were duly released. But then that publisher, too, lost all interest because of a personal crisis, and Chris and I were again lost at sea. We pulled up anchor again and found another publisher. Books 3 and 4 were released first to pacify our readers who'd been waiting endlessly, and Books 1 and 2 and the first novella collection were reissued in short order. Do you already know what I'm going to say at this point? This series had a death wish, and I think Chris and I were finally beginning to believe it might come true. Our new publisher, due to various issues, decided not to publish any new material. This happened while we were in the middle of edits on our second novella collection. The problems steamrolled and issues couldn't be resolved. Ultimately, the publisher gave us back the rights to the second novella collection.

Chris and I decided to discontinue the series, in part because I was working on so many other (solo) series at the time, in part because of the repeated publishing problems, and in part because three times unlucky was all we could handle. I'd already had two other novels in mind for the series, so the second novella collection had no sense of closure at all. Unanswered questions lingered in the main characters' lives and that bothered me too much to allow. Chris and I had started an open-ended series, but we'd fallen in love with the characters, as had our fans, and we didn't want anyone to feel disappointed or cheated by the abrupt end. So I went back into several of the stories in the second novella collection and provided happy endings and a sense of closure for all of the major characters.

Then, since the book had been professionally edited, I published it myself. Based on the feedback Chris and I received, readers were satisfied with the way the series ended as a whole, even if they (and we) were sad that it had to come to an untimely end. Luck struck finally when a new publisher accepted within a matter of hours my proposal to republish the series. The whole series was reissued from June 2012 to February 2013, and Chris and I have sold two brand-new novels in the series.

### AVOIDING INCONSISTENCY

In short, Oversights, Changed Premises, Technical Problems, Timeline and Production Issues, as well as Unanswered Questions are the five main categories all consistency problems will fall into. Avoid them by staying organized and planning the series as far in advance as possible. In chapter four, I'll talk about series organization, which should clear up the majority of these potential problems. I'll also create a checklist with these categories so you can go back into each story in your series when it's finished and ensure that you haven't inadvertently bungled something.

## OTHER CONSIDERATIONS WHEN WRITING A SERIES

No reference manual about writing a series would be complete without some tips from both readers and writers of series.

## SERIES READER TIPS

I've been "listening" to conversations about series on various online list-servs and forums. You might be interested in some of the comments I've heard from series readers. I won't use exact quotes, specific names, or titles/series referenced, but the gist of these comments are extremely revealing and worthy of noting so you can be sure to avoid the pitfalls and emulate the successes of series authors who have come before. Also notice that readers know almost as much about writing as authors do! Readers are savvy, and you forget that to your demise.

- I've read only a few series past seven books and still enjoyed them as much as I did the first. I enjoy spending time in those worlds. In all of these, the characters have grown, made mistakes, learned from their mistakes … and found a way to carry on and keep me interested. With other series, the later books start to drag. With the release of Book 12 of a certain author's series, the series seemed to undergo a resurgence, but I got really bogged down in Book 18 and found that I didn't care anymore about the next books in the series. Everything's starting to sound the same to me. For me, the only time a series can get too long is when the author is bored with it (it shows!), when the series is repeating itself, and when the scenarios feel forced. Most should probably stop at Book 5. Even though I'm going to miss these characters, I want to remember them before they outlive their welcome. I quail when I find a series that's really long. The investment in time and money to read the entire series is daunting. And sometimes you can't find the early books.

- What I hate about a series is the huge jump in characters. While I love all of a certain author's series, the ones over three books include huge character leaps in behavior—it's infuriating for a character to do something so *out* of previous character. Too many long series tend to go down that awful path of information dumps, genre shifts, mood swings, character assassinations (both literal and figurative), and off-the-wall changes that mean Book 12 doesn't vaguely resemble Book 1. I've read a certain author's series for years, but I'm getting weary of the premise now and wish the author would move in a new direction with the series.

- If I like a series, no wait is too long for the next book. Piers Anthony's final Incarnations of Immortality came out about fifteen years after the book before it, and it sold like hotcakes. Some people went back and reread the first seven books. If I love a series, I'll wait as long as I have to.

- I love when series books can be read separately but aren't quite complete without each other. I enjoy when previous characters in a series are mentioned or have brief cameos in new books. I get seriously overjoyed at this bit of "reality" when I'm given an insider moment, knowing these people from previous books.

- A decade ago, most readers preferred single titles as opposed to series. Today, series appear to be the rule rather than the exception. We seem to live in an instant gratification society. For me, the anticipation is part of the appeal ... but if I have to wait too long, I forget what I've read and can easily be distracted with something new.

- I'm not a fan of a series in which there are different characters in each story. I just don't buy the deep relationships that are established in such a short time.

- I love series, but, because I read so many series, it's too bad a short synopsis of what has happened before (kind of like a TV show that gives you a "what happened last week" refresher) can't be at the beginning of each new addition to a series. I don't like to be bored if I already know the basic setup introduced in earlier books in the series, but I also don't like to be confused if I've forgotten something from a previous book. If I'm given too many details about an earlier plot and then go back to read that story, the read is less satisfying because I knew too much. Even if the story is great, I don't like to peek at the end of the book before I start reading it.

- I love series, but one in particular crashed and burned for me when the author gratuitously killed off the main character. I threw all her books on my keeper shelf into the trash, and I'll never buy another one. I felt like it was a breach of trust. The act didn't follow the plot, it was random, and, based on what the author said later on her website about it, it was a conscious decision made to take the series in a different direction.

- I used to wait to get the books in a series until they were all available. But I realized that whether or not a book gets written sometimes depends on previous sales. If readers are waiting for all the books to come out before they buy them, then sales will be abysmal and the series could be shelved. Also, if you wait to buy the books until they're all out, some of the series titles will be harder to get. Some readers won't start a long series until they think it's over. But I've learned not to save up a series to read in one fell swoop.

- I have a love/hate relationship with series. I enjoy having the characters go on, but I hate having a book end in the middle of the story, before all the important plots are resolved. Then having to wait a year or more for the next one…. If you're going to have a series, the stories should stand on their own and *finish*.

I want to repeat that these are *reader* comments—not writers who got together and started punching in on the pros and cons of a series. Most of these comments are ones I think I've been steering toward in this book. However, though I often say that few rules can't be broken, when writing a series it's sometimes necessary to consider certain guidelines when it comes to satisfying savvy readers.

## SERIES AUTHOR TIPS

Experienced authors can also impart many pearls of wisdom to writers who are new to series. I've presented a list of them below in no particular order.

### SET YOUR OWN GROUND RULES FOR THE SERIES

CAT ADAMS: "*Don't cheat!* I can't stress that strongly enough. If you create a reality rule, it must *remain* a rule. Nothing will lose readers for you faster than allowing a character to do something you insisted in Book 1 could never happen. If you create a crisis that will get the hero/ine killed unless he or she breaks a world rule, then either the hero/ine must die or the crisis must change to allow for an out. This provides a logical reality where, even if the rules are weird, there *are* rules, and there are characters that are both interesting and fallible."

**CINDY SPENCER PAPE:** "You *never* change the basic premise—if the series is romance, don't throw in a book without a happy ending. If they're all mysteries, don't throw in a book with no suspense."

Whenever I start writing an Incognito Series book, I have a couple of ground rules for myself: First and most important, I want to remain true to the premise of the Network that I've established throughout the series, or, as a reviewer from Long and Short of It Reviews says, "to cleverly write within the rules of this world, yet manage to spin it on its axis, taking the reader on a new journey." Next, I want to offer something totally new and unexpected with each book, yet I always want to achieve what a reviewer from Once Upon A Romance Review said of the series: that I anticipate the reader's desires and am able to deliver the story she wants. Both of these ground rules are crucial to me. They'll never change.

## THINK BIG

**VIJAYA SCHARTZ:** "Make the scope of the series premise wide enough to give you room to create all sorts of new themes and stories and introduce new characters. Your publisher may want more than three books if the series is successful, and if you locked yourself into a small box, you may choke your inspiration, or there may not be room to grow. Patricia Cornwell did a fabulous job of taking a young, slightly flawed secondary character from *At Risk* and turning him into a chilling serial killer in *The Front*. Never assume that the last book of the series is the very last, unless you kill off all the main characters … and even then, in sci-fi, science can revive the dead, [or the dead can] travel through time. Series have a way of taking on a life of their own. I've been known to write prequels as well out of desperation, and I'm not the only one. Look what happened to *Star Wars* decades later."

**LUISA BUEHLER:** "Develop a series arc so you can think out your series in broad strokes. This helps you know if you have a trilogy or a longer series. Discover your passion for a type of character, place, avocation, and occupation (gardener, long-distance runner, curator, Colorado lodge, amateur sleuth) and create a story line that you can sustain throughout several books. *Live* with the characters and their lives."

**MARGARET L. CARTER:** "Choose a background and character situation complex enough to sustain multiple plots over the long term. If the character faces new challenges that evoke previously untapped resources within him, that aspect should take care of itself. Traumatic experiences can awaken emotional depths in a character and cause him to change believably, as can encounters with new places and different kinds of people he has never met before. Also, over a long-running series, the type of problem the hero has to solve can differ from book to book; as I've heard it suggested, if one book deals with his love life, the next might deal with his career or his family conflicts. The gravity of the problems, ideally, should escalate, but doing so can be difficult to sustain over a long stretch. If the hero reaches the stage of saving the universe, what can he do for an encore? In the hilarious opening chapter of *Callahan's Key*, Spider Robinson 'lampshades' this problem when the protagonist is told, 'We need you to save the universe.' He responds with an exasperated, 'What, *again*?'"

## TWISTS

**CHARLOTTE BOYETT-COMPO:** "Introduce both individual story and series plot twists so you ensure that you're not writing the same book over and over with each subsequent series title. First, you must have a unique concept. Be honest with what you are creating and come up with something that hasn't been done before. Yes, there have been vampires and werewolves for many years, but there is always something new you can incorporate into the rehashing of their legends. Create something new, an unexpected twist to the tale that will wow the reader."

**DENISE DIETZ:** "My readers expect originality and a twist ending, so I rarely go with my first impulse."

**N.J. WALTERS:** "It's tough to keep up with reader expectation over the long haul. You have to constantly push the envelope and come up with surprises. That can be harder to do when there are already 'rules' in place for a series. Each series book should be different from the last in some way. If you're simply recycling the same plot, you'll be bored and so will the readers."

## UP THE ANTE WITH THE PROTAGONIST, VILLAIN, AND THE ADVERSITIES THEY FACE

**CAT ADAMS:** "Create enough failings in the hero that he's always at a disadvantage. Or, if each book features a different character, create rules that keep the good guys from getting too powerful."

**CINDY SPENCER PAPE:** "When starting a series, it's important to create characters an audience can relate to. The characters need to be well-rounded and intriguing. If the series is based on secondary characters, the author needs to make those characters interesting enough that someone would want to read about them. Otherwise, the series dies with the first book. If your readers don't want to see more of these people, then a series is kind of pointless."

**P.A. BROWN:** "I think readers can get bored if the plot from one book to the next is a shallow copy of the previous. Each book must be strong on its own, and characters can't keep doing the same things or making the same mistakes. I know there are some well-known series I've read that I stopped reading for that reason. The main protagonist never changed and kept repeating her mistakes again and again."

**LUISA BUEHLER:** "I don't use a villain who appears in the last twenty pages. I like to develop the villain so he or she is worthy of my heroine's efforts. I think it's important when writing a long series to keep the plot moving and to introduce new characters the readers can warm to (or violently dislike!) so as not to let things stagnate."

**JANET ELAINE SMITH:** "If the characters are becoming boring to you, they probably are to the readers, too."

**MULTIGENRE AUTHOR DARRELL BAIN:** "I guess if a series is long enough readers could get bored. If the author is good enough, e.g., David Weber's Honor Harrington Series, it can go on a *long* time without boring readers. And he writes very long books, too! To keep readers from being bored, you have to introduce new characters to oppose your protagonist(s) and new situations that are unique to the series."

## CONSIDER THE RESEARCH NECESSARY FOR A SERIES

**LUISA BUEHLER:** "Determine your timeframe and make sure you're comfortable with the research needed—historical or modern day, there is much to learn. It's always what we don't know that gets us!"

## KEEP YOUR PROMISE TO THE READER

**MICHELLE LEVIGNE:** "Promises *must* be kept. There can be strings left dangling, but you should give strong hints that the loose ends will be resolved eventually, as well as hints about *how* they will be resolved. There are also certain conventions you must follow, depending on the genre. Romances demand a happily-ever-after. Follow the rules of your genre. Readers have certain expectations of genres. You must fulfill reader expectations and keep the promises you made in the opening pages of the book."

**N.J. WALTERS:** "The only thing that's a given for me is the happily-ever-after. I write romance and that means a happy ending. Plus, readers expect the hero and heroines to have certain codes of honor. They're certainly not perfect and, in fact, the more flawed they are the better. But there are lines they won't cross. Non-romance writers can certainly challenge any boundaries they want without expectation."

**MARY JEAN KELSO:** "Most important of all: Don't mess with the happily-ever-after! If I killed off Emma from *The Wallflower*, I'd have a revolt on my hands. Ditto the whole divorce thing. No matter how I personally feel about an old character, that happily-ever-after the readers want *must* remain in place!"

When you incorporate more than one genre into a story, you need to complete dual promises to readers. For instance, a romantic suspense must have equal parts romance and suspense ... but keep your audience in mind at all times. Generally, a female reader's demand for suspense and action/adventure is radically different than a man's requirements. While numerous male fans have enjoyed my Incognito Series, for the most part the suspense in each of the romances fulfills a *woman's* expectations. In other words, the suspense is just enough to enhance and validate the plot, but not so much as to overwhelm the romance. My audience is always women first, and I cater to them, though I believe men also appreciate my work.

## PLAY FAIR

**FRAN ORENSTEIN:** "I believe that readers can get bored with a series that is never-ending. Five books should be the maximum in a series that has a continuing theme that must be resolved. After that, the quest becomes sluggish and just fills space on the page. To keep readers interested, each book should present a new aspect of the characters and exciting events that are all designed to lead to the ultimate ending. I would never foreshadow the ending so that the reader can easily guess what's going to happen in the final book. The writer must use a cliff-hanger to lead into the next book and make the reader want to wait breathlessly for it to come out, but not to give away the ultimate ending."

**MICHELLE LEVIGNE:** "Victories have to be won fairly. If you're going to have a surprise ending, the reader has to say, in effect, 'I wasn't expecting that, but, looking back at everything that happened ... it's the only way the story *could* end.'"

**PARANORMAL AUTHOR M. FLAGG:** "In a romance, I'd never allow my hero to fall out of love with his soul mate. That one's a big no-no. Every character should have a level of predictability, but enough spice and depth to stay fresh. At the same time, you'll never peel an onion and find a peach pit at its center. In my series, good always trumps evil. That's a must."

Even in an inspirational series, where the characters are usually struggling to have the faith to trust God instead of their own efforts, the characters must find their own strength, their own willpower, their own logic for the choices they make. Nothing else would feel fair to the reader, who has to believe she also has the strength, faith, and willpower to make hard choices in her own life.

## DON'T KILL THE PROTAGONIST—OR ANY OTHER BELOVED CHARACTER IN YOUR SERIES—WITHOUT A DARN GOOD REASON!

In my interviews with authors and publishers of series, this was the number one no-no on nearly *everyone's* list. Only one author, Cat Adams, said the exact opposite: That you shouldn't be afraid to kill your "darlings" or, at the very least, in an action series, there *must* be a threat of disaster to create the crisis in the reader's mind. If nobody *ever* dies, there's no risk of loss. Even though you may love every single thing you've done and every character has value, people die senselessly, or, at the other end of the spectrum, with purpose and perhaps even honor. A character in *Star Trek* said that, essentially, how you deal with death is at least as important as how you deal with life. Writers need to have courage to take that leap—for the good of the series and for the enjoyment of the readers.

I take a fierce stand against killing important fictional players, but even I'm guilty of killing a beloved character in one of my series. Naturally, I think I did it in a smart way: I killed him before he became a crucial character in readers' minds. The characters all loved him, relied on him, held a sort of hero worship for him. But the reader hadn't yet invested herself in that character when I sent him to his death. In this way, the character's life and death was explored through the eyes of all the series characters over time, and the devastation was limited. I posted a review I received for the final book in that series earlier in this book: "In *White*

*Rainbow*, Karen Wiesner has come up with a powerful conclusion to her Wounded Warriors Series, one that will keep fresh the impact that the characters and books have had. I thank Karen Wiesner for the chance to connect with Wendy and Paul, Steve and Kristina, Gwen and Dylan, Gregg and Stormie, Jessie and Flint, and Tommie ... always Tommie in the background." I do think I succeeded in creating a beloved character without devastating readers with his death.

Readers have a very hard time letting go of characters they've come to love, especially over a period of several books and/or in relation to the main character in the series. I will probably never forgive J.K. Rowling for killing so many characters that I loved in the Harry Potter Series. To this day, I'm not sure why she needed to kill Harry's godfather—the first family Harry ever had. Did it add to the story/series, or would the story/series have been better if Sirius had lived? Honestly, I think she could have done this a dozen different ways and had a better story/series for it. For the most part, my distress over this stemmed from the fact that Harry had spent his whole life wanting a family of his own. She gave it to him, and then, two books later, she cruelly yanked it away. I kept hoping she would figure out some clever way of "extracting" Sirius from the arch he fell into and disappeared.

I also cried when Dumbledore was killed, but I will concede that it was necessary to the series as a whole. However, I don't think killing Dobby, Hedwig, Lupin and Tonks (new parents!), and Fred Weasley were at all necessary and could certainly have been avoided if the author had had more consideration for her readers. All of that is said with the earlier declaration that I love this series—I read it twice a year—but I suffer every time I read it because of these thoughtless, *needless* losses.

My grief aside, here are some other tidbits that reflect the majority opinion about this issue:

**MARY JEAN KELSO:** "Keep in mind that your readers don't want to let these characters go. If they did, you wouldn't still be writing about them. In the first draft of *The Homesteader's Legacy*, which I saw as only a sequel, I killed off the main character. My "first reader" got so upset I had to rewrite the first few chapters of the manuscript. And, of course, without the main character, I had no series. So don't get rid of a character permanently unless you are finished with the series or can dream up a way to bring him back."

**LINDA VARNER PALMER:** "What I would never do to a series is kill off the main character. There's no reader satisfaction in that."

**CHARLOTTE BOYETT-COMPO:** "You don't kill off a major character. *Ever!* That's a good way to lose readers. I did that in one book because I saw no other way for the character to go, and as a result I got many e-mails and letters from readers who were very vocal about their anger. Reviewers understood why I did what I did and even applauded it, but readers didn't like it one bit. I've since made the decision to never do that again … unless I find a way to bring the character back in a future book and give him a happily-ever-after."

## CAMEO APPEARANCES

**LINDA VARNER PALMER:** "Give evidence that the happy endings in earlier books are still in effect, i.e., characters show up in later books and are doing well."

## LOOKING FORWARD

**P.A. BROWN:** "If you write crime novels, put them in a place where interesting crimes can keep happening. Otherwise you end up with the Cabot Cove syndrome—where Jessica Fletcher is always running into the dead bodies of people she knows. That's not very realistic for a small, sleepy town anywhere. Also, be careful how unique you make a character. Some authors want to give their protagonist a problem or disability that comes back to bite them when they want to keep the series going. One that comes to mind is Josh Lanyon's Adrien English Series. He gave his main protagonist a weak heart that put him in constant danger of dying. He couldn't just drop the thread in later books and had to work around the fact that Adrien had this limitation on him. It's possible it prevented Lanyon from having Adrien do many physical things in future books. Another bit of advice: Do not make your character too old. If your character is an eighty-year-old woman in Book 1, her age is going to limit how much time may pass in future books. It would force the author to keep the character in near stasis—each book basically set in the same time—with no real changes taking place."

## KEEP READERS HOOKED FROM
## THE START OF A SERIES TO THE FINISH

**DIANA CASTILLEJA:** "You only have one chance, maybe two, to hook a reader on a series. Each book has to have its own value and purpose or the series will be ignored."

**JOANNE HALL:** "There's a lot to consider when you're trying to decide whether to write a series. First and foremost, does your first book have enough intrigue to make readers care to go further? If the first book isn't out-of-this-world phenomenal, chances are no one will want to follow you through a series. But, even if you do catch the reader's interest the first time, the second, even the fifteenth, you have to make sure every book is something a reader could pick up without first having read any of the other books in the series and still derive immense pleasure from reading. Ideally, they'll want to read the rest of the series. However, don't fall into the trap of writing three books when you could tell your story in one. Keep them hooked. Make sure you can maintain a decent level of drama and tension throughout your series. There will probably be something big and dramatic happening at the beginning and the end, but if you're writing a series, there will be an awful lot of words between the beginning and the end. Make sure you fill those thousands of pages with excitement! Middle books can often suffer from this. The payoff at the end has to be good. Reading a three-hundred-page book with an unsatisfying ending isn't nearly as annoying as reading five three-hundred-page books only to find at the end of it all that the ending is, in Internet parlance, 'a bit meh.'"

**ROWENA CHERRY:** "Each book in the series ought to be good value for the purchase price, not a glorified three-hundred-page trailer for the next installment. The writer needs to be sure the subsequent books in a series are just as exciting as the first one. We all get disappointed when we find the author coasting in the last books of a series."

**KIM RICHARDS:** "When you start the next book in a series, you need a clear, compelling reason for continuing the series. If there isn't that pressing a need, a series can quickly burn out the reader and stop them from caring."

**DEBORAH MACGILLIVRAY:** "Each book has to be great on its own. People will pick up Book 2 or 3 without having read the others, but each story needs to stand on its own two feet."

**CINDY SPENCER PAPE:** "Write a good story every time!"

**LINDA VARNER PALMER:** "Speaking from my own reading experience, I think readers can get bored, especially if the same villain shows up again and again."

**DIANA CASTILLEJA:** "I try to keep readers involved in the stories and the characters, to make them feel that 'What happens next?' question with each ending."

**J.M. SMITH:** "By the ninth or tenth book, the author is typically running out of ideas and writing for the sake of keeping the series going. But if the stories don't remain fresh and unique, then she'll lose her audience. Also, it depends on how many secondary characters you have to work with. It's possible to do a spin-off of the main series, starting with fresh ideas and new characters."

## Metamorphosing Series Characters (Pros and Cons)

**ROWENA CHERRY:** "Earlier books' heroes and heroines cannot morph into villains (because villains have to be punished, and that would mess with their happily-ever-after), but they can certainly be thorns in the sides of the next hero and heroine."

**DEBORAH MACGILLIVRAY:** "I don't like characters changing drastically within a series. I can think of three series where there were secondary characters who were the villains, and, suddenly, in other books in the series, they become heroes. This shift in character left me confused emotionally! I hated these men in the first books, yet suddenly they are warm and fuzzy down the road? I don't think readers can really come to love a character they have previously hated, especially if there was a very compelling reason for them to be villains. In the three series I saw do this, I was never convinced the hero was a *hero,* and it left those stories flat. In one series, a man committed rape, yet in the third book in the four-book series, he was the hero. I could never really commit to loving this man because I couldn't blot out what he had done in the first book."

I was actually surprised by how many series authors said that a villain in one book couldn't be the hero in the next. I don't agree at all, but I suppose there could be some precedent for it based on the severity of the villain's crimes. I've created three villains whom I've brought back later in a trilogy or series as heroes. In the first instance, the hero in a later book was unforgivably cruel (even emotionally abusive) to the heroine in the first book in the trilogy. In Book 3, this villain redeemed himself completely and became a hero because the reader understood that there was some justification for his behavior. (Of course on the part of the heroine in the first book, she wasn't able to see how cruelly she'd wronged this man.) I find this realistic because there are always two sides to every story, and I told them in two separate books.

In the second instance in which I turned a villain into a hero, the hero was a drug dealer and the heroine believed he cheated on her numerous times with other women. This was established in earlier books in the series, but in Book 5, the heroine learns several facts that change her mind and allow her and the reader to forgive this man. I might have cheated a bit on this example because, in fact, the hero was working for the DEA undercover and he never *actually* cheated on the heroine—he just made her think it for reasons that are learned over the course of the book. In any case, it was easy to forgive the previous misconceptions about him.

In the last instance of turning a villain into a hero, the heroine of the last book in the series had been painted scarlet throughout Books 1 through 5 in the series. She was totally guilty of every crime. But I redeemed her at the end. The reviewers loved it:

> "I was prepared to struggle to like Jessie based upon her very selfish and self-absorbed behaviors from the prior books. The emotion that Ms. Wiesner evokes is truly engaging. She has created characters that you root for and you care about. You want to know what happens to each character and, of course, you are glad when they overcome obstacles to reach a happy ending." (You Gotta Read Reviews)

I believe I've handled the redemption of these villains well. No rules except the ones you enforce, right?

## PREPARING FOR THE NEXT BOOK IN THE SERIES

**JENA' GALIFANY:** "Don't have too many characters active at the same time. If it gets too crowded, it gets too confusing. If the readers can't 'see the forest for the trees,' they'll put it down."

**B.J. DANIELS:** "Don't try to put every character from the series into every book. It's too cumbersome, confusing, and boring for the reader. Assume this is the first book a reader has picked up. Weave characters in only if they pertain to this book."

Don't neglect the need to establish main series characters in the first book because most readers are turned off past Book 1 by too many characters littering a single story. It's like squeezing a party into a phone booth. Too many characters, especially if they're not all well crafted and real enough to stand out, can bog down a story. In general, readers prefer to get into the heads of no more than two main characters per book; this allows them to get to know and love these two extremely well. In a series with a cast of characters, once all the major players are introduced (not point-of-viewed!) in that first book, many of them will, by necessity, fade into the background of the next stories until it's their turn to take lead roles. You can approach this in a lot of interesting ways, and many authors have opinions about how to do it. The way I usually handle it is to briefly introduce each series character in the first book, fleshing them out just enough to be compelling without locking myself into anything that I might want to change later. As paranormal author Liz Strange says, "Keep them simple enough for the reader to follow, and rich enough to set each character apart."

In the first book, the main characters naturally take center stage and character introductions come through them. Since I frequently write romances, my main characters are almost always the hero and heroine. I'll then choose one other secondary series character in the current book to be closest to these main characters. In my Wounded Warriors Series, the main series characters were Wendy, Paul, Steve, Gwen, Gregg, Brenda, Mitch, and Jessie. Tommie was a series character who died in Book 1 but played a role "in spirit" through all six books of the series. In Book 1 the main characters were Wendy and Paul. Wendy's brother Steve, in his connection to Wendy, played a larger role in Book 1 than most of the other series characters, and this whetted the readers' appetites for his book, which came next. In Book 2 Steve was the main character. Steve's friendship with another series character, Gwen (who was *not* the heroine in Book 2), was highlighted to get readers interested in Gwen's story. Gwen was the main character in Book 3, and her friendship with series character Gregg (again, not the hero in her story) was featured in a very natural way that prepared readers for Book 4, where Gregg was the main character with another non-series heroine. In Book 4 Gregg was connected to both Brenda and Mitch to prepare the way for their story in Book 5. In Book 5 Brenda had a connection with Jessie, who was the main character in Book 6, and so set up the next book. Nearly all of my cast-of-character series—whether the connection is between friends, family, colleagues, or co-workers—work this way, and it's an extremely efficient way of handling what could be a tricky situation.

If you know you're going to write a group of character series early enough (before or after the first book is written), it's always a good idea to sit down and figure out who the main series character is in each book and how you're going to introduce a secondary series character, who will become the main character, establishing them for the next book in the series. I'll talk more about this in chapter four.

## LEAVE SOME UNFINISHED BUSINESS AT THE END OF ONE BOOK ... BUT DON'T LEAVE TOO MANY QUESTIONS

**MICHELLE LEVIGNE:** "You want to leave a book hanging so the next one has to be read. Readers will complain, but they stand in line to buy the next one. A few loose ends make a reader want to come back to find out what happened next. Kind of like the cliff-hangers in the old serials they used to show in the theaters, where the hero was always in peril. You *knew* he would get out of danger because he was the hero, after all, but you came back to find out how he did it."

**CAT ADAMS:** "Don't leave too many questions at the end of the book. If the publisher goes under tomorrow, or the book doesn't sell well enough for the next book, the reader should never feel cheated. Sad or frustrated, yes (as is the author), but never cheated. I like to use *Star Wars* as an example. If *The Empire Strikes Back* had never made the screen (or the shelf), the reader/viewer would still have been satisfied because the Death Star was destroyed, the hero saved the day, and there was a hope for the future. Yes, there was still a war, but the battle was won and the good guys triumphed."

## GIVE 'EM WHAT THEY WANT

**CAT ADAMS:** "There's a very fine line between 'comfortable' and 'bored.' We readers ask a lot of authors. Give me more, but not *too* much more. Give me angst but don't hurt anyone I actually like. Give me different, but don't change things. The reader in me gives the author in me a headache sometimes."

## DON'T GIVE UP

**JOANNE HALL:** "Don't give up! Writing a book is daunting and tiring. Writing a series is even more so. It's a marathon effort. There will be times when you will be convinced it's never going to end. Don't think about the end of the whole sequence or even the end of the book. Think about the end of the chapter, the end of the page, the next five hundred words. If authors thought about what a massive undertaking writing a series is, the sane ones wouldn't even consider it! Luckily, you've chosen a profession not renowned for its sanity!"

The only way to truly learn how to write a series is to write a series. In a *Writer's Digest* interview, Sue Grafton reveals she doesn't know what she was thinking when she decided to write a twenty-six-book, alpha-murder mystery series. Averaging a book every two years, she's now four letters away from the culmination. But she doesn't think about how she'll get through it. "The next book—each new book—always feels like the first. I'm not going to worry about it. I'm like Scarlett O'Hara: I'll just worry about that tomorrow." Sue also offers advice to new writers, and I would add the same for new series writers: "Writing is really hard to master. You learn by failing over and over, but a lot of people don't care for that, thanks. I always wish new writers the greatest good fortune. It's a helluva journey—I'll tell you that."

## BUILD YOUR SERIES MUSCLES EXERCISES

1. What is your approach to writing a series? Is it character driven, plot loaded, or setting dominated? Defining your approach will decide how you begin the work of planning your series.
2. Using your individual approach, at this stage you really want to think about which characters will be taking the lead in the individual stories, as well as each character's internal conflicts, goals, and motivations. Think about plot conflicts that fit your particular characters. Finally, consider the settings that will

mesh with your characters and plot. If you can think of specific ways to do this, jot down notes now.

3. Go through several series of books you really enjoy, noting from Book 2 on how the authors reintroduced the premise of the series. Is the series premise immediately accessible? In other words, does the author include a description or other device that allows the reader to follow the current story without having to read any of the other books, but also sets the stage for what happened in the last book(s) and what's about to happen in the current one? Has the author tailored backstory specifically to fit the new story at hand? The more you study how this is done well, the easier it will be for you to become a master at reestablishing three-dimensional characters, settings, and premise/plot in only a paragraph or two.

4. Do you have any ideas about how you'll revisit characters, premise/plot, and settings in the second and subsequent books in your series? Make a note of them. Remember, you want to avoid information dumps and bring something new with each future book. If you've already written the first book in your series, look very closely at how you've introduced each aspect in your story. When you write the second and subsequent books in this series, ask yourself these questions: Do you have any information dumps? If you're not sure, try reading these sections out loud. Is one of your characters in a scene the cabbagehead who's made to endure the doling out of important information? Or, as you're reading, can you imagine a reader new to the series going "Huh?" every five seconds because you haven't given enough information to establish this particular story? What growth does your recurring character show from book to book? Can you make any notes on ways to grow him subtly, based on the plots in the individual series stories? If you've already written the first book in the series,

pay attention to ways the character has grown and how he'll continue to do so in the next book(s). How will you continue to make your plots and settings fresh for returning readers?

5. Consistency is crucial to a series. Though I won't define ways of keeping everything organized until the next chapter, I suggest you make a commitment now to stay consistent throughout your series. If you already have a lot of ideas for your series, you might have errors of consistency that could be of special concern. If you've finished the first book in your series, look at the major areas of inconsistency: Oversights, Changed Premises, Technical Problems, Timeline and Production Issues, and Unanswered Questions. Take notes to make sure you don't have any flubs. Use the checklist included in Appendix A to help you with this.

6. Are there any other things you considered in this chapter that stand out for you as crucial for your series based on the advice of series readers and writers? Write them down now so you keep them in mind as your series progresses.

Two things are absolutely necessary when it comes to creating a satisfying series: awesome characters and unflagging consistency. Now that you know you need them, you can build them into every book in your series. In the next chapter, I'll go over many ways to stay organized while writing each book in a series.

# CHAPTER FOUR

# SERIES ORGANIZATION

*"The last thing one discovers in composing
a work is what to put first."*

~T.S. ELIOT

Terry Brooks once said, "A writer seasons with each new book, becomes less wide-eyed and more calculating, and looks further ahead at the possibilities of his work." When writing a series, this truth becomes even more crucial. In general, the author realizes after completing the first book that he has a series on his hands. Ideally, he should start organizing now—before jumping into the second and subsequent books in the series—to make the process smoother. I'll discuss the many ways you can approach this in the course of this chapter.

## SERIES ORGANIZATIONAL TECHNIQUES

You should decide from the start how best to organize the crucial information in the series, such as details of character, plot, and setting. Establishing the basics for each book in the series can give you insight for further-reaching possibilities as you write each new book in untold ways; most important, doing so can also give you an edge when trying to sell the series. Therefore, organization is necessary to know where you're going with a series—especially if you've finished the first book and you plan to submit a proposal with series information.

You should note that small-press publishers and mass-market publishers have slightly different requirements for the submission process. Small presses want to see full blurbs for each book in your submission when you propose a series, while a mass-market publisher will want to know you've completed the first book, and you should submit the book as a stand-alone novel with series potential. Most mass-market publishers want to try one book before committing to more. However, if you're an established author, you or your agent will probably want to submit blurbs for the full series.

Christina M. Brashear of the small-press publisher Samhain added that "When a whole series is proposed, we'd like to see an outline of each book to know what is supposed to happen within each book. Knowing in advance how many books are planned, how the plot will develop, and the characters expected to be introduced with each title helps the editor help the author stay on course." Damnation Books and Eternal Press CEO Kim Richards wants the whole shebang: "If there is a series, I'm interested in how many [books] are completed, and I like to see a synopsis of each book in the series, [as well as] sample chapters of each. This tells me the writer actually has a series, rather than just plans for one. It also gives me an idea of how the overall series arc looks." The good news is that, once you've sold the first book and possibly another, most publishers will expect slightly less of their established authors. Debra Womack, the small-press publisher at Whiskey Creek Press, wants "blurbs at a minimum for new authors … and less for established WCP authors."

I'll take you through it step by step.

## STEP 1: BLURBING THE SERIES

The first step in figuring out where you're going with your series is to blurb the series. This should be done as soon as possible—as soon as you know you'll be writing a series. By putting the plot into blurb form, you may even hone in on aspects of the series arc you hadn't considered before.

The series blurb should tell readers how all the books in that series are connected. If the series blurb is done well enough, those sentences will accurately reflect what every book in the series is about in a concise, intriguing summary. Remember, you're not focusing on individual stories at this point (you'll start blurbing the separate stories in the next step)— you're looking at the series as a whole, attempting to give readers the gist of what the *series* is about. You started this task at the end of chapter two:

Define your series tie(s):

> Recurring Character Series
> Central Group of Characters Series
> Premise/Plot Series
> Setting Series
> Combination of These (list them here)

In developing your series blurb, your tie will in many cases help you figure out what needs to be included in the blurb. In as few sentences as possible, define your series arc by putting it into the series arc equation. Try to do this in a single sentence, if possible, following the "leads to" logic. Note that resolutions are not always needed in the series blurb since you don't want to defuse the intrigue or tension, but sometimes a resolution will work well in the overall series blurb. Play with it and test out all the alternatives.

Introduction → Change → Conflicts →
Choices → Crisis → Resolutions

Note that if you have a central group of characters, you *won't* name each main character specifically in the series blurb. Instead, you'll sum up the overall premise of the series and how it affects the group as a whole. Additionally, I spoke earlier about open-ended series and whether it was wise to come up with a series arc for them. While a series arc is optional in this case, it's always a good idea to blurb your series anyway because you'll need to use a blurb in your submissions and promotion. In Appendix B, check out the variety of series blurbs in the open-ended examples. You might get an idea for how to handle yours by studying others.

At this stage, it's fine to have something as simple as "Cast of Characters will find soul mates," or "College professor follows the trail to an ancient artifact that could save the world or destroy it." You'll build on this jumping-off point as you go along, fleshing it out as much as possible. The example below uses my Kaleidoscope Series and the series arc formula discussed in chapter two. Keep in mind, this series is lighthearted romance and the series blurb reflects that—and should. In this one, I've included a rare resolution—most series blurbs won't have or need one.

> Kaleidoscope Office Building provides employment to nine hot, young singles **(Introduction)**—all about to make a love connection. **(Change and Choices)** Working 9 to 5 has never been so complicated **(Crisis)** ... or so much fun! **(Resolutions)**

Treat your blurb like a work in progress; tweak it multiple times until it's just right. Consider adding intrigue by making the blurb a question or an exclamation. Adding ellipses can also whet the reader's appetite for more. Some tips to keep in mind while you hone your series blurb:

1. The genre(s) specific to your series should be apparent. If you have a romantic paranormal, you should allude to both the romance and paranormal aspects in the blurb. Connect the genre(s) of your series and your blurb in your mind, and evaluate whether each genre is effectively portrayed.

2. Most series blurbs range from one to four sentences. Shorter is better. Sum up an entire series in a single, fascinating sentence that encompasses your whole series effectively. If it's short and punchy, it's guaranteed to be intriguingly memorable.

3. The series blurb must match the tone of the story genre. In other words, if it's a romantic comedy series, your blurb should portray that aptly—it should be funny or at least amusing enough to pull a smile from the reader. If it's a paranormal, your blurb should feel eerie, maybe even a little scary. Suspense in any form should induce tightness in your chest as you read the blurb.

4. Quite simply, your blurbs should captivate your readers. A series blurb should make you say "Huh!" or "Wow!" If your blurb doesn't

elicit intrigue or the desire to read the books in the series, it's not effective. It's true that while you're in the process of organizing a series, you may be the only person reading the blurbs you come up with—but don't underestimate the importance of intriguing *yourself*. When I begin writing a new series blurb, I can't imagine a more exciting time for me. Blurbing the actual stories only adds to my exhilaration. Your blurbs should elicit enough excitement about writing the series and the individual stories that it'll be hard to resist jumping into each one *immediately*.

As the first step to getting organized, a series blurb is crucial, but you can also use the series blurb for submissions and marketing. Below, you'll fill out your series organization worksheet (Appendix A):

---

## SERIES ORGANIZATION WORKSHEET, PART 1: SERIES BLURB

**SERIES TITLE:**

**SERIES GENRE:**

**SERIES TIE:**

   *If Recurring or Cast of Characters Series, list:*

   **MAIN SERIES CHARACTER(S):**

   *If Premise/Plot Series, list:*

   **MAIN PREMISE/PLOT:**

   *If Setting Series, list:*

   **MAIN SETTING(S):**

**SERIES BLURB:**

---

Below, I provide series blurbs I've used for my books that I think effectively convey what the series is about as a whole. Remember, what you focus on with the series blurb is usually the series tie, which will determine what aspect of the worksheet you fill out.

**SERIES TITLE:** Incognito Series

**SERIES GENRE:** Action-Adventure/Romantic Suspense

**SERIES TIE:** Premise/Plot

> **MAIN PREMISE/PLOT:** The Network is the world's most covert organization with underground headquarters in Chicago beneath a front technology company called ETI. Having unchallenged authority and skill to disable and destroy criminals, the Network takes over where regular law enforcement leaves off in the mission for absolute justice. The price for that justice is high, requiring the life of every man and woman who serves. For them, there is no life and no love, only duty.

**SERIES BLURB:** Men and women who have sacrificed their personal identities to live in the shadows and uphold justice for all—no matter the cost.

**SERIES TITLE:** Shadow Missions (spin-off from the Incognito Series)

**SERIES GENRE:** Action-Adventure/Romantic Suspense

**SERIES TIE:** Premise/Plot

> **MAIN PREMISE/PLOT:** The Network is the world's most covert organization with underground headquarters in Chicago beneath a front technology company called ETI. Having unchallenged authority and skill to disable and destroy criminals, the Network takes over where regular law enforcement leaves off in the mission for absolute justice. The price for that justice is high, requiring the life of every man and woman who serves. For them, there is no life and no love, only duty.

**SERIES BLURB:** Return to Karen Wiesner's award-winning Incognito Series, where you first met and fell in love with these intriguing operatives in an interconnected trio of novellas, along with the epic conclusion of this long-running series. Six Network operatives and three dangerous undercover missions to take down one terrorist organization that wants to right the wrongs tainting life, liberty, and the pursuit of happiness.

**SERIES TITLE:** Family Heirlooms Series

**SERIES GENRE:** Inspirational Romance

**SERIES TIE:** Central Group of Characters and Setting

> **MAIN SERIES CHARACTER(S):** Samuels family siblings, including Tamara, Joshua, Peter, Samantha, Jay, and Marcus
>
> **MAIN SETTING(S):** Peaceful, Wisconsin (fictional)

**SERIES BLURB:** Nuggets of faith can be passed down as family heirlooms from parent to child, sibling to sibling, spouse to spouse.

**SERIES TITLE:** Friendship Heirlooms Series (spin-off from the Family Heirlooms Series)

**SERIES GENRE:** Inspirational Romance

**SERIES TIE:** Central Group of Characters and Setting

> **MAIN SERIES CHARACTER(S):** Secondary characters introduced in the Family Heirlooms Series, including Zoë Rossdale, Lee-Ann Wagner, Michael Fremont, Jasmine Pepowski, Wesley Horace, Chad Feldmann, Winnie McBride, Elaina Houston, and Ethan Lynwood
>
> **MAIN SETTING(S):** Peaceful, Wisconsin (fictional)

**SERIES BLURB:** Return to the quaint little town of Peaceful, Wisconsin, from Karen Wiesner's award-winning Family Heirlooms Series, where you first met and fell in love with these colorful, lovable friends. Now you can read the stories of those secondary characters in an all-new spin-off series. Nuggets of faith can be passed down as heirlooms from friend to friend, heart to heart, soul mate to soul mate.

**SERIES TITLE:** Wounded Warriors Series

**SERIES GENRE:** Women's Fiction

**SERIES TIE:** Central Group of Characters

> **MAIN SERIES CHARACTER(S):** Tommie Nelson, Wendy Thomas, Paul Randall, Steve Thomas, Gwen Nicholson, Gregg Stevens, Brenda Bennett, Mitch Taylor, and Jessie Nelson

**SERIES BLURB:** Women who have faced pain, loss, and heartache. They know the score and never back down. Women who aren't afraid to love with all their passion and all their strength, who risk everything for their own little piece of heaven. Men who live their lives on the blade's edge. Knights in black armor. The only thing more dangerous than crossing these men is loving them...

**SERIES TITLE:** Woodcutter's Grim Series

**SERIES GENRE:** Romantic Horror/Paranormal

**SERIES TIE:** Setting

    **MAIN SETTING(S):** Woodcutter's Grim, Wisconsin (fictional)

**SERIES BLURB:** For the ten generations since the evil first came to Woodcutter's Grim, the Guardians have sworn an oath to protect the town from the childhood horrors that lurk in the black woods. Without them, the town would be defenseless ... and the terrors would escape to the world at large.

**SERIES TITLE:** Cowboy Fever Series

**SERIES GENRE:** Contemporary Romance

**SERIES TIE:** Combination of Central Group of Characters and Setting

    **MAIN SERIES CHARACTER(S):** Ranchers from a cooperative group of ranches in (fictional) Fever, Texas: Wings "Mac" Mackenzie, Lance Olsen, Jared Chapman, Shawn Jacobs, Ken Abrams, and Maggie May

    **MAIN SETTING(S):** Fever, Texas (fictional)

**SERIES BLURB:** Return to cowboy country in Fever, Texas, where the heat isn't the only thing causing a fever! See if you can find the heirloom wedding band.

**SERIES TITLE:** Denim Blues Mysteries/Red Velvet Mysteries

**SERIES GENRE:** Inspirational Romantic Mystery

**SERIES TIE:** Combination of Central Group of Characters, Premise/ Plot, and Setting

**MAIN SERIES CHARACTER(S):** Shamus "Den" McHart, Orlando Bateman, Tyler Shaw

**MAIN PREMISE/PLOT:** Each story in the trilogy has something "denim blue"/"red velvet" in it.

**MAIN SETTING(S):** Briar's Point (fictional)

**SERIES BLURB:**

**FIRST TRILOGY:** Briar's Point is a whimsical little town with its fair share of colorful characters, crime, and Cupid suffering from the denim blues ...

**SECOND TRILOGY:** Briar's Point is a whimsical little town with its fair share of colorful characters, crime, and a Cupid celebrating hundred-proof red velvet romance...

**SERIES TITLE:** Bloodmoon Cove Spirits Series

**SERIES GENRE:** Paranormal/gothic inspirational romances

**SERIES TIE:** Setting

**MAIN SETTING(S):** Bloodmoon Cove, Wisconsin (fictional), in Erie County (fictional)

**SERIES BLURB:** Don't close your eyes.

## STEP 2: BLURBING INDIVIDUAL SERIES STORIES

Now that you've written your series blurb, you must come up with story blurbs for each book you have in mind (this may grow as the series progresses, but as soon as you know another story in the series is coming up, try to blurb the story and give it connections to the previous books). Brainstorming is so important when you're in the earliest stages of a series, and if you get your mind going on the individual stories early enough, you could conceivably have most of the stories planned in your head before you begin work on them in the physical sense. Stories on the back burner of your mind can become amazing things!

Most authors have heard of the story blurb because it's little more than a back cover blurb. But let's go into a bit more detail. This kind of blurb is made up of concise, tantalizing sentences (no more than one to four paragraphs; as with the series blurb, the shorter the better) that sum up your entire story, as well as the conflicts, goals, and motivations of the main character(s). No easy task. Your story blurb should begin with a high-concept blurb—which is a lot like a series blurb. You want to condense this down to a single sentence. Here's a simplified explanation of what your high-concept blurb needs to contain:

A character (who) wants (what) a goal because he's motivated (why), but he faces conflict (why not).

Your premise/plot or setting might also come into this sentence. Come up with a simple sentence that defines your story in this way. Tweak it (possibly by making the sentence into a question or exclamation, or by ending with ellipses) until it's intriguing.

Now, flesh out your story blurb by filling in the blanks for each of the main characters in your story (unless you find the blurb is more effective with just one of the main characters):

_____(name of character) wants _____ (goal to be achieved) because _____ (motivation for acting), but faces _____(conflict standing in the way).

Keep honing your story blurb until it's intriguing (again, making the last sentence a question or exclamation or by ending with ellipses). This is the story blurb for my inspirational romance/chick-lit *Clumsy Girl's Guide to Falling in Love*, Book 1 of the Friendship Heirlooms Series, with the conflicts, goals, and motivations tagged:

> *They were two abnormal peas in an even stranger pod...* (**high-concept blurb**)
>
> Zoë Rossdale (**name of character**) is the clumsy girl who always has her elbows, feet, eyes, and brass-red hair going in the wrong directions. She floats around in her own world, comfortable there alone, only to be jarred back into the real one when her obliviousness gets her in trouble again. After a lifetime of being

evaluated critically—first by her own father, and then by everyone around her—and found wanting, she's trying to change … for her own good. She's reaffirmed her commitment to Christ and vowed not to do any of the stupid, possibly illegal, things she'd done for years on the pitiful excuse of surviving. After nearly being fired from the only job she could get to keep her from starving and living on the streets **(motivation(s) for acting),** she's going to school once more and trying to do better for her über-patient boss. And she's allowed her best friends to talk her into getting contacts, some new clothes, and a more flattering hairstyle. They tell her she looks beautiful, but she feels more like a dodo bird than ever before—until she literally runs into the only man she's ever gone loopy over.

Curt Bertoletti **(name of character)** has spent years trying to forget the seriously messed-up Zoë and her embarrassing ways. The only person who'd ever approved of the ditzy klutz was his mother, and his mother has become relentless in her cause to get him married and settled down. Surely that's what conjured the appearance of Zoë … Zoë, who looks so little like the girl he remembers. Even as he vows that he won't stray again—out of weakness or whatever it was that had him stone-gone over her before—he can't help remembering how well he and Zoë fit together. **(motivation(s) for acting)** No other woman had ever gotten that misty look in her eyes when she looked at him, or kissed him like she'd forgotten anyone or anything else existed. No other woman made him so happy, so mad, so sad, and so content. Though he's walking stronger in the Lord than he ever has before and he finally knows what he wants in life, he's convinced Zoë Rossdale is not *it*—matchmaking mother or no matchmaking mother. So why can't he forget her and be done with it?

For better or worse, Zoë will always be Zoë—the clumsy girl with her dress tucked into her pantyhose, toilet paper stuck to her shoe and trailing in her wake, the girl whose idea of falling in love is to stand at the edge of the precipice, throw out her arms, and confidently jump into a free-fall. If Zoë will always be

Zoë, the only question left is, can they both live with that fact? Forever? **(goal to be achieved)**

What elements should and shouldn't be included in a story blurb, and how long should it really be? Ideally, you want to weave all the long-term threads into the blurb—as concisely as possible. If a character is a *main* character, that's a strong reason to include him or her; however, I don't think it's necessary in every case.

If you can reduce your blurb to just a few sentences, you've really mastered this (check out Jane Toombs's blurbs in Appendix B—talk about tight!). Keep in mind, though, that a *too*-short blurb can be less than dazzling. Instead of being memorable, it can lack details to capture true interest in readers. Remember, if the blurb doesn't make you want to read the story, it's ineffective. The goal is to get readers to pick up the book.

Sometimes highly effective blurbs don't fit into formulas. The formula is designed to help you find your way, but if you produce something phenomenal using a free-form approach, go with it.

Below, I provide examples of blurbs (my own) from a variety of genres because I believe example is more effective than instruction alone. Remember the pointers I gave you in the last section: You should see the genre in your story blurbs. Next, the story blurb should match the *tone* of the story genre. Finally, short is *usually* but not always better. Ultimately, all blurbs should intrigue you to the point of wanting to write (and read) the story.

*Until It's Gone,* Book 5 of the Wounded Warriors Series (romantic suspense)

*You don't know what you've got ... until it's gone.*

Mitch Taylor has been playing a very dangerous game, and the lines between black and white, good and evil, saint and sinner are all blurred. Just when he thinks the stakes can't get any higher, in steps the only woman who could ever hurt him and the only one who can heal him. In the space of a skipped heartbeat, he can't imagine having more to gain ... and more to lose.

*Falling Star,* Book 1 of the Angelfire Trilogy (contemporary romance)
*A man of God, a fallen angel. Two different worlds, one undying love ...*

For the first time in her life, Rori Mason is independent, supporting herself as a stripper; she has friends who love her, and—most importantly—she respects herself. She's vowed never to allow a man to hurt her again.

Nate Jovanovich broke the heart of a younger, less cynical Rori by marrying her rival. Eleven years later, Nate has lost his wife, gained a child and, at the end of it all, realizes Rori is still the woman of his heart.

---

*Moonlight and Roses,* Book 2 of the Red Velvet Mysteries Trilogy (inspirational romantic mystery—private investigators)

*Love is in the air ...*

Den and Sylvia McHart are celebrating their first Valentine's Day as husband and wife. With business slow at their private investigating firm, there's plenty of time for *amour* ... until a painfully shy wallflower of a woman comes in asking them to find out if the man sending her red velvet heart cutouts is a lover—or an enemy.

---

*The Deep,* Book 8, A Woodcutter's Grim Series Novel (inspirational romantic paranormal horror)

*Very loosely based on* Metamorphoses: The Story of Pygmalion and the Statue *by Ovid*

Cheyenne Welsh can't forget her past and the disappearance of her younger sister. When she returns to Woodcutter's Grim to sell the family property she grew up on, she's confronted with all the nightmare realities of her childhood, still alive and well, still right where she left them—down in the darkness the Deep dwells inside. Her home ...

*Bounty on the Rebel's Heart,* Book 3 of the Incognito Series (action-adventure/romantic suspense)

*Rebel Porter is a man on the edge. His wife was killed to silence evidence he uncovered on a dangerously corrupt man of power. Now Reb is in hiding, and he's as afraid to lose someone else to the bounty on his head as to lose his heart to another woman.*

Corrupt head of Network operations Giles Jameson has gone MIA. As a boy, he'd been brought in with the choice: join or die. Giles joined, vowing secretly to bring down the Network. Working with an organized crime ring, Giles had killed a senator. The son of that senator was Rebel Porter, who grew up to be an investigative reporter who spent his life searching for Giles and the covert organization he believed Giles headed. When Reb disclosed his findings on public radio, Giles covered up the breach and silenced Reb by arranging to have his wife killed. Now, sixteen years later, Giles has begun his lifelong mission to destroy the Network for good.

Network operative Natalie Francis goes undercover, posing as Reb's former lover—investigative journalist Adrienna Kelly—to find Reb and his evidence against Giles Jameson and the Network. Together they uncover a conspiracy that could upset the wrong people and silence both of them for good. And when Natalie realizes she's fallen for the man she's been protecting, she considers the impossible—escaping the Network.

*Shadow Boxing,* Book 2 of the Family Heirlooms Series (inspirational romance)

*Joined before God and family out of a sense of responsibility? Or love?*

As a teenager, Justine Morris's escape from the pressures of caring for her dying father was stolen moments with Joshua Samuels. But their tender, desperate liaison found them facing teen pregnancy. Afraid of their Christian families' responses to the situation, they married quickly and built a life for their child.

But now that their daughter is ready to fly the nest, Justine can no longer ignore the truth: She and Joshua haven't had a real marriage for a long time. Maybe they never had one at all.

Joshua is only too aware that his busy, professional attorney wife is an independent woman who never really needed him. After nearly two decades of marriage, he's quit trying to get more than a piece of her at a time. Without their daughter holding them together, he knows the chasm between them will grow to epic proportions.

Their empty nest looming, they face the hard questions. Had they married in love ... or out of a hasty sense of responsibility? Was it God's will for them to be together? And now, is it worth the effort to learn to become one as the Lord intends for a man and a woman ... or better to simply let go?

---

*The Fifteenth Letter*, Book 3 of the Falcon's Bend Series {with Chris Spindler} (mystery/police procedural)

*Sins of the father ...*

For the past fifteen years, on the anniversary of his arrest for armed robbery, Zeke Carfi has received a threatening letter signed by the wife of his deceased partner in crime.

Zeke's daughter Amber, Falcon's Bend Police Department's newest patrol officer, has spent fifteen years holding onto a secret that could further condemn the father she'd worshipped as a child. When Zeke is released on parole, Amber finds herself questioning everything she's ever believed. Is Zeke the good man she once knew? How could the father who'd made her the center of his world for the first seven years of her life be a criminal? Is it possible to turn from a life of crime, or is it true that once a criminal, always a criminal?

Their reconciliation is cut short when Amber discovers the fifteenth letter ... and the key to a fifteen-year mystery that could lead to murder.

*Return to Bloodmoon Manor,* Book 4 of the Bloodmoon Cove Spirits Series (gothic inspirational romance)

*Back into the mouth of hell ...*

Daniel and Hannah Reynolds are newly married with their first child on the way when a notice comes from a lawyer saying that the remaining member of the Bonavaris clan has returned to her ancestral home in Syria and willed Bloodmoon Manor and all its possession to Hannah, her former maid. While Hannah can't fathom the reason for the bequest, the notion of selling the house and the valuable items inside it begins to grow inside her like an obsession. She and Daniel have begun their married life with little more than outstanding debts from his medical education—debts that come due around the same time as the birth of their baby. After a lifetime of poverty, Hannah refuses to allow her children to face the kind of scavenging, hand-to-mouth existence that had led to her employment at the horrible Bloodmoon Manor in the first place.

Unable to convince his beloved wife to forget about returning to Bloodmoon Cove to secure the future for their family, Daniel has no choice but to follow her into what he aptly recalls as "the mouth of hell"—a place Hannah just barely escaped with her life last time.

Daniel's worst fears are justified when the doors of Bloodmoon Manor slam shut behind them. They've been lured here deliberately, and the ghosts that haunt the dark, evil castle aren't willing to let them leave ever again ...

Tweak your story blurb until it's concise and targeted, and, of course, utterly captivating. You'll find a worksheet for developing series and story blurbs in Appendix A.

Once you know your series tie and you've blurbed your series and the individual stories, you should see a clearer picture of where your series is going. But you're not done yet. I suggest you build your individual stories on the series organization worksheets. Remember back in the last chapter, I explained how to introduce the character, premise/plot, and setting in subsequent stories without including an information dump? Well, this early in a series, it's a very good idea to figure out how you're going to introduce each of these in a way that will help you before you begin work on the stories. You can do that with your series organization worksheet. You'll find a blank worksheet for your use in Appendix A.

## SERIES ORGANIZATION WORKSHEET, PART 2: INDIVIDUAL STORY BLURBS

**TITLE OF BOOK:**

**BOOK NUMBER IN THE SERIES:**

**STORY GENRE (IF DIFFERENT FROM THE SERIES):**

   **MAIN STORY CHARACTER(S):**

   **MAIN SECONDARY CHARACTER(S):**

**STORY BLURB:**

Below, I've filled out the worksheet with examples from one of my own series. This series uses the central group of characters tie, and therefore there are lines in the form for both main series characters as well as secondary characters. You'll notice that for the first story and subsequent stories, usually the previous main character(s) makes a *brief* appearance in the current story, as well as the main character(s) in the upcoming story (who will likely play a larger role as secondary character(s) in the current one). This accomplishes two things: Readers glimpse the continuation of the previous character's happy ending, and they become interested in the upcoming main character(s).

## SERIES ORGANIZATIONAL WORKSHEET: SERIES BREAKDOWN EXAMPLE

**SERIES TITLE:** Kaleidoscope Series

**SERIES GENRE:** Contemporary Romance

**SERIES TIE:** Central group of characters: All the co-workers at Kaleidoscope Office Building find true love.

> **MAIN SERIES CHARACTERS:** Co-workers at Kaleidoscope Office Building, including: Keri Woods, Angela Lewis, Aimee Cooper, Rob Channing, Dex Everett, Roni Spencer, Billy LaPointe, Shayna Cavanay, and Jolie Everett.

**SERIES BLURB:** Kaleidoscope Office Building provides employment to nine hot, young singles—all about to make a love connection. Working 9 to 5 has never been so complicated ... or so much fun!

**TITLE OF BOOK:** *Perfect Cadence*

**BOOK NUMBER IN THE SERIES:** Book 1

**STORY GENRE (IF DIFFERENT FROM THE SERIES):** same as series

**MAIN STORY CHARACTER(S):** Keri Woods (a series main character) and Joshua Lewis

**MAIN SECONDARY CHARACTER(S):** Angela Lewis and Rob Channing

**STORY BLURB:** Thirty-year-old Keri Woods has had it with her no-commitment, no-way boyfriend Rob. Planning to get her head on straight, she accepts her boss Angela's offer to use the Lewis family's cabin for a two-week skiing vacation over the Christmas holiday. Little does Keri realize that her boss's cousin, Joshua Lewis, is already occupying the very same cabin at the very same time. Ten years earlier, Keri and Joshua had shared a single, unforgettable day and night together that ended with a kiss that left them both desperately smitten. Yet Joshua's life had been too complicated. At only twenty-six, he'd realized that there could be no long-distance, long-term relationship between them. He hadn't been ready to have his whole life happen to him at once. His decision to leave and never see her again had come back to bite him in the butt. For years after confiding to his closest friend, Dandy—the foreman on his father's cattle ranch in Fever, Texas, and the true father figure in his life—Joshua had had to listen to the old man encourage and berate him for not following his heart with Keri Woods. Joshua has come to the family cabin after the recent death of Dandy, who'd made him promise to return to the cabin to "mend old regrets." The last thing Joshua expects to find is the drop-dead beautiful woman he'd regretted abandoning a decade earlier naked in his bed.

**TITLE OF BOOK:** *In Cahoots With Cupid*

**BOOK NUMBER IN THE SERIES:** Book 2

**STORY GENRE (IF DIFFERENT FROM THE SERIES):** same as series

**MAIN STORY CHARACTER(S):** Angela Lewis (a series main character) and Kiowa Mackenzie

**MAIN SECONDARY CHARACTER(S):** Keri Woods and Aimee Cooper

**STORY BLURB:** Angela Lewis, owner of Kaleidoscope Office Services and its companion business Lewis Graphics by Design, has devoted her life to seeing that everyone she cares for is happy. But when she returns home to Fever, Texas, for a wedding, she remembers the one instance where she'd turned her back on something she wanted for herself. Kiowa Mackenzie is five years younger than she is and had pursued Angela with the energy of a stallion when they were younger. Even now, he seems to have no inclination to stop, though she insists she's too old for him and she's not interested in falling in love again. Best man Ki has every intention of tackling the bridesmaids to make sure maid of honor Angela catches the bride's bouquet!

**TITLE OF BOOK:** *Behind Amethyst Eyes*

**BOOK NUMBER IN THE SERIES:** Book 3

**STORY GENRE (IF DIFFERENT FROM THE SERIES):** same as series

**MAIN STORY CHARACTER(S):** Aimee Cooper and Rob Channing (both series main characters)

**MAIN SECONDARY CHARACTER(S):** Dex Everett, Billy LaPointe, Roni Spencer, Shayna Cavanay, and Angela Lewis-Mackenzie

**STORY BLURB:** Amethyst-eyed, bespectacled Aimee Cooper has had a secret crush on muscle-bound accountant Rob Channing for years—even while one of her best friends dated him. When Aimee's father dies after years with Alzheimer's, she's left to mourn and sort out the complicated mess his estate has fallen into. In life's strange serendipity, this tragedy gives her an "in" to get close to the man of her dreams. But what does a lifelong freckle-faced wallflower know about capturing the interest of a bean-counting playboy?

**TITLE OF BOOK:** *Jordana's Chair*
**BOOK NUMBER IN THE SERIES:** Book 4
**STORY GENRE (IF DIFFERENT FROM THE SERIES):** same as series
**MAIN STORY CHARACTER(S):** Dex Everett (a series main character) and Jordana DeSoto
**MAIN SECONDARY CHARACTER(S):** Jolie Everett-Myrick (Dex's sister), Aimee Cooper, Rob Channing, Roni Spencer, and Billy LaPointe
**STORY BLURB:** Soulful-eyed heartbreaker Dex Everett has been intrigued by his neighbor since she moved into his building a year ago—though, or perhaps because, she's nothing like the made-up glamour girls he's used to dating. Jordana DeSoto barely speaks English, has worn the same two handmade outfits in all the time Dex has known her, and has never bothered with, nor needed, makeup. The few times he's helped her carry furniture up to her apartment, he's noticed that her living space is basically empty. No one he's ever known before has been content with so little or displayed such joy over a new chair simply because she earned it on her own. Jordana captures Dex the way no other woman ever has. Is this ladies' man officially off the market?

**TITLE OF BOOK:** *Paper Tiger*
**BOOK NUMBER IN THE SERIES:** Book 5
**STORY GENRE (IF DIFFERENT FROM THE SERIES):** Romantic suspense
**MAIN STORY CHARACTER(S):** Roni Spencer and Billy LaPointe (both series main characters)

**MAIN SECONDARY CHARACTER(S):** Shayna Cavanay, Rob Channing, and Dex Everett

**STORY BLURB:** Billy LaPointe's wife died only a couple of years after they married, leaving him with a son to raise on his own. Nine years later, he's found love again with Veronica Spencer, and his teenage son, Damian, is just as smitten with her. But after years of hearing Roni hedge on his marriage proposals, Billy is desperate. Determined to make her his forever, he offers her an ultimatum that he soon regrets. What he doesn't know is that Roni has a secret past she doesn't want to look back on or confront—a past that may have come back to haunt her. Can she risk losing Billy and Damian because of what could be a true threat ... or merely a paper tiger?

**TITLE OF BOOK:** *Cabin Fever*
**BOOK NUMBER IN THE SERIES:** Book 6
**STORY GENRE (IF DIFFERENT FROM THE SERIES):** same as series
**MAIN STORY CHARACTER(S):** Shayna Cavanay (a series main character) and Dakota Loring
**MAIN SECONDARY CHARACTER(S):** Angela Lewis-Mackenzie, Aimee Cooper, Rob Channing, and Jolie Everett-Myrick

**STORY BLURB:** Shayna Cavanay divorced her lying, cheating, deadbeat husband three years ago and she's sure of only one thing: The only good thing her husband ever did for her was give her their seven-year-old son, Ty. As a single mother, Shayna divides her time between working to provide for her and her son and making up for the vast multitude of deficiencies in Ty's poor excuse for a father. When Ty begins to exhibit an inability to cope with the lack of a father figure in his life, his elementary school teacher reaches out to Shayna. But Shayna has been burned by do-gooders before. It's up to hunky Dakota Loring—and Ty—to prove he's the real deal.

**TITLE OF BOOK:** *The Longest Night*
**BOOK NUMBER IN THE SERIES:** Book 7

**STORY GENRE (IF DIFFERENT FROM THE SERIES):** same as series

**MAIN STORY CHARACTER(S):** Jolie Everett-Myrick (a series main character) and Jag Myrick

**MAIN SECONDARY CHARACTER(S):** Dex Everett (but all series cast of characters—and spouses—make an appearance in the last scene, for a series closure that gives a fitting, highly satisfying, happily-ever-after send-off)

**STORY BLURB:** When Jolie Everett married Jag Myrick, she was a reluctant model eager to settle down and have a family, and he was a restless photographer eager for his big break. They both got what they wanted—separately. After three short years of a marriage spent mostly apart, Jolie has decided to get the child she wants and forget the naïve illusion of marital bliss. But Jag is nowhere near ready to let his beloved bride go. During one endless night, he tries to convince her he's in their relationship for the long haul while she tries to distract him with every sweet seduction in the book. Unfortunately, their first night back together in almost two years starts out badly ... and only seems to be getting worse.

After reading this example of the Series Organizational Worksheet for my Kaleidoscope Series, you should have a feel for each story in the series, as well as the series as a whole. Remember, I filled this out before I ever wrote any of the stories, so I had a very good idea of the series arc, as well as how the individual stories would play out. Once you fill out your own worksheet, I highly recommend you print a copy to go into your series bible, which I'll tell you how to create next.

## STEP 3: CREATING A SERIES BIBLE

While it's true that the writer should try to reread all the previous books in her series before starting a new one in order to refresh herself on the tone, mood, character flavors, and so on, if the series is a long one, that might not always be possible. Pausing to look up things you need to know from the previous books while trying to write a new one can get insane. I sometimes feel I've memorized every word of my stories (especially when I realize an editor has changed something without asking me first!), but without fail, when I really need to know something that was established in previous books in the series, like hair color (that little detail that eludes my every attempt to find it, even when I use the search function in the computer files), I turn to my series bible. The more a series grows, the more tedious it becomes to flip through countless pages of book after book in search of the information I need.

Of all the series organizational techniques mentioned in the author and publisher interviews I did for this book, creating a series bible was the one that hit nearly every series author's list of necessities. Even those authors who didn't blurb each story in the series beforehand found the series bible crucial to staying organized throughout the course of their series. The series bible can easily be compiled in a large binder with tabbed divider pages, in a file on your computer (and backed up on a disk or flash drive), or even in a three- to five-subject notebook with section dividers. You can also store the series bible in an index card file box with separate sections.

I put my completed series organizational blurb worksheets in the front of all my series binders. Then I include tabbed divider pages and label them as follows: Characters, Settings, Premise/Plot Specifics, and Miscellaneous/Research. You can use more or fewer section headers depending on the requirements of your specific series. If your series bible is on the computer, create one overall series folder and store subfolders within this folder, using the labels I've indicated. The same approach can be applied to using a notebook. If the notebook isn't already divided into sections that you can label, label and attach self-stick tabs to pages along the vertical edge.

How you initially create the series bible is your choice. I tend to start each project by outlining the story. Within that outline, I include all character and setting descriptions, as well as any research I've done for the story placed directly in the listing of the scene I need it for. If the research material is sizable, I'll put it in a separate section of my series binder so I can easily use it when I need to. Additionally, I can transfer character and setting sketches into the series binder for later use. Or I might wait to create my series binder information either as soon as I finish a book or just before I begin a new one. Just before I start a new book in a series, I'll go through the last book in the series I finished (preferably after it's gone through editor revisions), and fill out information sheets (by cutting and pasting directly from the story file into a blank one) that include things such as main or secondary series character descriptions, setting descriptions, specific plot information I might need to reuse, or any miscellaneous research that I could use for future stories. You can do this at any point that works best for you.

In Appendix A, I've included a variety of worksheets you might find useful in putting together your series bible. Use the ones that are helpful to you. All of them are fairly basic and self-explanatory and can be remodeled to your own preferences and needs.

Be sure to update your series bible frequently. If it doesn't include the stuff that's canon to the series, it's of little use in helping you find the facts you need and avoid inconsistencies.

As I said, I don't personally use a lot of worksheets for this step, since mainly I cut and paste from previous books into a single document that has the basic breakdowns listed above. As an example, here are some notes I made just before I started writing *Foolish Games*, Book 3 of my Family Heirlooms Series. Each of these categories were filled out on separate pages, and then I printed them and inserted them into my series folder or binder so I could easily reference them when I was ready to start working on the next book in the series.

---

## SERIES ORGANIZATIONAL WORKSHEETS: SERIES BIBLE EXAMPLE

### CHARACTERS:

*For main characters who were secondary characters in previous books, I'll cut and paste actual descriptions from those other books here:*

- Kimberly Wolfe was the picture of a Barbie Doll with her long blond curls, exotic blue eyes, rosebud-pink mouth, and killer body. Her optimistic outlook on life and precocious wisdom were blessings to her friends and acquaintances, but Justine knew her upbringing had left scars that obscured any chance of optimism for herself.
- Kimberly had a way of wiggling into places other people couldn't enter. Once her head was in, that was it. She'd zero straight to the heart of the matter in no time.
- Kimberly owns a Suzuki Sidekick.

*For series characters who play small roles in later books in the series, I might just put something like this:*

Descriptions of Tamara in *Baby, Baby*: pages 12 and 24
- Tamara and Peter Samuels are twins. They're 39 years old in *Baby, Baby*; 40 in *Shadow Boxing*, 41 in *Foolish Games*.
- Marcus Samuels is 2 years younger than Tamara and Peter; he's 37 years old in *Baby, Baby*; 38 in *Shadow Boxing*; 39 in *Foolish Games*. He works as a missionary for a Christian outreach organization overseas.

**SETTING:**

*The descriptions below were previously gleaned from descriptions in Books 1 and 2 in the series:*

They live in Peaceful, Wisconsin. Peaceful was an apt name for the friendly Midwestern town located in central Wisconsin with a population of around 3,500 citizens. Filled with old-fashioned, barely modernized business fronts along the main street, lush green grass, and an abundance of brightly colored trees lining most of the residential roads, the town had nevertheless had many new commercial and private businesses crop up to make it much more self-sufficient in the last few years. It had to be one of the last places in the world that remained utterly safe, even after dark. Has a skating rink. The only swanky restaurant in town, The Pier. Few people were out and about this morning, which wasn't a surprise. Peaceful didn't usually wake on Saturdays until ten, eleven o'clock in the morning. For that reason, the local restaurants served breakfast for most of the day all weekend.

The church Stephen Samuels pastors is about two miles from their home. The church is a picturesque, old-fashioned structure set into a neatly trimmed lawn, fragrant apple trees, and numerous bushes and flower beds.

Descriptions of Kimberly's apartment from *Baby, Baby*:

- Her apartment building was one of the nicest ones in Peaceful, filled with families and even a little playground he knew Kim frequented and joined in the activities. In an ideal world, one where she hadn't been scarred by their parents' mistakes, she would've been married to one of the many guys who would have given a lot to make her his wife. Kim was designed for babies and kids. They flocked to her everywhere she went. She hadn't married and had the kids she was meant to because of their old man. Despite how obvious it seemed, Robert realized that for the first time now ...

- Climbing the stairs to the third floor and following the scent of cinnamon, he wondered if she'd shut the door in his face or tell him to go away. He couldn't imagine his sister doing that, but she'd been testy enough lately to do it this time. He knocked and heard only silence in response. He hadn't taken a glance into her garage to see if her car was here. Maybe she'd gone out ...

- Robert nodded before they entered her colorful living room with enough throw pillows to choke a horse. He sat on the sofa, pushing a stack of pillows aside. On the oak coffee ta-

ble in front of him, he saw three baskets, all in various stages of development. She'd been weaving for Tamara again ...
- Curled up in the overstuffed white suede chair across from him ...

## PREMISE/PLOT SPECIFICS:

It'd been a tradition as long as anyone could remember for the whole Samuels clan—those who lived in the area, that was—to get together after church at their parents' house for the day. He and his wife had brought forth a large family, with Tamara and Peter, the eldest. Marcus worked as a missionary for a Christian outreach organization and was currently stationed overseas. Then came Joshua and another brother, thirteen years younger than him, Jay, who'd joined the Marines last year. The baby of the family was Samantha. She'd graduated high school the previous year with Tamara and Robert's oldest son.

- On Mondays, Kimberly volunteers at the elderly home.
- On Tuesdays, Kimberly is involved in a Bible study. Samantha and Kimberly walk at the high school track.
- On Wednesdays, Kimberly has a prayer meeting social in her apartment building.
- On Thursdays, Kimberly, Justine, and Tamara meet at Michael's restaurant for lunch.
- On Fridays, Kimberly sometimes babysits Cora—when Priscilla is on a date with her new boyfriend.
- Every Sunday the Samuels family has a potluck (Kimberly is always invited).
- She used to have Fridays off, now works most days of the week except Sunday.

## MISCELLANEOUS/RESEARCH:

Timeline Information:
- *Baby, Baby*, Book 1 started on September 16, 2006, and ended in October 2006. Tamara's brother Peter's wife, Lydia, was

diagnosed with a brain tumor that month. She died around the holidays.

- *Shadow Boxing*, Book 2 started June 22, 2007, and ended July 3, 2007.
- *Foolish Games*, Book 3 starts December 30, 2007, and ends the night before Valentine's Day 2008.

Miscellaneous information that pertains to *Foolish Games*, taken from *Baby, Baby*, Book 1:

Kimberly and Robert had come from a supposedly Christian home, but one in which their father had been an utter tyrant who took his role as man of the house to the extreme. He refused to allow his wife the slightest amount of freedom from the two-foot chain he fastened ruthlessly around her neck. Kimberly had been the result of his continued rape of the woman he claimed to love, an act committed in order to ensure his wife remained settled with another child that would keep her with him. Somehow, it'd worked, but Kimberly's mother died a broken woman with her daughter privy to every one of her horrible secrets in her journals. And Kim hated her father with a passion, especially when he'd tried to put that chain around her neck.

Miscellaneous information that pertains to *Foolish Games*, taken from *Shadow Boxing*, Book 2:

Joshua was finitely aware that his brother had lost his wife only six months ago. Lydia's brain tumor had been inoperable and took her in her sleep. Since then, Pete had barely looked up, though he'd cared for their children alone and admirably. At first, he'd accepted help from family, but he hadn't for a while, as if knowing he had to move forward if for no other reason than for Brenna and James. Lydia home-taught them since they started formal schooling, but Pete had decided to put them in public school and both had done well there. He'd relied on Kim more and more to take over the store when he couldn't function under his grief.

*I hired a lawyer to help me with some of the parole facts I needed for a secondary character in* Foolish Games, *so I interspersed the research she gave me with my story information here (and, incidentally, also used parts of this for Book 4):*

Question 2: Would Ryder be eligible for Extended Supervision (ES) at the time *Foolish Games* opens?

I think you probably have enough latitude for that to happen. *You need to see which degree of sexual assault fits your story facts because that determines the class of felony—which determines the sentence. If your story involves sexual intercourse without consent by use or threat of force or violence, that's a 2nd degree sexual assault and Class C felony.* (See statutes, page 8-9 for the official definition of sexual assault and Chapter 973, Sentencing for confinement and extended supervision sentences.)

Wisconsin adopted a new Truth in Sentencing system for crimes committed after 12/31/99. You said Samantha's rape was three years ago, so I'm assuming the new system governs. It uses a bifurcated sentence. *That means the sentence is a term of confinement followed by a period of extended supervision (ES).* The statute eliminates parole for all crimes committed after 12/31/99. Here's where you see the classification system at work: *for a Class C felony, the "term of confinement" may not exceed 25 years, with up to 20 years of supervision—which follows confinement. The supervision period can't be less than 25% of the confinement.*

When I asked the series authors I interviewed for any organizational tips they might have, I received some interesting ideas that I'll include here in no particular order:

**MARILYN MEREDITH:** "I keep 3" × 5" cards with notes about each series character."

**JANET ELAINE SMITH:** "I keep a disk with the new ideas that come to me in any series (a separate disk for each series). Some of the characters in my series even have their own websites (or they appear on my main website) and upcoming books are listed there. My basic problem is that my characters run me, and it should be the other way around. I often feel like a stenographer instead of a creator."

**FRAN ORENSTEIN:** "I do a preliminary story line for each book in a series and then an 'erasable' storyboard of the characters and locations."

**CINDY SPENCER PAPE:** "I'll do family trees, and I'm a big believer in Microsoft Word tables."

**JANE TOOMBS:** "When I conceive a series, I have only a general idea what it will be about. I do a pretty detailed synopsis for the first book, and I invent names for as many books as I believe the series can contain. After I finish this synopsis, I sometimes can see what some of the other books will be about. Also sometimes the titles of the individual books I choose show me what the plot needs to be about."

**LUISA BUEHLER:** "When I get to the end of one book, I immediately write broad stroke notes for the next one while the events of the current book are fresh in my mind. You'd be amazed how quickly the subtle nuances fade when you begin the left-brained work of preparing and marketing for the book's launch. I have folders with notes and even bits of dialogue that I know (because of the series arc) will fit a future book. I wrote seven lines of dialogue three years ago that are finding their way into the book I'm writing now."

**MARY JEAN KELSO:** "I maintain a list of who's who in the series—who is related to which character, the color of their eyes, other pertinent information that can easily get mixed up."

**MYSTERY AUTHOR LORIE HAM:** "I keep a calendar of events for every book. I also have 3" × 5" cards for each character, store, etc."

**C.R. MOSS:** "For a planned series, it's a matter of creating a bible of sorts in a notebook or on the computer—a section on the characters, a section on setting, an outline of each story, and a page or two focusing on the overall premise and arc of the series."

**REGAN TAYLOR:** "When I start a new book, I also start a notebook for the book and pretty much carry it everywhere with me. I describe my characters—all of them, even ones who make a brief appearance, like the receptionist in the dentist office that they may walk through—on their own page. I never know when one of them will pop up again and by having them drawn out I don't have to worry about remembering them. I have their physical descriptions, foods they like, where they live, a bit of their history, even a few details like a favorite movie or museum exhibit. For the Descendants of Earth Series, because it is set in the future on another planet, I created its own dictionary to match up with what words would be on Earth."

**MICHELLE LEVIGNE:** "I have maps of my made-up towns and countries hanging on the wall of my office to help me keep straight where people have to go to get from A to B, and how long it should take. Sometimes there's no organization because it grows organically. Other times I have lots of files, lots of help. Maps, calendars. The OneNote [note-taking software] system is invaluable because I have a folder for a series and then subfiles for each book, files for locations and people and organizations that apply to all the stories in the series, files for timelines, files for rewrites, and more. With OneNote, I just click on the tab to open the page so I can essentially have them all open at one time to look back and forth. I've looked at other organization systems, but they just don't work for me, or they're too much work to learn them. [That's] time I need to spend on writing!"

For my fictional towns, I make up my own maps so I can visualize where everything is—and this information can be recycled and reused throughout the series. Sometimes, if my setting is a specific building (like the Network compound and the ETI skyscraper apartments above it, or the police department in Falcon's Bend), I'll create my own blueprints so I know if my characters need to go up, down, or sideways to get where they need to go. I envy authors who have professional maps and blueprints made up for their characters' worlds (either by fans, publishers, or by their own commission).

## STEP 4: DEVELOPING A SERIES, STORY, AND PLANT ARC PLAN

In chapter two I talked about the importance of series, story, and plant arcs. If you don't have some idea of where you're going with all of these, you might miss valuable opportunities not only in a story but in the entire series. Now that you know all about these arcs, try to create a breakdown of each one and then plot the course of each individual arc.

Keep in mind that a series is a work in progress. You probably won't finish filling out this worksheet before you write each individual story. The idea is to give yourself some jumping-off points. In general, get the worksheet started now and fill out what you can each time you complete another book in the series.

The basic headings on this worksheet are as follows:

> Overall Series Arcs
> Individual Story Arcs
> Series Plant Arcs

I set up this form as a table with three columns and numerous rows, with a separate form for each individual book, including the title and book number in the series at the top. For now, fill out a form for each expected story in your series:

## SERIES ORGANIZATIONAL WORKSHEET: SERIES, STORY, AND PLANT ARCS

[TITLE OF STORY]

BOOK 1 IN [THE NAME OF THE SERIES]

| OVERALL SERIES ARC | INDIVIDUAL STORY ARCS | SERIES PLANT ARCS |
|---|---|---|
| | | |
| | | |
| | | |
| | | |

In Appendix A, you'll find a blank worksheet for this step. The filled-in example I've provided for this step (using the Harry Potter Series) is very long and detailed, and you'll find it in Appendix B.

## STEP 5: SERIES FACT-CHECKING

I talked about a variety of inconsistencies that can crop up in a series. On the next page, I've created a fact-checking checklist that incorporates all of these inconsistencies in one place. Ideally, during the revision of your story, you will go over the entire story, evaluating descriptions, timelines, characters, premise/plot, and settings, in order to ensure that you've stayed true from one book to the next. You can use the checklist against your series bible (which you need to keep accurate by frequently updating it) or the actual books you've written to make sure all of the details are correct and as they should be.

Unfortunately, it's nearly impossible for any author to stay completely organized on his own. At one point or another, something will be forgotten, neglected, or screwed up. You may not see some issues because you're too close to the project (or sick of it). That's why it's so important to turn each book in your series over to a critique partner (or three) for a critical read before you hand it over to an editor or agent. Critique partners can be found through writing groups or online groups of authors. If you don't have at least one critique partner, start asking around. Your work will only improve from the feedback.

But don't stop with getting one or more critique partners—get *good* critique partners. While it is important to have people who simply love to read your work and tend to be fanatical about knowing every little detail about a series from one book to the next, a professional author needs an equally professional (in the layman-author sense of the word) critique partner. You want someone who has the experience and expertise to spot structural problems with the story, as well as any series issues that might have gone awry or amiss, and you also want someone honest enough to tell it to you straight. In essence, it's vitally important for a series author to find a genuine fact-check reader.

After you've gone over your own series stories with this checklist, you might also want to send it to your fact-check reader so she can mark things off as she works (or after she finishes the book).

# SERIES ORGANIZATIONAL CHECKLIST: CONSISTENCY ISSUES

❑ **OVERSIGHTS**

Anything in a plot line, character, or setting that concerns illogical, unexplainable, or unrealistic courses of action and plot holes, including coincidence contrivance (writer needs it to work and so creates the groundwork "on the spot" to patch up a means to get it to work) and convenience justifications (it was the only way to pull off what I needed to happen, so I had to do it, didn't I?)

> **EXAMPLE:** Your hero is mortally afraid of snakes, starting in Book 1. In Book 5 you need him to get rid of a snake so he can pass into the cave. He does so without blinking an eye.

❑ **CHANGED PREMISES**

Anything concerning character, plot, or setting that conflicts with something that was previously established.

> **EXAMPLE:** In Book 1 you determined that all off-world humans can't breathe the air of the planet, then in Book 3 you have a human who breathes it easily with no explanation of how he does so.

❑ **TECHNICAL PROBLEMS**

Anything dealing with equipment and technical oddities, inadvertently or indiscriminately jumping into alternate viewpoints, descriptions, dialogue, names, or jobs of characters, or the setting changes from what was previously mentioned.

> **EXAMPLE:** A character's eye color was green in Book 1 of the series. In Book 4 her eyes are blue.

❑ **TIMELINE AND PRODUCTION ISSUES**

Production errors that creep up as a direct result of not checking information in previous books in the series or the series bible, and timelines that are uncertain, overlap, or even become erroneous in the course of a series if not rigorously maintained and upheld.

---

**EXAMPLE:** In Book 2 you establish that the hero was attending college three years ago. In Book 6 it says three years ago he took a trip to Italy for a year, foregoing school for the time being.

❑ **UNANSWERED QUESTIONS**

While each book in the series must have satisfactory individual story arcs, all series arc questions must be answered at the end of a series.

**EXAMPLE:** At the beginning or middle of your series, your heroine is bitten by a werewolf, and in all subsequent books she's waiting in horror for something to happen because of this ... but by the final book in the series, nothing happens and no explanation is ever given for whether or not she escaped her fate, or how it was possible.

---

In this chapter, you learned five steps to make the process of writing a series easier and set yourself up nicely for submitting your series to publishers. In the next chapter I'll talk about how to get "branded" when it comes to marketing your series.

## BUILD YOUR SERIES MUSCLES EXERCISES

Go through the five steps of organizing your series as soon as you know you'll be writing a series:

- Blurb the series.
- Blurb individual stories.
- Create a series bible.
- Develop a series, story, and plant arc plan.
- Always fact-check your series when you finish a book. If you can find a critique partner or three to do the same, you've got it made!

# CHAPTER FIVE

# SERIES MARKETING

*"There is no method but to be very intelligent."*

~T.S. ELIOT

Once you've written the first book in a series, both you and your publisher will want to begin marketing. In this chapter I'll talk about some essentials for doing this.

## SERIES MARKETING TIPS

While an author may have little or no control over the process of the publication of his series, he can still influence the outcome and specific areas of consideration in order to achieve success. The place to start is with branding.

### BRANDING

In her article "The Basics of Author Branding,"[1] author Theresa Meyers talks about building an image or perception that's used to create a loyal readership. This is called "branding." Essentially, branding is name recognition, creating a distinction for what you're offering. I'd go so far as to say that every author should have an "author branding statement" that

---

[1] This article is currently available at http://ultimatepromotionsclass.blogspot.com/2006/03/basics-of-author-branding-by-theresa.html. However, things disappear quickly on the Internet, so if this link no longer works, try searching by title and author.

she uses in every piece of promotion she puts out. For instance, my branding statement is *"Creating realistic, unforgettable characters one story at a time ..."* In this statement is a concise summary of what I'm most known for as an author: realistic, hauntingly memorable characters. This simple sentence captures the essence of everything I've ever written and everything I will ever write.

Branding is very much an implied promise to consumers that you'll continue to offer something similar and consistent to what you've offered in the past. It takes quite a bit of time and effort to build brand recognition. Theresa mentions ten impressions an author can make on readers through her books, advertisements, interviews, or word of mouth in her article, but I've heard it's closer to fourteen these days simply because the market is so saturated and consumers are harder to entice. The state of the economy plays a huge factor in purchasing habits. It's essential that branding is put in place immediately—as soon as you realize your book is part of a series. The proper branding can propel the author onto best-seller lists, which means the publisher is happy. And when a publisher is happy, authors prosper.

While patrolling listservs for series readers, I overheard comments such as:

- "I always check any information on the author or books on their websites, especially if I need to know the order of the series. I don't want to start in the middle and miss any inside jokes or cool continuities."
- "Author websites are the first thing I check if I'm interested in a new series."
- "I think it would pay for authors and publishers to make it easy to know if a book is part of a series and where each title fits in that series, since each story prepares you for the coming books."

It's logical for publishers and authors to make it as easy as possible to determine whether a book is part of a series and to make it as easy as possible to purchase all of the books in a series. But in reality it sometimes seems like they're doing the opposite.

Unfortunately, authors don't always have a lot of influence over branding methods, but even if your publisher doesn't back your series with an aggressive marketing track, nothing is stopping you from discussing these issues with your editor or publisher to get branding running hot and fast. You can also offer as much as you can to your fans on your own website or blog. For each rule below, I include methods that authors can employ to promote branding, even if publishers don't cooperate.

## RULE 1: ASSOCIATE THE SERIES WITH EACH TITLE

To me, this one is so out-and-out obvious, I feel foolish even mentioning it. If your readers don't know your book is part of a series, what's going to prompt them to look for the next one and the next one and the one after that? Believe it or not, this is the number one series rule I see broken most frequently, and it's such a missed opportunity. Book distributors are guilty of this time and again: Go to many book distributors' websites and you'll likely have a hard time determining whether a book is even part of a series. A few publishers are diligent about advertising a series as such, but most don't bother.

Make sure the title of the book is always, always, *always* associated with the series. In other words, never allow yourself or your publisher (if you can help it) to include just the title of your book. For instance, I never refer to my book *Shards of Ashley* simply by its title. I always refer to it as *Shards of Ashley*, Book 5 of the Family Heirlooms Series. Notice that I include the title of the book, the book number in the series, and the series title. In this way, new readers and long-time fans immediately recognize the information they need to know. For those readers who try to follow a series, it's extremely helpful to include the book number in the series whenever you talk about a particular title. On the listservs I patrol, I've heard a huge number of series readers say they won't skip around in a series—they start at the beginning and read chronologically. Very few readers skip around. Having the book number associated with the title (and even on the spine and/ or front and back cover, as I'll address soon) ensures that readers know exactly where this book falls in the series.

As I mentioned in the introduction of this book, I capitalize the word *series* (or *trilogy*, *saga*, and the like) in every instance it is used in this book. This is a crucial point, and I realize it'll take a shake-up in the publishing industry before it becomes a standard practice. However, *series* is actually part of the series title, and you want readers to know immediately that this story *is* part of a series. Doing so further solidifies the branding. In other words, I never refer to my Incognito Series as simply Incognito. Always, I add the "Series" tag because this is the full series title and the most effective way to brand it to my readers. If you lowercase the word *series*, you're downplaying the importance of the full series title. Worse, if you leave it off the title altogether, series readers won't know what they're missing (but you might when your sales aren't what you hoped for). Start this habit now and make a point of being consistent in the use of the title of each book and trilogy/series name. Underline or highlight it, but whatever you do, don't forget this rule: Make sure the *whole* title of the book is always associated with the series.

In the process of working with your editor, continue to reinforce that you see all the stories as part of the series—one book cannot be separated from the others because they all belong together.

You wouldn't believe how often I have to chase my own publishers to make sure they include the title of the book with the series name and the book number in all the places the book is promoted and distributed. Only one of my publishers consistently uses both the book title and series without fail, and out of all of my publishers, I believe this is the only one who truly understands the power of branding a series. The others must be sick of hearing me complain about this issue, but only after I've complained substantially do I get results. I believe it's important enough to keep asking until it gets done. It's true that small-press publishers put out my fiction, but the mass-market publishers fail to practice this form of branding as well. I expect above all that large publishers must realize that series sell, and they sell better when the book's series title and book number are made clear on every piece of marketing literature, every word-of-mouth recommendation, and every website mention.

While publishers use distributors for getting the books out to the customers, publishers provide all the information necessary for distributors to sell the books. It's the publishers who tend not to provide series information at all, or incompletely, along with the basic book information. Talk to your editor/publisher about associating the series name and book number for every single title. Make sure this information makes it to distributors consistently.

If your publisher isn't diligent in this regard, you can change your information at amazon.com, barnesandnoble.com, and other online distributors. While you're logged in to these sites, the page for your book may have a section labeled with something like "Update This Information." Sometimes publishers won't allow anyone to change the book information, but if you find that you can change it yourself, do so!

Take my advice: If your publisher won't follow through on this particular branding, rigorously follow this advice yourself: For every scrap of promotion you do for the series, make sure you include the complete series information for every title. Then make sure you do it for your website as well. You might even consider putting a list of series on your website with the title in each series and the book number—and maybe even making this list printable. That way, your most avid followers can get the information they need without too much hassle. Remember, you can lose sales by making basic information hard to come by.

## RULE 2: UTILIZE SERIES BLURBS

Earlier I discussed creating a series blurb. All of my series have a series blurb I use for promotion. It's necessary to utilize the series blurb as much as possible to create brand awareness for your series. Don't underestimate the appeal of the series blurb. New and longtime series readers alike want to know how the current book connects with others in that series. If the series blurb is effective, those sentences will accurately reflect the premise of every book in the series in a concise, intriguing summary. Series blurbs can sell books just as surely as story blurbs can. An author would never consider skipping a story blurb—a publisher wouldn't either. While some publishers write and use their own series blurbs instead of using the one the author writes, the series blurb is often underrated and underutilized—to the author's detriment.

This the second most common branding rule I see broken. In this case, it's not only publishers who neglect to utilize the series blurb. Recently I wanted to find more information about a certain best-selling author's series. The series had been around for a while, and several books were already available. I went to the publisher's website, the author's website, and even to distributor websites and tried desperately to find out what the series was about. The story blurbs were fine, but they didn't tell me enough about the connections between individual books to appeal to me. In addition, none of the books had numbers, so I had no idea what the order of the series was, and worse, which book to start with.

When I buy a series, I look first at the series blurb—it tells me what I'm getting into. If that blurb entices me, I'll read individual story blurbs (starting with the first book and continuing in consecutive order). If I like those, I'll make a purchase. Unfortunately, in the case I described above, the information I needed was nowhere to be found. I got tired of chasing after it, and the author of this series lost the sale—possibly of many titles.

I do feel bad about that because I know authors have little if any control over aspects of publication when working with mass-market (and sometimes even small-press) publishers. But that particular author did have control of her own website, and she failed to give me the information I needed to make a purchase enticing or even inevitable.

Getting your series blurb out there is critical to branding. It is part of what convinces a consumer to begin your series. If she likes what she reads, she may buy every book in the series. But if she doesn't know what she's getting into, she probably won't bother. A series isn't like a single-title book. If you lose readers from the beginning or anywhere in the series, you've lost them forever. That's a major ruin some series authors never recover from.

Talk to your publisher about everything I've addressed here. If you can't get her to act, at the very least make sure you provide easily accessible and compelling information about your series on your website.

## RULE 3: ENCOURAGE SERIES RECOGNITION

I was talking to a friend of mine who grew up reading Harlequin Super-romances. From what I could gather from my friend, this series imprint puts out numerous "continuity miniseries" that include books from several of their most popular authors. The main thing my friend could remember about this particular series was the logo on the spine. I did some research and found that this logo was featured on the back covers of the books as well, along with a very tight, one-sentence series blurb. After my friend read a couple of these titles, she began to search for the series logo on the spine of the books whenever she needed a new book to read. She was initially drawn in by reading a single book, but seeing the series logo sucked her in every time. A logo! A tiny, readily identifiable graphic on the spine of a book! It's a brilliant concept ... and unfortunately one that many publishers underutilize.

This conversation with my friend reminded me of a reader letter I'd perused in an issue of *RT Book Reviews* in 2010. This reader had been following a particular book series, and she'd been trying "for ages" to put together a complete list of all the books in the series. The publisher, who had many imprints, published the books in this series across several of the various imprints. At the time this reader was actively purchasing these series books, the publisher had used a little symbol on the spine of all the books in the series, making it easy for her to locate the related books on the shelves in the bookstore. But then the publisher abruptly abandoned that practice, and the reader couldn't find the necessary information on the publisher's website, possibly because older books weren't listed or available there. (Harlequin/Silhouette books don't stay on bookstore shelves for long, and that's probably why they also disappear from the publisher's website quickly.) Because the series was written by many different authors, the reader couldn't search for upcoming books in the series. She had no idea which author's book would be released next. This was a loyal reader who became addicted to a series and went to great lengths to get every single book in that series. The publisher did absolutely nothing to help her gather the information she needed to make purchases. Have you ever heard of anything so sad? Or so avoidable?

So many publishers (and authors) fall off the branding bandwagon in this regard, and I can't fathom why. The use of a recognizable series logo to go with the series blurb can create instant sales. My friend had loved all previous books in the particular series, and she placed any new ones on her automatic-buy list. If you can get your publisher to go the extra mile and design a series logo for you that can be placed on the spines and covers of each book in the series, you'll find that it really does help increase your sales.

Also, having similar cover art for each book is a huge help in creating instant recognition for that series. Of my current books, I've designed all but one cover (a perk of working with small-press publishers), for which I've been nominated for cover design awards. For my series, I create a series logo and make sure the book cover designs are similar from one to the next. For my Incognito Series, all the books are portrayed in black and white, with a third of the front cover devoted to a vertical black panel that contains the title of the book in a very colorful font (all the books use the same font—the colors for each book are different). The series logo is placed beneath the title. On the spine I include the book number at the top, the book title and my name down the middle, and a smoking gun near the bottom. The back cover is the same format from one book to the next. When all the books are lined up on a bookshelf, you know instantly that they're part of the same series. The layout for almost all of my series books is very similar from one book to the next, helping to create cover art recognition. I encourage you to check out my website at karenwiesner. com and click on the button that says "Author's Cover Designs" to see examples of series cover similarities and series logos that create branding.

One way of taking this a step further is to include information *inside* each book that allows the reader to follow the series easily. In all of my series books, I include a list of all currently available books in the series with ISBNs, as well as a teaser blurb for the upcoming book in the series with the release date.

It's worth a phone call or e-mail to your publisher to ask about getting logos, covers, and front matter that will create the instant recognition of your series.

While you probably won't get these things until you're on the best-seller lists, a lot of publishers do create author name recognition logos. In other words, on the covers of all of Nora Roberts's books, her name is big and bold—and her name is actually a recognizable logo that her publisher created in an effort to encourage branding.

Finally, another way to create recognition for your series is to come up with similar titles for the books in your series. Take Nora Roberts again: For her Born In Trilogy, the titles were *Born in Fire, Born in Ice,* and *Born in Shame.* Fans would have found these easily—especially since the series title and order of books were not only listed on the front covers and some of the back covers, but also just inside the front covers and possibly on the spine as well. Jane Toombs also uses similar book titles with many of her series: For instance, the Temple of Time Series has *Forbidden, Forsaken, Forlorn,* and *Forsworn* (she's also planning a final book called *Forever*).

Again, while authors have little or no control over whether readers will recognize a book in their series, it doesn't mean you can't push for it as much as possible. If your publisher won't help you in this regard, the least you can do as the author is provide all the information the reader needs on your website or blog.

Writing for small-press publishers, I don't have the money to spend on a website with all the bells and whistles, so I do what I can with what I'm capable of working with. I have separate pages on my website for each of my series (including a hot-linked button to each one on the main page). The individual books in the series contain comprehensive information and enticing series and book blurbs so readers can easily determine which series the book belongs to, as well as its number, availability, and distributor details. If the book is available, I include links to several places where it can be purchased—instant gratification is key! My website also provides multifaceted search pages, which make navigation of my sometimes-overlapping series as easy as possible for my readers. The search pages include an alphabetical character search (which lists all of my major and minor characters and how they're linked in my various books and series, along with a list of, and links to, the titles each character is featured in), a location search (a list of the major settings in my books and the titles they're featured in), a series search (a basic listing of each title in my many series), a genre search (a list of all my titles grouped by genre), and a printable book list with ISBNs, which a reader can print out and take to the bookstore.

Nora Roberts is another series-oriented author who knows how to keep fans from getting confused. Her website includes everything necessary to follow her many series—and it's easily navigated.

Of course, the best thing that can happen for a series writer is for his series to garner an official companion in which everything you ever wanted to know about that series is published. Examples include *The Official Nora Roberts Companion*, *The World of Shannara* (Terry Brooks), *The Outlandish Companion* (Diana Gabaldon), which has a second volume in the works, and my own, *The World of Author Karen Wiesner: A Compendium of Fiction*.

## RULE 4: TIME SERIES RELEASES WISELY

Something else to consider when marketing a series is the release schedule. What makes more sense? Back-to-back releases or releases that come out at the same time once or twice a year? I talked to a slew of authors and publishers about this, and they offered several different opinions, listed in no particular order:

**LINDA VARNER PALMER:** "Releasing books back to back or even one per year should keep the reader intrigued. Longer than a year apart is just cruel!"

**MARILYN MEREDITH:** "My books are usually released one a year. That's plenty, as promoting two books a year takes a lot of time."

**P.A. BROWN:** "I think back to back might be too close together, but one a year might be too much time these days. People are less patient about waiting. I don't really write mine on a timetable. And I try to do other writing in between series books. One of the crucial things for a writer is to have your backlist available."

**MARISSA ST JAMES:** "Releasing books back to back might make creativity difficult. At the same time, to do it once a year or so could create impatient readers. You take a chance either way."

**JANET ELAINE SMITH:** "I think if you wait too long in between books of a series, people are apt to lose interest. That doesn't mean that the future books can't sell, but you have to start your marketing all over again. It's much easier to build on something that people still remember and can relate to."

**SPECULATIVE ROMANCE CO-AUTHORS STELLA AND AUDRA PRICE:** "I like when series books come out two a year. It gets me into the series more and helps keep my interest. We try to put out at least four books a year between two different series. Readers enjoy it and so do we."

**FRAN ORENSTEIN:** "By releasing series books regularly, the reader will not lose the impact of the book and will keep the reader craving more. Wait too long and the reader will move on. With a children's book series, you have to tighten the time between books or the kids will outgrow them very quickly, just like their clothes and shoes, and definitely move on and away from your books. Kids also don't have the attention span most adults have, and they can't wait as long for the next book."

**CHRISTY POFF:** "Releasing back to back depends on the way the stories run, but I believe in some cases it's detrimental because the second release may pull everyone away from the one before it. With e-publishing, it's okay to release one or two in a year's time because the medium supports doing so (print takes a lot longer). Any longer and I would think the readers might forget the ones before, though I can see it boosting sales for those who do not have the preceding volumes. I'm reading one series where the books came out like clockwork, then two came out over the next ten years because the writer had several other series going. His last release was last August (five years after the previous one, which was five after its predecessor), and the next one comes out this August—a year later. Had I not loved the series, I may have given up on it. In this day and age, we can't afford to have that happen if we expect to be successful."

**CHARLOTTE BOYETT-COMPO:** "A book a year is really pushing reader commitment. They tend to get very frustrated when they have to wait that long and are liable to look for a writer who releases books quicker. As a reader, I prefer the author bring out a new book in a series at least three times a year. I can handle twice a year, but I really don't like to. There are series I follow faithfully, and I am anxious to read the latest development as soon as possible. Conversely, I think if you bring out a book in a series every other month or so, readers get overwhelmed. The answer to that is to break up the series with another series so the reader can go back and forth between core characters and new stories being written for the old ones. It's like having spaghetti one night and lasagna the next. You wouldn't want to eat the same thing night after night. You'd get jaded, so you have to stagger what you eat."

**LUISA BUEHLER:** "The books have to be well written and create the word-of-mouth buzz every author hopes will occur. With the first book of a series, if it takes off, the second one needs to be coming out soon enough to keep the buzz going. It's lovely to have books coming out back to back, but it's tough to write that way if you're not writing full time. One a year is difficult to do if you're not writing full time—sometimes even if you are. My books come out about eighteen months apart. Readers are realistic people, and they are willing to wait about a year for a new release. If they're hooked on the series, they'd like the books on the shelf! I tell my readers to slow down, savor, and don't speed-read through Grace's adventures because I can't write that fast!"

**MARY JEAN KELSO:** "Promotion is everything. Branding is optimal! Until an author makes the bestseller lists, it is a struggle. As long as you can keep your name in the forefront, it helps. I try not to release more than a couple of Andy books a year because I want the reader to eagerly look forward to the next. I was releasing the Homesteader Series at [a rate of] a book a year but, because of all the other books I write, this time has stretched considerably."

**N.J. WALTERS:** "The advantage of releasing series books back to back is that readers don't have time to forget about it. The disadvantage is the writer can't work on anything else. It really pushes you into a time crunch and can make you sick of writing the series. The same goes for the series where you write one a year, but in reverse. Advantage: Lots of time to write and work on other projects. Disadvantage: Readers might forget about the characters and lose interest."

**M. FLAGG:** "My series [books are] releasing a year apart. I'm not entirely happy with that. I would have preferred back to back. I think the closer a series releases, the more it builds momentum and a firm reader base. Then again, I've picked up the first book in a series long after it was written and went on to read all the books in the series. Who knows, right?"

**VIJAYA SCHARTZ:** "Faster sells better. Readers are not patient. Unless writers are so prolific that they can release four or five books a year (I know a few who do it), individual authors cannot gather the same kind of momentum for their [books]. Their promotion finances are also limited. It's simple math. Still, series sell better than single titles because the author can build on each book and build readership."

**DIANA CASTILLEJA:** "My deepest objection is to the back-to-back monthly releases. There's no time to find a strong reading market before you're throwing more [books] at the shelves, [which are] likely to be ignored and then returned because time wasn't given to let them draw the readership necessary to prolong them."

**ANN TRACY MARR:** "I suspect that flooding the market with a series is as bad as having them come out too far apart."

**REGAN TAYLOR:** "I find a good number of authors lose steam by Book 3. They lose interest or come upon a deadline they didn't plan for or are just ready to move on. As a result, the books can get sloppy. Released too soon, the books may be badly written. Released one per year, readers move on to another hot book or series."

**MICHELLE LEVIGNE:** "Staying visible, letting people know what's new, and getting them to try [a book] is the most important part [of promotion]. I can't say what the advantages or disadvantages are [of relcasing series books close together], except that from a reader's stand-point with favorite authors, I *love* having more than one book per year available. When I get into a series that I love, I don't want to wait for the next one—especially not a whole year. I think that having to wait a year until the next book comes out may contribute to readers losing interest. Readers might forget they're waiting for the next installment because they've become interested in so many other stories and au-thors in the meantime. It helps being e-published with many different houses because you can have multiple releases throughout the year. You might have one per year with each publisher, but if you have six publishers, that's six hits you had in the year. Keeping your name out there keeps the readers coming back."

**DANA MARIE BELL:** "Just because the book is on the shelves does not mean readers are aware that it's there! Advertise! As a (primarily) e-published author, I've had back-to-back releases and not so back-to-back releases. In the first case, the book sold well, but my backlist didn't. Not enough time had elapsed for people to look for the backlist. With the releases spaced more evenly apart, my backlist sold much better."

**PUBLISHER J.M. SMITH:** "I think spacing titles in a series is really impor-tant. Leaving a six-month gap or more between the titles makes the reader anticipate the next—and anticipation is important. Some of our series release two titles per year, while others release one per year. It depends on the author's writing pace, the audience of the particu-lar series, and how the genre itself is doing overall."

**PUBLISHER LAURA BAUMBACH:** "As a reader, I think a year is too long to wait for a new book. I think three to four months is fairer for a series. As an author, I couldn't write a book every four months if I wanted to, [in addition to running] a business and having a family life. So the author must either write the stories all at once and present them to a publisher, or the publisher must be prepared for the possibility that the books will get released as the author manages to finish them, *if* she finishes them. As a publisher, I rejected a third book in a series because the sales numbers for the second book were so small as to be barely accountable. The author was disappointed, but so far no readers have commented on its disappearance."

If you're a prolific author the way I am, you'll have to spread your work around to various publishers so they can keep up with you. At the end of 2011, I was working more than a year ahead of my releases. In other words, I'd completed all my 2012 releases and all but three of my 2013 releases. At that time, I was juggling seven series of vastly different genres and a few single titles, along with quite a few reissues, so I was expecting a release every single month in 2012 (more than one per month, in fact). But I had titles from each of these series coming out several times a year, allowing me the time to make sure every single book I offered was of the highest quality while giving my fans time to anticipate what was coming up and satisfying their need for more reading material.

In late 2007 Harlequin established a new marketing strategy of releasing trilogy books back to back: three books in three consecutive months. This practice has become popular with all types of romance series, and publishers of other genres are jumping on the bandwagon as well. Readers get the instant gratification they desire, and the author gains recognition and a boost in sales (meaning print runs soar and the books go into multiple printings), and usually all of the books will be on store shelves at the same time. Sales feed off each other. A lot of publishers say they use this strategy to avoid a lag in excitement and momentum, which can sometimes happen with back-to-back releases. Publishers most often consider this strategy for the books of authors who already have fan bases, but many find great success using the books of debut authors as well since the beginning momentum for the author can be phenomenal.

The big problem with this strategy is that some authors simply can't write that quickly. Obviously a publisher will work with an author in this manner only if he proves he can meet the challenge. It helps if all the books have been written before endeavoring to release them back to back (i.e., close together). While most of my interviewees said one year was too long between releases, they also frowned upon releasing books in quick succession because momentum for the first book is still growing by the time the second book is released. In general, releasing two books a series per year is good, but three can also work well. Constant promotion during that time is as important as completing the series books. You have to write a book in order to promote it, but you also have to promote to sell the book before moving on to the next—unless you're writing far ahead of your releases. The fact that I'm currently a year ahead of my releases usually allows me adequate time to promote my many new releases as well as to write the con tracted works I need to. If you want to find out how to get ahead, consult my books *First Draft in 30 Days* for the goal-setting chapter and *From First Draft to Finished Novel* to learn about working in stages. Both will help you produce books that balance quality with quantity. You can learn more about how to promote effectively in my book *The Power of Promotional Groups*. Writing and promotion work hand in hand in furthering an author's career.

Ultimately, authors (especially those who have mass-market publishers) have little control over when their series titles will be released. The decision is based on how quickly the author writes, how well the books sell with each new title, and the climate of the economy from one point in time to another. Promotion is key, and if the series is well received by fans, you may find that you have more say in the matter. Once one of the books in your series sells well, you should consider approaching your publisher about getting your series books released more frequently as long as the quality of your writing can be sustained.

When all is said and done, the four rules outlined here come down to one blatantly obvious requirement: If you want readers to follow and purchase your series, make the series as easy to find and as enticing as possible!

## BUILD YOUR SERIES MUSCLES EXERCISES

To create branding for your series:

- Always associate your series with the title and specify where each book falls within the series. Ask your publisher to do the same, especially when it comes to distribution.

- Utilize your series blurbs as often as you can, everywhere you can—but especially on your own website and blog. Talk to your publisher about using a series blurb in all distribution and promotion.
- Create series recognition through the use of logos, familiar covers, similar titles, and interior book material if at all possible. If your publisher doesn't do any of these things, at the very least include comprehensive series information on your website.
- Quality and quantity go hand in hand in writing any book. If you are a prolific writer and you write well, you can aggressively promote many releases. If sales numbers are solid, you may be able to influence your publisher to increase the number of books you release per year.

In this chapter, I detailed the most important aspects of marketing a series in order to make it memorable and easily accessible to fans and series-searching readers. In the next chapter, I'll explore series endings.

# CHAPTER SIX

# PREPARING FOR THE CONCLUSION OF A SERIES

*"In my beginning is my end. ... What we call the beginning is often the end. And to make an end is to make a beginning. The end is where we start from."*

~T.S. ELIOT

When parents send a child off on his own, they often experience a sense of loss and of hope, a sense that they're not prepared for the child's departure. Ultimately the emotions they feel are as individual as they are. It's the same way with ending a series. The author may not be prepared to let go of the characters and their situations, and may have mixed emotions or very definitive ones. In part, these emotions can reflect how long or short the series is, how frequently the books are released, and how it was decided that the series would end.

## SERIES ENDINGS

The series authors I spoke with and whose blogs I read voiced many different feelings when it came to the ending of a series, feelings that I think most authors can understand. Micqui Miller says that, as an author, she suffers terrible separation anxiety for days, sometimes weeks, after she finishes a book. The characters have a place inside her heart and she misses them terribly.

Says Joanne Hall, "I found it very hard to let go of the New Kingdom Trilogy at the end. So much so that I chose to do *gasp!* housework, rather than sit down and write those last few pages. It was only when my partner caught me taking down the net curtains to wash them that he called me on it, forced me into a chair, and basically stood over me until I wrote 'The End.' Without him, the book would still be unfinished!"

On the other hand, Jane Toombs has this to say: "When I'm done, I'm done, and the series is ended. I'm always glad to finish a novella or novel, and a series is no different. I need to let it go when I feel I have no more stories for that series."

Like me, Jane is the author of many series, and like Jane, I think the more an author has written, the easier it is to let go of characters and stories and to move on to other projects. Frequently, I feel relieved to have a series (especially a long one, like my Incognito Series with twelve hefty novels) completed and officially under my belt. If I'm not relieved to end it, a spin-off series is usually born. Celtic historical romance/ fantasy author Kelley Heckart told me she was relieved when her Dark Goddess Trilogy ended. "I was free to move on to something else," she said. "I did not leave anything open, but I never say never because there is always something more to explore in the world I've created if I decide to go back to it."

Janet Elaine Smith says this about ending a series: "My biggest problem with writing a series is that I get started with too many of them at one time and I don't have enough hours in the day. I hear from readers all the time; those who keep bugging me to get the next books in any of the series out. I know you are supposed to leave them wanting more, but there has to be a limit. At this rate, I'm going to have to stick around until I'm at least 124 years old to get all of my series done. Of course, by that time other ideas will have invaded my brain!"

Letting a series go is hard, but sometimes it's the best option for the author. L.A. Banks said it best in an interview with *RT Book Reviews*: "You want to leave the game while you're on top. I want people to say, 'Man, all the way to the end you got a slammin' read.'"

## RESOLUTIONS: THE (ABSOLUTE!) END OR OPEN-ENDED?

Writing a series can be a win/lose situation. While you'll find many pros to doing one, a few cons exist as well. Once you start a successful series, you've locked yourself in. Unless you're a writer who can churn out a lot of quality material in a short time, you may end up focusing exclusively on the series because it'll consume your attention. You'll have to work harder with every book to keep the series fresh for the reader and for *you*. To me, that's been the hardest part of being a series author.

On her website, author Charlaine Harris tells fans of her Aurora Teagarden novels that she's not discrediting the idea of more stories for that series in the future. But she's moved on to other series, and time has become a consideration in whether she'll continue. Kelley Armstrong says the same thing about her Nadia Stafford books. With two other series that keep her busy, she would have to write another in her free time ... something of which she has little.

When I started my Incognito Series, I didn't imagine it would ever end. I had story ideas for most of the characters I had introduced in the early books. The first book in the series came out in mid-2005. Starting in 2006, my publisher began releasing two books a year—usually one in March and the next in October. At first, this thrilled me, especially because at that time I had finished only the first two books in the series. The next nine were sold practically on mere speculation. I had titles and the main characters for Books 3–12 in the series, nothing more. Mind you, this series was far from the only series I was writing at that time (I think I was juggling six or seven others), so I was writing about a half dozen books a year, in addition to at least that many novellas. I started to get burned out on the Incognito Series by Book 5, the writing of which came very hard for me. Luckily, Books 6 through 8 emerged fairly easily, and I thought I'd gotten over the "hump." I believe I was able to complete those stories because I'd had a lot of ideas for them over the course of many years. The next four books were nightmarish. Remember when I said I had only a title and main characters for each book when I signed contracts? I'd been writing so many books in various series back to back that I didn't have time to brainstorm much on any of them. So there I was, attempting to pull rabbits out of hats.

In retrospect, I don't know how I wrote those books or how they turned out good, but luckily they did, and my streak of five-star reviews continued. I only knew that by the time I finished Book 8, I was exhausted and *beyond* ready for the end of this series. Somehow I had to write the stories of eight more key players in the series over the course of four more books. Without those, the series wouldn't feel finished. Though I'd planned on writing an additional three books beyond the twelve contracted ones, I was able to let them go easily. I'd never made those six characters key to the overall series, so it was possible to leave them out. I felt a little like Sir Arthur Conan Doyle with his Sherlock Holmes character. I knew that if I didn't stop the series soon, I would be killing all of my characters off just so I could escape. I had planned for the end of the series as I led up to it, and Book 12 ended on a note in which the conclusion was neatly gift wrapped, the series came full circle, and the end was satisfying. While I made it clear that this was the final book I would be writing for the series for some time, I still left a tiny gap in the series as a whole because I knew someday (when I wasn't so burned out) I might want a way to get back in.

On the same topic N.J. Walters says: "I love completing a series. If I'm not ready for it to be over, then it's not done, and I'll write another book. I ended the Dalakis Passion Series when the stories surrounding the main family were done. It took five books to do that. Readers have asked for more, but I know in my heart that the series is complete. On the other hand, a writer never says never."

I tried to say "never again" to my Incognito Series, but the day I wanted to get back in came sooner than I expected. In 2011 I started brainstorming on those last three stories I'd considered writing. The series felt unfinished to me, regardless of how I had tried to tie it up in Book 12. However, I wasn't 100 percent sure I was ready to commit to three more novels or to open the door wide again. In fact, I knew I wanted closure with this series as much as I believed my fans did. The idea of doing an interconnected spin-off trilogy with an overarching series arc came to me then. However, when I submitted the proposal for Shadow Missions, I felt like I still hadn't completely tied up the series in a way that allowed me to walk away forever. The decision to include a bonus story called "Out of the Shadows," The Final Mission in the Shadow Missions Series, sealed the deal—and the end of the series for good. That decision felt like perfect timing and a satisfactory resolution for me, and, when it comes out at the end of 2016, I expect my fans to be happy with it as well.

Vijaya Schartz agrees that a writer can creatively reopen a portal previously closed: "I always mourn my characters at the end of a book, and I miss the world where I spent so much time. It's always difficult to say good-bye. I like to tie all of the loose ends with the known characters, but sometimes I'll leave out a group of people to settle somewhere for a new beginning. It could become the starting point of a spin-off series in the future. But usually, by the time I finish a series, I have another series or a story brainstormed and I'm ready to write it, so I just bury myself in that new world with those new characters."

Personally, I always have something else going on, so I don't feel an overwhelming sense of loss when I finish a book or series anymore. But when I finished my Kaleidoscope Series, I knew I wanted to revisit the town I'd created in Book 2. (Incidentally, this town had its start in Book 5 of my Incognito Series.) The majority of the characters were waiting to have their stories told based on my two previous journeys there. The spin-off series, Cowboy Fever, reignited my passion in a new direction that didn't depart too greatly from where I'd left off with the other two stories. Sometimes a spin-off of a previous idea, setting, or character is an easy way to keep things fresh and alive for the author and the readers.

As N.J. Walters says, "Any series is always open. A good writer can find a way back in. With my Project Alpha Trilogy, I knew going in that it was only going to be three books. I tied up the major story line in the final book. It was done! But the characters and the futuristic world I created still existed, and still exist today. If I wanted to, I could start another series in that world and give readers a glimpse of the characters from the trilogy."

I often think that starting with a smaller number of books or working in stages makes a world of difference in keeping things manageable for authors as well. After writing four books in my six-book Family Heirlooms Series, I came up with the idea for a seven-book series in the same world. Many characters within the first series clamored for their own books. If I'd started out with a thirteen-book Family Heirlooms Series, I doubt I would have completed the last seven books. Writing a spin-off series allowed me to keep things very manageable. I remembered only too well how intimidating the twelve-book Incognito Series became toward the middle and end of writing it. But since I planned only six books and then came up with the idea for additional books, I felt like I'd achieved something major when I completed the Family Heirlooms Series. The last book felt as fresh to me as the first one. I could hardly wait to start the spin-off series, Friendship Heirlooms. This series doesn't feel like something that will go on and on with no end in sight. I'm handling the series in definable chunks so I don't get burned out the way I did before.

Sir Arthur Conan Doyle wasn't able to kill off Sherlock Holmes in the minds of his readers. The outcry was so great, the author had no choice but to pick up where he left off, literally. And he had to literally resurrect this character from the dead, giving him a new life that lasted for quite a long time, to the relief of avid readers. While I'm sure Doyle was annoyed at first, isn't this what all authors want? Characters who have become so real that readers absolutely refuse to let them go?

## THE (UNNATURAL) DEATH OF A SERIES

What if the *author* doesn't want the series to end, but the publisher goes out of business while the author is in the middle of writing a series? What if the publisher gets bored with the series or changes the formats, covers, or style, and/or distributors put the books in another section so readers can no longer find the upcoming books in that series? What if readers taper off (God forbid!), sales drop, and the publisher decides to pull the plug? Unfortunately, this is happening with more and more regularity, and it's what gives most series authors nightmares. To have a series left dangling in this way can put an author in a very awkward position, especially if she has readers on tenterhooks that become skewers when the announcement of this series' unnatural death comes.

Due to declining sales, Shanna Swendson's popular Enchanted, Inc. Series ended abruptly at Book 4, and she was informed that her series would be discontinued after she wrote that book. She had no chance to wrap up the existing plots in Book 5 as she had originally planned. While Swendson hasn't given up all hope that the final book in the series will someday be published, she and her publisher have moved on.

Ann Tracy Marr says, "My publisher was not very interested in my series. The company was sold between Books 2 and 3. I am shopping Book 4 elsewhere, with fear that it is dead." (Incidentally, she has continued her series—good news for her fans!)

Historical author J.M. Hochstetler says she sold the first two books in her American Patriot Series to Zondervan, but before she signed the contract, the acquiring editor left. She'd given verbal acceptance at that point, and her agent encouraged her to honor the agreement. She signed the contract, but the editor who took over wasn't interested in historical novels and gave Hochstetler's books minimal attention. They didn't sell well and Zondervan canceled the series. For a long time after the contracts were terminated, no other publishers would consider the series, but J.M. did eventually find a new publisher for the series. Walker & Co.'s mystery division went belly up before Denise Dietz had completed her series with them. She ended up selling the paperback rights to Worldwide Library Mysteries, and even though the press runs sold out in less than three months, it took her five years to find a publishing house that would continue the series.

Author Marilyn Meredith, who also writes as F.M. Meredith, says, "My Tempe Series has had three publishers. The first four books were published by a small regional publisher and, sadly, she died. I'd retained my e-rights, and another publisher took on the books as e-books and published an earlier book as an e-book and trade paperback. Now all the books are with Mundania Press. Most of my readers don't care about the change of publishers. They just want to know when the [next] Tempe Series title is coming out. My first Rocky Bluff book was published [as an e-book] in the dark ages of e-publishing before any kind of e-reader existed. It languished. Later it was picked up by another e-publisher who [published] it and the second in the series and published trade paperbacks. Though the publisher had the next two books, they were never published. I took the series back. The next publisher published the next two books both as e-books and trade paperbacks and then went out of business. Oak Tree Press put the previous books on Kindle and published the latest two for Kindle and trade paperback."

"After *L.A. Heat* was sold," says P.A. Brown, "I wrote Book 2 and submitted it through my agent. The publisher rejected it. Before I could ask if they wanted to do another, my editor left the company and my agent retired, so I was left without a publisher. At first I was stunned, then annoyed, then I tried to get another agent, but most were reluctant to take on a new book midseries. I finally found my current publisher without an agent, and we republished Book 1 and all subsequent books. I actually wrote *L.A. Mischief* as a filler for the publisher who put out *L.A. Heat* in e-book form, and it was very well received."

Fran Orenstein says, "After publishing *The Wizard of Balalac* in the Book of Mysteries fantasy series and *The Ghost Under Third Base* in the mystery series, the publisher ran off with the money and went bankrupt, leaving 165 authors in the lurch. I went through a very depressing ten months and tried several times to self-publish the books and the others in the series but failed because of technology. The books are still listed on Amazon and will be forever, but there are no copies available. I finally found a wonderful publisher, Sleepytown Press, that republished Book 1 of each series under different names and with different covers because of the Amazon listings. Book 2 from each series is also published with the new publisher. It was difficult when I ran out of my own copies of the first books because I could no longer do book signings or provide books for people who wanted them. Series are particularly hard hit because readers are waiting for the next book and when it doesn't appear, they move on."

Charlotte Boyett~Compo says, "Readers have followed me from one publisher to the other and for that I am very grateful. That tells me they like what I write and are willing to look for it with other publishers."

Lorie Ham says, "While my publisher is still in business, it became difficult to work with and set too-high prices on my books. It also gained a bad reputation. Because of this, I decided to self-publish the final book. I did it for the sake of my fans so the series could have an ending and be resolved."

I've been in the unfortunate position of experiencing many of the things other authors have spoken of in this book. The original publisher of my Wounded Warriors Series lost all interest in the series after the publication of Book 4. I did write Book 5 and waited more than a year, hoping for something to happen. When it didn't, I packed up the slew of awards and excellent reviews I'd received for the series and took it to another publisher, who agreed to release the entire series again, starting with Book 5, backtracking with Books 1 through 4, and finally releasing Book 6. The series is enjoying a resurrection of renewed interest, selling better than ever, and getting all new rave reviews that push sales. (Incidentally, when the contracts were up with this publisher, I moved the whole series to yet another publisher that's been putting out all my reissues for the past several years. The newest revised versions will be reissued in 2013. In today's book world, publishing and republishing the same books is becoming an everyday practice.) The same waning publisher put out the three books in my Angelfire Trilogy. I finally pulled the trilogy and resold it to another house. I was very glad to re-edit these books, and now the trilogy is enjoying a resurgence of interest, so I've decided to write the second trilogy set I'd always meant to write for new and old fans of the series (all three will come out between 2014 and 2015).

The publisher of my Family Heirlooms Series suddenly lost interest after I submitted Book 4, though the series itself had received starred reviews, won awards, and was growing in sales. They asked if I would be willing to go along with a whole new concept and marketing strategy with the series—essentially, they wanted me to start over—while refusing to offer me contracts for Books 4 through 6. Though the publisher was offering me a great opportunity, fans of the series were beginning to drop off because of the extended period of time they'd been kept waiting for the next book. I knew I couldn't go into an arrangement that wouldn't guarantee contracts for the final books in the series. Too much damage had already been done by the lengthy lag between Books 3 and 4. For the good of the series and for my eager, loyal fans, I asked for the return of the rights to the first three books. The publisher was extremely generous and allowed this. I've since sold this series to another publisher of mine, and the fourth book came out in February 2011, with Books 1 through 3 reissued in April, May, and July

2011. Books 5 and 6 were released September 2011 and March 2012. With a resurgence of publisher interest, I got back on track with the series and gave it a fresh start, the same way I had with Wounded Warriors. I also sold the spin-off series to this publisher, and its publication should keep interest alive in both series for quite a long time.

On the opposite side of the spectrum, Cat Adams (the joint pen name of authors C.T. Adams and Cathy Clamp) told me that fan reaction to the possible end of the Sazi Series convinced their publisher to agree to continue the series. The support of the fans also helped sales, and ultimately it is all about sales. One of the most publicized series' deaths was young adult author Mari Mancusi's Blood Coven Vampire Series. Her publisher decided not to publish the fourth book in the series for reasons that had to do with distribution and bookseller issues. The bottom line was money or lack thereof. A Save the Blood Coven campaign ensued. Books 4–6 were released in the next couple of years. Book 7 was released in 2012.

Fans of Brenda Joyce's Deadly Series were also able to save the series from ending in the middle of nowhere. Her publisher had decided that paranormals were no longer selling, and Brenda reluctantly moved on to other books and series. The outcry from fans led the publisher to ask the author to write a ninth book (possibly more, based on the note Brenda has posted on her website, which states that she wants to write three more stories in the series, and her publisher is interested provided the level of enthusiasm in the current releases and the actual sales warrant it—no definitive decision has been made at the time of this writing).

While a mass outpouring of support for a series can lead to its continuation, this happens only infrequently and many a series is left to die an unnatural death. During a phone interview I did with editor Alicia Condon, who works for Kensington Brava, she said without a hint of compunction that she would end a series in the middle of it. "Definitely! We discontinue if a series isn't selling well and also if we find that a series can't go beyond the three to five book mark without readers feeling like they're missing something—that they have to go back and get caught up again or initially to really enjoy them." Publisher Christina M. Brashear of Samhain Publishing also didn't get misty eyed at the prospect of abandoning a series: "Certainly I don't think any publisher hasn't been in the situation where the series didn't live up to expectations in one way or another. Sales are certainly a factor, but it can also be that the follow-up book(s) weren't the same quality as the preceding titles. We would prefer to end a series gracefully, but that's challenging to accomplish."

Vijaya Schartz was involved in Triskelion's publisher series Operation: Pleaides with several other authors in the same series. Vijaya had just turned in the last book of the series when the publisher went out of business in 2007. Her book was never published. Triskelion authors spent a year in court to get their rights back. But since that time Vijaya has started a new series on her own with the last book she wrote for the Operation: Pleaides Series. Talk about turning a lemon into lemonade!

The bottom line is that publishing is a business. Unfortunately, if the sales aren't there, an author has to accept that his fans may never get to finish out the series with him … or he can take a risk by pulling the series and striking out anew with it.

For whatever the reason, sometimes a series must end, and authors have to deal with the ramifications the best way they can. Can you prevent the end if it should come prematurely? Unfortunately, the answer is probably not. The best any series author can do to prevent a premature end is to write a killer book every single time, one that has a story arc that is self-contained (even if series arcs can't and shouldn't be). Don't let a series book lag or grow stale or boring. Especially in particularly saturated genres, authors of series must set their series apart from the slew of others already out there.

Ask yourself what makes your series different. Why should a reader follow your series versus another author's? What's your selling point that separates you from the masses? What is everyone else writing, and how can you do something different to interest readers? Readers may become very choosy about what they read, especially when the market is flooded with the same old, same old that works for one author but doesn't work for the ones who jump on the bandwagon. It's too easy for the truly exceptional to get lost in the fray, but truly exceptional books and series will usually rise to the surface. The ones that stand out are the ones that put a twist on the predictable, the ones that invigorate and live on in the minds of the readers until they simply must have another and another and … on and on.

## SERIES WRAP

The ultimate test of a good novel and whether it should become a series is when you dread beginning the last chapter. While writing a series, live up to your promise to your readers by providing intriguing stories that become *more* exciting as the series progresses, by creating characters that grow and have lives that readers want to follow obsessively, and by offering something new with each book. Write the best book you're capable of—every single time. Love your characters and your fans will love them too.

Series author Elaine Coffman says, "I suppose the biggest plus to writing a series is the reader response, for they truly come to love these characters as much as the author does, and they don't mind telling you. How can you find pleasure in the praise of those you hope to entertain? What idiot wouldn't sit up at night typing because her readers are waiting to find out what happens to the next character in the series, when anyone with an ounce of sense would have gone to bed or out to dinner?"

Allow your readers to become invested in your series in a way that takes over their minds and hearts, and they'll always be waiting eagerly to join in a quest with the friends they've made. These books will live on.

The series tiger has sprung. Will your readers be "devoured" enough to stand in line in the middle of the night to get the next offering?

### BUILD YOUR SERIES MUSCLES EXERCISE

Before you begin your series, spend some time thinking about what sets your series apart from countless other series. Why should a reader follow your series versus another author's? What separates your book from the masses? What is everyone else writing, and how can you do something different to interest readers? The unique hook is the one that catches readers—and you want to catch them in droves. Brainstorm ways to lure those readers in.

# SERIES ORGANIZATION WORKSHEETS FOR YOUR USE

Download printable versions of all worksheets at writersdigest.com/fiction-series.

## WORKSHEET 1:
## SERIES AND STORY BLURB DEVELOPMENT

### SERIES BLURB

**STEP 1:** Define your series tie(s):

> Recurring Character Series
>
> Central Group of Characters Series
>
> Premise/Plot Series
>
> Setting Series
>
> Combination of these (list)

*Your series tie(s) will frequently help you figure out what needs to be included in the series blurb.*

**STEP 2:** In one to four sentences, define your series arc by putting it into the series arc equation. Try to do this in a single sentence, if possible, following the "leads to" logic.

> *Remember, resolutions are not requisite in the series blurb since you don't want to defuse the intrigue or tension, but sometimes a resolution works for the overall series blurb. Play with it.*

> Introduction → Change → Conflicts →
> Choices → Crisis → Resolutions

> **EXAMPLE:** *Men and women* (**Introduction**) *who have sacrificed their personal identities* (**Choices**) *to live in the shadows* (**Change**) *and uphold justice for all* (**Conflicts**)—*no matter the cost.* (**Crisis**)

**STEP 3:** Keep tweaking your series blurb (possibly by making the sentence into a question or an exclamation, or ending with ellipses) until it's intriguing.

### STORY BLURB

**STEP 1:** Your story blurb should contain a high-concept blurb. For instance: A character (**who**) wants a goal (**what**) because he's motivated (**why**), but he faces conflict (**why not**). Your premise/plot or setting might also appear in this sentence. Come up with a simple sentence that defines your story in this way.

**STEP 2:** Flesh out your story blurb by filling in the blanks for each of the main characters in your story (unless you find it more effective to use just one main character):

_____ (name of character) wants _____(goal to be achieved) because_____ (motivation for acting), but faces_____(conflict standing in the way).

**STEP 3:** Keep tweaking your story blurb until it's intriguing (again, by using a question or exclamation to end the blurb, or by ending it with ellipses). Remember, your story blurb should fit the genre and tone of the story, and it should be short enough to be memorable but detailed enough to capture interest.

> **EXAMPLE:** An unsuspecting nurse is lured to an ancient family man-sion said to hold both ghosts and horrifying secrets in order to care for three orphaned children. **(high-concept blurb)**
>
> Amberlyn Lyons **(name of character)** has recently suffered a devastating miscarriage that has torn her marriage apart and shaken her faith **(motivation for acting)**. She quietly takes a nanny position at an isolated mansion in Bloodmoon Cove without electricity, telephone, or ease of passage. The moment she walks into Bloodmoon Manor, Amberlyn deduces that things aren't as they seem. The eerily similar owners distrust doctors who, in thirty years, have been unable to cure their severely deformed daughter Kat-erina. Katerina both idolizes and despises Amberlyn for her beauty. Childishly cruel, Katerina enjoys tormenting the orphans by telling them tales of the malicious ghost that haunts the decaying mansion. Amberlyn discounts the paranormal legends as made-up stories until she hears the shuffling of footsteps in the cold, dark halls and feels that she's being watched at every turn. She knows the ghost

is real and she must protect the children.  But when she discovers a graveyard behind the mansion filled with babies who died at birth or shortly thereafter, she realizes the ghost of Bloodmoon Manor is really a family curse, and she was brought there to uphold the family legacy of that curse. **(conflict standing in the way)** Either she finds a way to escape with the children ... or she becomes the next bloodmoon bride. **(goal to be achieved)**

## WORKSHEET 2: SERIES BREAKDOWN

## SERIES BLURB

**SERIES TITLE:**_____

**SERIES GENRE:** _____

**SERIES TIE:** _____

*If Recurring or Cast of Characters Series, list:*

    **MAIN SERIES CHARACTER(S):**_____

*If Premise/Plot Series, list:*

    **MAIN PREMISE/PLOT:** _____

*If Setting Series, list:*

    **MAIN SETTING(S):**_____

**SERIES BLURB:**_____

_____

_____

## INDIVIDUAL STORY BLURBS

**TITLE OF BOOK:**_____

**BOOK NUMBER IN THE SERIES:** _____

**STORY GENRE (IF DIFFERENT FROM THE SERIES):**_____

*If Recurring or Cast of Characters Series, list:*

    **MAIN SERIES CHARACTER(S):**_____

    **SECONDARY CHARACTER(S):**_____

*If Premise/Plot Series, list:*

    **MAIN PREMISE/PLOT:** (if different from the series)

_____

*If Setting Series, list:*

    **MAIN SETTING(S):** (if different from the series)

_____

**STORY BLURB:** _____

_____

_____

## WORKSHEET 3:
## SERIES BIBLE: CHARACTERS

*You can use separate worksheets, tablets, index cards, or word-processing files for each subject in your series bible.*

*In free-form essays, detail:*

## CHARACTERS

### Character Descriptions:

NAME:_____

_____

_____

NAME: _____

_____

_____

NAME: _____

_____

_____

### Other Important Character Information:

NAME: _____

_____

_____

NAME: _____

_____

_____

NAME: _____

_____

_____

## WORKSHEET 3A:
## SERIES BIBLE: CHARACTER SKETCH

## GENERAL CHARACTER SKETCH

**CHARACTER NAME:** _____

**NICKNAME:** _____

**BIRTH DATE/PLACE:** _____

**CHARACTER ROLE:** (hero, heroine, secondary character, villain) _____

_____

_____

_____

**PHYSICAL DESCRIPTIONS:**

      **AGE:** _____

      **RACE:** _____

      **EYE COLOR:** _____

      **HAIR COLOR/STYLE:** _____

      **BUILD (HEIGHT/WEIGHT):** _____

      **SKIN TONE:** _____

      **STYLE OF DRESS:** _____

      **CHARACTERISTICS OR MANNERISMS:** _____

**PERSONALITY TRAITS:** _____

_____

_____

**BACKGROUND:** _____

_____

_____

**INTERNAL CONFLICTS:** _____

_____

_____

**EXTERNAL CONFLICTS:** _____

_____

_____

**OCCUPATION/EDUCATION:** _____

_____

_____

**MISCELLANEOUS NOTES:** _____

_____

_____

## CHARACTER DIALOGUE SHEET

**1. CHARACTER:**

    **DIALOGUE SPECIFICS:** _____

    _____

    _____

    **OTHER MANNERISMS OR CHARACTER TAGS:** _____

    _____

    _____

**2. CHARACTER:**

    **DIALOGUE SPECIFICS:** _____

    _____

    _____

    **OTHER MANNERISMS OR CHARACTER TAGS:** _____

    _____

    _____

## WORKSHEET 4:
## SERIES BIBLE: SETTINGS

*You can use separate worksheets, tablets, index cards, or word-processing files for each subject in your series bible.*

*In free-form essays, detail:*

## SETTINGS

**NAME OF SETTING:**

    **DESCRIPTION:** _____

_____

_____

_____

_____

    **OTHER IMPORTANT SETTING INFORMATION:** _____

_____

_____

_____

_____

## WORKSHEET 4A:
## SERIES BIBLE: SETTING SKETCHES

## GENERAL SETTING SKETCH

**STORY TITLE:**_____

**NAME OF SETTING:** _____

**CHARACTERS LIVING IN THIS TIME PERIOD AND REGION:**_____

_____

_____

_____

_____

**YEAR OR TIME PERIOD:**_____

**SEASON:**_____

**STATE:** _____

**CITY OR TOWN:** _____

**MISCELLANEOUS NOTES:** _____

_____

_____

_____

_____

## CHARACTER SETTING SKETCH

**STORY TITLE:**_____

**CHARACTER NAME:** _____

**GENERAL SETTINGS FOR THIS CHARACTER:**_____

_____

_____

_____

_____

**CHARACTER'S HOME:**

    **CITY OR TOWN:** _____

    **NEIGHBORHOOD CHARACTER LIVES IN:** _____

**STREET CHARACTER LIVES ON:** _____

**CHARACTER'S NEIGHBORS:** _____

_____

_____

_____

**CHARACTER'S HOME (APARTMENT, HOUSE, MANSION, TRAILER, RANCH):** _____

_____

_____

**HOME INTERIOR:** _____

_____

_____

_____

_____

**CHARACTER'S WORKPLACE:**

**CITY OR TOWN:** _____

**BUSINESS NAME:** _____

**TYPE OF BUSINESS:** _____

**NEIGHBORHOOD:** _____

**STREET:** _____

**INDIVIDUAL WORKSPACE:** _____

**CO-WORKERS:** _____

**MISCELLANEOUS NOTES:** _____

_____

_____

_____

_____

_____

_____

_____

_____

_____

## WORKSHEET 5:
## SERIES BIBLE: PREMISE/PLOT SPECIFICS

*You can use separate worksheets, tablets, index cards, or word-processing files for each subject in your series bible.*

*In free-form essays, detail:*

**PREMISE/PLOT SPECIFICS:** _____

_____

_____

_____

_____

_____

_____

_____

_____

_____

_____

_____

_____

_____

_____

_____

_____

_____

_____

_____

_____

_____

_____

_____

_____

_____

_____

_____

_____

_____

_____

_____

## WORKSHEET 5A:
## SERIES BIBLE: PLOT SKETCH (SIMPLE)

**STORY TITLE, SERIES NAME, AND BOOK NUMBER:** _____

*Where you see the arrows, insert the words "leads to."*

Introduction → Change → Conflicts →
Choices → Crisis → Resolutions

Refer to the chart in chapter two.

*In free-form essays, detail:*

**CHARACTER INTRODUCTION:** _____
_____
_____

**CHARACTER CHANGE:** _____
_____
_____

**CHARACTER CONFLICTS:**

    **DEFINE/DISCUSS SERIES ARC:** _____

    **DEFINE/DISCUSS STORY ARC:** _____

    **DEFINE/DISCUSS SUBPLOT #1:** _____

    **DEFINE/DISCUSS SUBPLOT #2:** _____

**CHARACTER CHOICES:**

    **DEFINE/DISCUSS FINAL DOWNTIME (OR CRISIS POINT):** _____
_____

**CHARACTER CRISIS:**

    **DEFINE/DISCUSS THE BLACK MOMENT (OR EPIPHANY):** _____

    **DEFINE/DISCUSS THE SHOWDOWN:** _____

**CHARACTER RESOLUTIONS:** _____
_____
_____
_____

# WORKSHEET 5B:
# SERIES BIBLE: PLOT SKETCH (DETAILED)

**STORY TITLE, SERIES NAME, AND BOOK NUMBER:** _____

**WORKING GENRE(S):** _____

**WORKING POV SPECIFICATION:** _____

**ESTIMATED LENGTH OF BOOK:** _____

**HIGH-CONCEPT BLURB:** _____

## BEGINNING STORY CONFLICT:

_____

_____

_____

_____

## IDENTIFYING THE MAIN CHARACTER(S):

### Character Overviews

**FIRST CHARACTER:** _____

_____

**SECOND CHARACTER:** _____

_____

### Description (Outside POV)

**FIRST CHARACTER:** _____

_____

**SECOND CHARACTER:** _____

_____

### Description (Self POV)

**FIRST CHARACTER:** _____

_____

**SECOND CHARACTER:** _____

_____

## Occupational Skills

**FIRST CHARACTER:** _____

_____

**SECOND CHARACTER:** _____

_____

## Setting Descriptions

**FIRST CHARACTER:** _____

_____

**SECOND CHARACTER:** _____

_____

## Character Internal Conflicts

**FIRST CHARACTER:** _____

_____

**SECOND CHARACTER:** _____

_____

## Evolving Goals and Motivations

**FIRST CHARACTER:** _____

_____

**SECOND CHARACTER:** _____

_____

## External Plot Conflicts: _____

_____

_____

_____

## MIDDLE EVOLVING STORY CONFLICT:

## Character Internal Conflicts

**FIRST CHARACTER:** _____

_____

**SECOND CHARACTER:** _____

_____

## Evolving Goals and Motivations

**FIRST CHARACTER:** _____

_____

**SECOND CHARACTER:** _____

_____

## External Plot Conflicts:

_____

_____

_____

_____

# END RESOLVING STORY CONFLICT:

## Character Internal Conflicts

**FIRST CHARACTER:** _____

_____

**SECOND CHARACTER:** _____

_____

## Evolving Goals and Motivations

**FIRST CHARACTER:** _____

_____

**SECOND CHARACTER:** _____

_____

## External Plot Conflicts

_____

_____

_____

_____

## WORKSHEET 5C:
## SERIES BIBLE: PLOT SKETCH (IN-DEPTH)

**STORY TITLE, SERIES NAME, AND BOOK NUMBER:** _____

## PART I: THE BEGINNING

1. Conflict is introduced

    **DETAIL THE MAJOR CONFLICT:** _____

    _____

2. Story and series arcs are introduced

    **DETAIL THE MAJOR STORY GOAL:** _____

    _____

    **DETAIL THE MAJOR SERIES GOAL:** _____

    _____

3. Characters Are Outfitted for Their Task

*List and briefly describe the characters involved in the story goal and the conflict. List each character's strengths and weaknesses.*

    1. _____

    _____

    2. _____

    _____

## PART II: THE MIDDLE

1. Characters Design Short-Term Goals to Reach the Story Goal

    **CHARACTER 1:** *Briefly describe his first short-term goal and how he'll go about reaching it.* _____

    _____

    **CHARACTER 2 (OPTIONAL):** *Briefly describe his first short-term goal and how he'll go about reaching it.* _____

    _____

2. Quest to Reach the Story Goal Begins

*Briefly detail the events that take place.* _____

_____

3. First Short-Term Goals Are Thwarted

*Briefly detail the events that take place.* _____

_____

4. Characters React With Disappointment

**CHARACTER 1:** *Briefly describe his reaction.* _____

_____

**CHARACTER 2 (OPTIONAL):** *Briefly describe his reaction.* _____

_____

5. Stakes of the Conflict Are Raised

*Detail new stakes of the conflict and how they affect all subplots.* _

_____

6. Characters React to the Conflict

**CHARACTER 1:** Briefly describe his reaction to the conflict. ____

_____

**CHARACTER 2 (OPTIONAL):** Briefly describe his reaction to the
conflict. _____

_____

7. Characters Revise Old or Design New Short-Term Goals

**CHARACTER 1:** Briefly describe his new short-term goal and how
he'll reach it. _____

_____

**CHARACTER 2 (OPTIONAL):** Briefly describe his new short-term
goal and how he'll reach it. _____

_____

8. Quest to Reach the Story Goal Is Continued

*Briefly detail the events that take place.* _____

_____

### 9. Short-Term Goals Are Again Thwarted

*Briefly detail the events that take place.* _____

_____

### 10. Characters React With Disappointment

**CHARACTER 1:** *Briefly describe his reaction.* _____

_____

**CHARACTER 2 (OPTIONAL):** *Briefly describe his reaction.* _____

_____

### 11. Stakes of the Conflict Are Raised

*Detail new stakes of the conflict and how they affect all subplots.* \_

_____

### 12. Characters React to the Conflict

**CHARACTER 1:** *Briefly describe his reaction to the conflict.* _____

_____

**CHARACTER 2 (OPTIONAL):** *Briefly describe his reaction to the conflict.*

_____

*Repeat Steps 7–12 as many times as necessary. During the final cycle, skip Steps 11 and 12 and continue with Step 13.*

### 13. Downtime Begins

*Detail the events that lead to downtime.*

**CHARACTER 1:** *Briefly describe his reaction to these events.* _____

_____

**CHARACTER 2 (OPTIONAL):** *Briefly describe his reaction to these events.* _____

_____

14. Characters Revise Old or Design New Short-Term Goals With Renewed Vigor

> **CHARACTER 1:** *Briefly describe his desperate short-term goal and how he'll go about reaching it.* _____
>
> _____
>
> **CHARACTER 2 (OPTIONAL):** *Briefly describe his desperate short-term goal and how he'll go about reaching it.* _____
>
> _____

15. The Quest to Reach the Story Goal Continues, But Instability Abounds

> *Briefly detail the events that take place.* _____
>
> _____

16. The Black Moment Begins

> *Briefly detail the events that take place and how they affect all subplots.*
>
> _____
>
> _____

17. The Characters React to the Black Moment

> **CHARACTER 1:** *Briefly describe his reaction.* _____
>
> _____
>
> **CHARACTER 2 (OPTIONAL):** *Briefly describe his reaction.* _____
>
> _____

## PART III: THE END

1. A Pivotal, Life-Changing Event Occurs

> *Detail this event and how it affects all subplots.* _____
>
> _____

2. Characters Modify Short-Term Goals One Last Time

**CHARACTER 1:** *Briefly describe his final short-term goal and how he'll go about reaching it.* _____

_____

**CHARACTER 2 (OPTIONAL):** *Briefly describe his final short-term goal and how he'll go about reaching it.* _____

_____

3. The Showdown Begins

**SHOWDOWN DETAILS:** *(including all main characters who are in-volved)* _____

_____

4. The Opposition Is Vanquished and the Conflict Ends

**DETAILS:** _____

_____

5. The Story Goal Is Achieved

*Detail resolution plot and all subplots.*

1. _____

_____

2. _____

6. Characters React to the Resolution of the Plot and Subplots

**CHARACTER 1:** *Briefly describe his reaction to the end of the conflict.* _____

_____

**CHARACTER 2 (OPTIONAL):** *Briefly describe his reaction to the end of the conflict.* _____

_____

7. The Relationship Black Moment Is Addressed (only for romance novels)

**CHARACTER 1:** *Briefly describe his reaction.* _____

_____

**CHARACTER 2:** *Briefly describe her reaction.* _____

_____

8. Characters Revise Their Life Goals

**CHARACTER 1:** *Briefly describe his life goal.* _____

_____

**CHARACTER 2 (OPTIONAL):** *Briefly describe her life goal.* _____

_____

## WORKSHEET 6:
## SERIES BIBLE: MISCELLANEOUS/RESEARCH

*You can use separate worksheets, tablets, index cards, or word-processing files for each subject in your series bible.*

*In free-form essays, detail:*

**MISCELLANEOUS INFORMATION:** _____

_____

_____

_____

_____

_____

_____

_____

_____

_____

_____

**RESEARCH SPECIFICS:** _____

_____

_____

_____

_____

_____

_____

_____

_____

_____

_____

_____

_____

_____

## WORKSHEET 6A:
## SERIES BIBLE: MISCELLANEOUS/RESEARCH
## FACT SHEET

STORY TITLE, SERIES NAME, AND BOOK NUMBER: _____

| PAGE OR CHAPTER | CHARACTER | LOCATION | FACT |
|---|---|---|---|
| Example: page 7 | Police Department staff | Police Department | Police department employs: 12 full-time patrol officers (including Jensen, Bradley, Rosch, Folksmeyer); 6 reserves; patrol sergeant (Chopp); chief (Vanderwyst); administrative assistant (Maggie Sheppard); 2 investigators (Ezra and Ben). |
|  |  |  |  |
|  |  |  |  |
|  |  |  |  |
|  |  |  |  |

# WORKSHEET 6B:
# SERIES BIBLE: MISCELLANEOUS/RESEARCH
# BACKGROUND TIMELINE

**STORY TITLE, SERIES NAME, AND BOOK NUMBER:**_____

| PAGE OR CHAPTER | CHARACTER | AGE/YEAR(S) | FACT |
|---|---|---|---|
| Example: page 105 | Zeke and Violet | Zeke is 19; Violet 16. 1987. | She gets pregnant. At the time, Zeke is working part time at handmade furniture factory. They marry; he takes a full-time job. When Amber is born, Zeke is a wonderful father, but he's growing increasingly restless. He's beginning to think of escape—about easy money ... |
| | | | |
| | | | |
| | | | |
| | | | |

# WORKSHEET 6C:
# SERIES BIBLE: MISCELLANEOUS TIMELINE

**STORY TITLE, SERIES NAME, AND BOOK NUMBER:** _____

| PAGE OR CHAPTER | CHARACTER | LOCATION) | TIMELINE FACT |
|---|---|---|---|
| Example: page 85 | Terry | Nightclub and Witmer Park | It takes 12 minutes to get from the nightclub to Witmer Park, so if Terry left the nightclub at 3:15, she'd reach the park by 3:30 at the latest. |
| | | | |
| | | | |
| | | | |
| | | | |
| | | | |
| | | | |

# WORKSHEET 6D:
## SERIES BIBLE: CRIME TIMELINE

STORY TITLE, SERIES NAME, AND BOOK NUMBER: _____

FIRST/SECOND/THIRD/ADDITIONAL MURDER: _____

(ACTUAL WITNESS ACCOUNT): _____

VICTIM: _____

DETAILS ON HIS/HER DEATH: _____

| PAGE OR CHAPTER | CHARACTER/SUSPECT | LOCATION AT THE TIME OF THE CRIME | DAY AND TIME | SPECIFIC INFORMATION |
|---|---|---|---|---|
| Example: page 12 | Killer | Nightclub/ dressing rooms 2 and 3 | Thursday, 2:15 A.M. | During first dance break, the killer sneaks into dressing room 3 and gets Lori's ipecac, then sneaks into dressing room 2 and poisons Terry's snack. |
| | | | | |
| | | | | |

# WORKSHEET 6E:
# SERIES BIBLE: MOTIVES AND ALIBIS SHEET

**STORY TITLE, SERIES NAME, AND BOOK NUMBER:**_____

**VICTIM:**_____

**DETAILS:**_____

| SUSPECT | CHARACTER | ALIBI |
|---------|-----------|-------|
| Example: Blaine | Terry thought he would run away with her, so she put him under pressure. | Around midnight at the club, when Lori sprained her ankle, he was there; still, she could have sneaked out, driven home, and killed Crystal, all in less than twenty minutes. |
|  |  |  |
|  |  |  |
|  |  |  |
|  |  |  |
|  |  |  |

# WORKSHEET 7:
# SERIES, STORY, AND PLANT ARC BREAKDOWN

TITLE OF STORY: _____

BOOK 1 IN [THE NAME OF THE SERIES]: _____

| OVERALL SERIES ARC | INDIVIDUAL STORY ARCS | SERIES PLANT ARCS |
|---|---|---|
|  |  |  |
|  |  |  |
|  |  |  |
|  |  |  |

TITLE OF STORY: _____

BOOK 2 IN [THE NAME OF THE SERIES]: _____

| OVERALL SERIES ARC | INDIVIDUAL STORY ARCS | SERIES PLANT ARCS |
|---|---|---|
|  |  |  |
|  |  |  |
|  |  |  |
|  |  |  |

**TITLE OF STORY** _____

**BOOK 3 IN [THE NAME OF THE SERIES]** _____

| OVERALL SERIES ARC | INDIVIDUAL STORY ARCS | SERIES PLANT ARCS |
|---|---|---|
| | | |
| | | |
| | | |
| | | |

**TITLE OF STORY** _____

**BOOK 4 IN [THE NAME OF THE SERIES]** _____

| OVERALL SERIES ARC | INDIVIDUAL STORY ARCS | SERIES PLANT ARCS |
|---|---|---|
| | | |
| | | |
| | | |
| | | |

*Fill out a table for every book in your series, but keep in mind that it's unlikely that the final book in your series will have any new series or plant arcs, since the last story is the one that will provide resolutions to all of these. You'll focus almost entirely on providing closure, so you'll be dealing with story arcs.*

## FACT-CHECKER CHECKLIST: CONSISTENCY ISSUES

❑ **Oversights**

Plot, character, or setting details that are illogical, unexplainable, or unrealistic, including coincidence contrivance (writer needs a certain plot point or detail to work and so creates the groundwork "on the spot") and convenience justifications (it was the only way to get it to work, so I had to do it, didn't I?)

> **EXAMPLE:** Your hero is mortally afraid of snakes, starting in Book 1. In Book 5 you need him to kill a snake so he can pass into the cave. He does so without blinking an eye.

❑ **Changed Premises**

Anything concerning character, plot, or setting that conflicts with something that was previously established.

> **EXAMPLE:** In Book 1 you determined that all off-world humans can't breathe the air of the planet, but in Book 3 a human character breathes the air easily with no explanation of how he does so.

❑ **Technical Problems**

Anything dealing with equipment and technical oddities; inadvertently or indiscriminately jumping into alternate viewpoints, descriptions, dialogue, names, or jobs of characters; setting details that change from what was previously mentioned.

> **EXAMPLE:** A character's eye color was green in Book 1 of the series. In Book 4 her eyes are blue.

❑ **Timeline and Production Issues**

Production errors that creep up as a direct result of not checking information in previous books in the series or the series bible; timelines are uncertain or overlap or become erroneous in the course of a series.

**EXAMPLE:** In Book 2 it's established that the hero was attending college three years ago. In Book 6 he says that he took a trip to Italy for a year and skipped out of school during that time period.

## ❏ Unanswered Questions

While each book in the series must have satisfactory individual story arcs, all series arc questions must be answered by the close of a series.

**EXAMPLE:** At the beginning or middle of your series, your heroine is bitten by a werewolf, and in all subsequent books she's waiting in horror for something to happen ... but by the final book in the series, nothing happens and no resolution is given for whether or not she escaped her fate or how she did so.

# CASE STUDY EXAMPLES OF POPULAR SERIES

## CASE STUDY 1: YOUNG ADULT/CHILDREN'S

With this example, it's interesting to note that I had a hard time find-ing a story blurb for each story. Most blurbs that I did find (on the author's website, stepheniemeyer.com, or on distributor websites) focused on the author and the popularity of the series and sometimes incorporated reviews. It's as if the individual story blurbs for these books have become inconsequential. But those who want to read the popular series need information about each book—and a series blurb would be nice, too—regardless of whether an author has "legions of fans." I honestly can't understand why finding this information was so difficult, even impossible. It reminded me of the time I was told by a local dentist that they didn't need my business because they already had enough clients to be profitable. Since when does a business not need new clients? Can books become so popular that they no longer need new fans? The blurbs I did manage to find were imbued with the story genre, tone, and the incredibly intense, obsessive passion between Bella and Edward.

**SERIES TITLE:** The Twilight Saga by Stephenie Meyer

**SERIES GENRE:** Young Adult Paranormal Romance

**SERIES TIE:** Combination of Recurring Character, Premise/Plot, Setting

    **MAIN STORY CHARACTER:** Isabella "Bella" Swan

    **MAIN PREMISE/PLOT:** Vampires and werewolves

    **MAIN SETTING:** Forks, Washington

**SERIES BLURB:** None available

**TITLE OF BOOK:** *Twilight*

**BOOK NUMBER IN THE SERIES:** 1

**STORY GENRE (IF DIFFERENT FROM THE SERIES):** same

**STORY BLURB:** Isabella Swan's move to Forks, a small, perpetually rainy town in Washington, could have been the most boring move she ever made. But once she meets the mysterious and alluring Edward Cullen, Isabella's life takes a thrilling and terrifying turn.

Up until now, Edward has managed to keep his vampire identity a secret in the small community he lives in, but now nobody is safe, especially Isabella, the person Edward holds most dear.

The lovers find themselves balanced precariously on the point of a knife—between desire and danger. Deeply romantic and extraordinarily suspenseful, *Twilight* captures the struggle between defying our instincts and satisfying our desires. This is a love story with bite.

**TITLE OF BOOK:** *New Moon*
**BOOK NUMBER IN THE SERIES:** 2
**STORY GENRE (IF DIFFERENT FROM THE SERIES):** same
**STORY BLURB:** For Bella Swan, there is one thing more important than life itself: Edward Cullen. But being in love with a vampire is even more dangerous than Bella could ever have imagined. Edward has already rescued Bella from the clutches of one evil vampire, but now, as their daring relationship threatens all that is near and dear to them, they realize their troubles may be just beginning ...

Legions of readers entranced by *The New York Times* bestseller *Twilight* are hungry for the continuing story of star-crossed lovers Bella and Edward. In *New Moon* Stephenie Meyer delivers another irresistible combination of romance and suspense with a supernatural twist. Passionate, riveting, and full of surprising twists and turns, this vampire love saga is well on its way to literary immortality.

**TITLE OF BOOK:** *Eclipse*
**BOOK NUMBER IN THE SERIES:** 3
**STORY GENRE (IF DIFFERENT FROM THE SERIES):** same
**STORY BLURB:** As Seattle is ravaged by a string of mysterious killings and a malicious vampire continues her quest for revenge, Bella once again finds herself surrounded by danger. In the midst of it all, she is forced to choose between her love for Edward and her friendship with Jacob—knowing that her decision has the potential to ignite the ageless struggle between vampire and werewolf. With her graduation quickly approaching, Bella has one more decision to make: life or death. But which is which?

**TITLE OF BOOK:** *Breaking Dawn*
**BOOK NUMBER IN THE SERIES:** 4
**STORY GENRE (IF DIFFERENT FROM THE SERIES):** same
**STORY BLURB:** When you loved the one who was killing you, it left you no options. How could you run, how could you fight, when doing so would

hurt that beloved one? If your life was all you had to give, how could you not give it? If it was someone you truly loved? To be irrevocably in love with a vampire is both fantasy and nightmare woven into a dangerously heightened reality for Bella Swan. Pulled in one direction by her intense passion for Edward Cullen and in another by her profound connection to werewolf Jacob Black, a tumultuous year of temptation, loss, and strife have led her to the ultimate turning point. Her imminent choice to either join the dark but seductive world of immortals or to pursue a fully human life has become the thread from which the fates of two tribes hang. Now that Bella has made her decision, a startling chain of unprecedented events is about to unfold with potentially devastating, and unfathomable, consequences. Just when the frayed strands of Bella's life—first discovered in *Twilight*, then scattered and torn in *New Moon* and *Eclipse*—seem ready to heal and knit together, could they be destroyed ... forever? The astonishing, breathlessly anticipated conclusion to the Twilight Saga, *Breaking Dawn* illuminates the secrets and mysteries of this spellbinding romantic epic that has entranced millions.

## CASE STUDY 2: ROMANCE

Wow! Getting information for this series was like pulling teeth! The author's website (debbiemacomber.com) includes the titles in the series but absolutely no story or series blurbs, or information pertaining to the order of the books in the series. The website is, however, very easy to navigate. Distributor and publisher websites are more like fanzines in this case. Back cover blurbs contain only reviews and praise for the author, as if the individual stories were of little consequence. I finally found a website that included the order of the books in the series (based on release dates and not true chronological order) along with actual story blurbs, but keep in mind that you'll find them listed in a different order at various distributor websites, some with vastly different blurbs for more than one book in the series.

**SERIES TITLE:** Dakota Series by Debbie Macomber

**SERIES GENRE:** Romance

    **SERIES TIE:** Combination of Cast of Characters and Setting

    **MAIN SERIES CHARACTER(S):** Lindsay Snyder, Gage Sinclair, Maddy Washburn, Jeb McKenna, and Margaret Clemens

    **MAIN SETTING:** Buffalo Valley, North Dakota

**SERIES BLURB:** Buffalo Valley, North Dakota, a close-knit farming community struggling to survive in an increasingly industrial world, has become a good place to live—the way it used to be. People here feel confident about the future again. Thanks to the arrival of enterprising newcomers, the once struggling farming town of Buffalo Valley is now enjoying a revival.

**TITLE OF BOOK:** *Dakota Born*

**BOOK NUMBER IN THE SERIES:** 1

**STORY GENRE (IF DIFFERENT FROM THE SERIES):** same

**MAIN STORY CHARACTER(S):** Lindsay Snyder and Gage Sinclair (both series characters)

**MAIN SECONDARY CHARACTER(S):** Maddy Washburn

**STORY BLURB:** Buffalo Valley is dying. But its citizens won't give up on the town where generations have lived, loved, raised families, worked hard, and died. When Savannah-born Lindsay Snyder decides to accept the teaching position in Buffalo Valley, she brings a breath of fresh air with her. Lindsay is trying to escape a stalled romance and learn more about her family, especially her grandmother, Gina, who lived her entire life in the tiny town. Buffalo Valley has its share of characters, including Hassie Knight, the matriarch of this small community; Buffalo Bob Carr, the ex-biker who won the local watering hole in a poker game; and Gage Sinclair, the handsome farmer whose roots are deeply planted in the fertile soil of this North Dakota village. But Gage refuses to believe that Lindsay will find any reason to stay so far from the bright lights of the big city she recently called home. And Lindsay despairs that Gage will never comprehend that she has the best reason to remain—love, for him.

**TITLE OF BOOK:** *Dakota Home*

**BOOK NUMBER IN THE SERIES:** 2

**STORY GENRE (IF DIFFERENT FROM THE SERIES):** same

**MAIN STORY CHARACTER(S):** Maddy Washburn and Jeb McKenna (both series characters)

**MAIN SECONDARY CHARACTER(S):** Lindsay and Gage Sinclair

**STORY BLURB:** Buffalo Valley, North Dakota, has found new life. People have started moving here—people like Lindsay Snyder who came for one year to work as a teacher and stayed, marrying local farmer Gage Sinclair. And now Lindsay's closest friend, Maddy Washburn, has decided to pull up stakes and join her in Buffalo Valley, hoping for the same kind of contentment. And the same kind of love ...

Jeb McKenna is a rancher, a man who's learned to endure, as the Dakota earth endures. He's raising bison and, by choice, lives a solitary life. Maddy, unafraid and openhearted, is drawn to Jeb, but he rejects her overtures—until one of North Dakota's deadly storms throws them together. These few days and nights bring unexpected consequences for Maddy and Jeb. Consequences that, in one way or another, affect everyone in Buffalo Valley.

**TITLE OF BOOK:** *Always Dakota*

**BOOK NUMBER IN THE SERIES:** 3

**STORY GENRE (IF DIFFERENT FROM THE SERIES):** same

**MAIN STORY CHARACTER(S):** Margaret Clemens (a series character) and Matt Eilers

**MAIN SECONDARY CHARACTER(S):** Lindsay Sinclair and Maddy Washburn

**STORY BLURB:** Stalled lives are moving forward. People are taking risks on new ventures and on lifelong dreams. On happiness. And one of those people is local rancher Margaret Clemens, who's finally getting what she wants most: marriage to cowboy Matt Eilers. Her friends don't think Matt's such a bargain; neither does her father. But Margaret's aware of Matt's reputation and his flaws. She wants him anyway. And she wants his baby ...

**TITLE OF BOOK:** *Buffalo Valley*

**BOOK NUMBER IN THE SERIES:** 4

**STORY GENRE (IF DIFFERENT FROM THE SERIES):** same

**MAIN STORY CHARACTER(S):** Carrie Hendrickson and Vaughn Kyle

**MAIN SECONDARY CHARACTER(S):** Lindsay Snyder, Gage Sinclair, Maddy Washburn, Jeb McKenna, and Margaret Clemens

**STORY BLURB:** Buffalo Valley, North Dakota, has discovered a will to survive, to prosper. And the outside world has discovered Buffalo Valley. A large retail conglomerate, which would surely destroy the small independent businesses that have begun to succeed, plans to move in. And it might even destroy the town.

It's a season of change for a man named Vaughn Kyle. He discovers that he's at an impasse. Just out of the army, he's looking for a place to live, a life to live. As Christmas draws near, he decides to visit his family in Grand Forks, North Dakota, while he waits for his reluctant fiancée to make up her mind. Vaughn decides to visit Buffalo Valley and Hassie Knight, the old woman who owns the pharmacy there. His parents named him after Hassie's son who died in Vietnam. Although he and Hassie have never met, she thinks of him almost as family, as a surrogate son. He arrives at her pharmacy one snowy day and finds not Hassie but a young woman named Carrie Hendrickson ...

As he begins to love Carrie, as he grows close to Hassie, Vaughn has to question his feelings for the woman he thought he loved. He knows now that he wants to stay in Buffalo Valley and fight for its way of life, a life that's all about friends and family—not just at Christmas, but every day of the year.

## CASE STUDY 3:
## HORROR/PARANORMAL

Jane Toombs is the author of so many books and series that her website, (janetoombs.com) has been designed with easy navigation in mind. But since she contributed most of these particular novellas below to promotional group Jewels of the Quill anthologies (before Books 1 through 5 were put in a series collection), the group's website at jewelsofthequill. com includes all the detailed information necessary to follow this series. Unfortunately, you can't find this information anywhere else. Notice that

Jane's blurbs are straight to the point and intriguing—she's the queen of being concisely fantastic.

**SERIES TITLE:** North of Nonesuch Series by Jane Toombs
**SERIES GENRE:** Paranormal Romantic Suspense
**SERIES TIE:** Combination of Premise/Plot and Setting

> **MAIN PREMISE/PLOT:** Paranormal elements
>
> **MAIN SETTING(S):** Michigan's Upper Peninsula

**SERIES BLURB:** North of Nonesuch—a magical place in the wilds of Michigan's Upper Peninsula, where the real world can be invaded by strange occurrences. From shifters to djinns to vampires to ghosts, anything may happen here. Danger, suspense, and love happen to all who live in or enter this wonderful world.

**TITLE OF BOOK:** *The Turquoise Cat*
**BOOK NUMBER IN THE SERIES:** 1
**STORY GENRE (IF DIFFERENT FROM THE SERIES):** same
**STORY BLURB:** When an eccentric great-aunt dies, Olivia Sumner unexpectedly inherits an old mansion on Lake Superior, plus an odd turquoise curio of a creature half human, half cougar. With no idea of what this talisman means, she faces a terrible danger, one she never dreamed could exist. Is Raoul DeKalb, the enigmatic DNR officer, on her side, or is he part of the danger?

**TITLE OF BOOK:** *The Turquoise Talisman*
**BOOK NUMBER IN THE SERIES:** 2
**STORY GENRE (IF DIFFERENT FROM THE SERIES):** same
**STORY BLURB:** Grandma Toivi always told Ella Rose that trouble comes in threes. Ella decides her grandmother was right when a great-uncle's death brings her the bequest of an ancient Eastern dagger with a turquoise hilt, a mysterious stranger shows up claiming he's a gift of the dagger, and danger stalks her.

**TITLE OF BOOK:** *Turquoise Twilight*
**BOOK NUMBER IN THE SERIES:** 3
**STORY GENRE (IF DIFFERENT FROM THE SERIES):** same

**STORY BLURB:** Talissa Hunter takes her dream-of-a-lifetime trip to European vampire country and is disappointed not to meet any "creatures of fantasy," as her friend calls them. In a romantic encounter on the way home, she rescues what she believes is a wounded man. What a pleasant surprise when he turns up at her place in North of Nonesuch Country! But what will happen when she discovers what he really is?

**TITLE OF BOOK:** *Let My Bones Rest*

**BOOK NUMBER IN THE SERIES:** 4

**STORY GENRE (IF DIFFERENT FROM THE SERIES):** same

**STORY BLURB:** Archeologist Andrea Johansen reaches the wilderness mounds along the Ojibway River earlier than intended, hoping to be able to measure them before the inevitable Native American representative shows up to make sure she doesn't disturb possible native remains. But Hart Blackstone, ex-marine and Anishinabe medicine man, arrives on her heels. Though attracted to each other, Andrea's and Hart's goals are opposite. But when a vicious grave robber poses a threat not only to the site, but to them personally, they join forces to try to save themselves and the mounds. The odds against them seem impossible—how can they survive?

**TITLE OF BOOK:** *Capricorn Capers*

**BOOK NUMBER IN THE SERIES:** 5

**STORY GENRE (IF DIFFERENT FROM THE SERIES):** same

**STORY BLURB:** Krystal Kapp is lured from a ski run by a voice in her mind she can't resist. She reaches the winter lodge of Shadrach Capprich just as a storm hits, and she winds up taking the strangest journey of her entire life, one she may not survive.

**TITLE OF BOOK:** *Are You Listening?*

**BOOK NUMBER IN THE SERIES:** 6

**STORY GENRE (IF DIFFERENT FROM THE SERIES):** Young Adult Paranormal

**STORY BLURB:** A six-year-old's wish to have her daddy back for Christmas uncovers a dark secret.

**TITLE OF BOOK:** *The Turquoise Heart*

**BOOK NUMBER IN THE SERIES:** 7

**STORY GENRE (IF DIFFERENT FROM THE SERIES):** Romantic Saga

**STORY BLURB:** When Milo Saari inherits half of a turquoise heart, she knows the odds are stacked against her ever encountering the man who has the other half. And, even if she did meet that man, they'd have no way to recognize each other as holders of the heart. Are the two halves doomed to forever remain unattached?

**TITLE OF BOOK:** *The Nonesuch Curse*

**BOOK NUMBER IN THE SERIES:** 8

**STORY GENRE (IF DIFFERENT FROM THE SERIES):** Gothic Historical Paranormal Romance

**STORY BLURB:** "My name is Falana, I am a fae, and Ruthven blood I curse this day..." For five generations, the wood witch's curse has killed all Ruthven males on their thirtieth birthdays. When Trilla Pasanen falls in love with Rom Ruthven, she discovers that the only way to save him is to believe in the power she hasn't been able to accept as her own. If she fails, Rom will die at thirty just as every Ruthven male has since Falana pronounced her evil curse.

**TITLE OF BOOK:** *The Charmer*

**BOOK NUMBER IN THE SERIES:** 9

**STORY GENRE (IF DIFFERENT FROM THE SERIES):** Romantic Horror

**STORY BLURB:** Who is the charmer and who the charmed? It's a very difficult distinction to make. If Will Pasanen fails to solve the problem, more than his love for Lily Fowler is doomed ...

# CASE STUDY 4:
# MYSTERY/SUSPENSE/THRILLER

Author Barbara Colley's website (barbaracolley.com) is very well done. The only thing missing is a series blurb ... but since most of the story blurbs include what can be considered a series blurb, this author has given fans everything necessary to follow her series. Incidentally, Barbara's brilliant back cover blurbs perfectly fit the character of Charlotte LaRue.

**SERIES TITLE:** Charlotte LaRue Mysteries by Barbara Colley

**SERIES GENRE:** Cozy Mystery

**SERIES TIE:** Combination of Recurring Character, Premise/Plot, Setting

    **MAIN STORY CHARACTER:** Charlotte LaRue

    **MAIN PREMISE/PLOT:** Housecleaning and amateur sleuthing

    **MAIN SETTING:** New Orleans' historical Garden District

**SERIES BLURB:** See individual story blurbs

**TITLE OF BOOK:** *Maid for Murder*

**BOOK NUMBER IN THE SERIES:** 1

**STORY GENRE (IF DIFFERENT FROM THE SERIES):** same

**STORY BLURB:** In New Orleans' historic Garden District, life is all about attending the right parties, impressing the right people, and making the right amount of money (a lot!). It's an attitude fifty-nine-year-old Charlotte LaRue has never really understood. She leads a quiet, simple, practical life—and it suits her just fine. Business is booming at her housecleaning service, Maid for a Day—and in her downtime, she loves reading mystery novels and hanging out with her parakeet, Sweety Boy. Everything's perfect. Well, almost everything ...

Charlotte doesn't mind polishing silver, scrubbing toilets, or dusting bookcases—but she can't stand dealing with her rich clients' dirty laundry. And when it comes to the much-talked-about Dubuisson family, there's an awful lot of it—especially since Jackson Dubuisson was found murdered in his study.

Now this exclusive enclave is abuzz with all kinds of gossip—and some very sinister speculation. A chatty socialite keeps hinting that Jackson's extramarital affair may have been the death of him. His mother-in-law, who's quite possibly senile, has revealed more of the Dubuisson family's secrets than Charlotte ever wanted to know. And then there's Jackson's widow, Jeanne. Charlotte refuses to desert her in her time of need—but suspects she may have something to hide. One thing is certain: Someone wanted Jackson dead—and that someone is not coming clean ...

Surrounded by possible suspects and hounded by a tenacious police detective, Charlotte wishes she could stick to her own policy of staying out of clients' personal business. Problem is, she's never been able to walk away from a mess. And this is the biggest one she's ever seen.

**TITLE OF BOOK:** *Death Tidies Up*
**BOOK NUMBER IN THE SERIES:** 2
**STORY GENRE (IF DIFFERENT FROM THE SERIES):** same
**STORY BLURB:** It's October in New Orleans, and most residents of the city's historic Garden District are rejoicing in the brief reprise of cooler fall weather—a rare occurrence in steamy south Louisiana. But murder-solving maid Charlotte LaRue isn't one of them—not this year...

Between running her maid service (the successful Maid for a Day) and fretting about her upcoming birthday (the dreaded 6-0), Charlotte LaRue doesn't have much time for gossip. But New Orleans' latest dust-up is hard to ignore—especially since it involves Marian Hebert, one of Charlotte's new clients. Turns out Marian's now-deceased husband once worked for his best friend Drew Bergeron's real estate agency—and when the business deal soured, so did the friendship. The whole sordid affair came to an unfortunate end when Drew died in a plane crash—and Bill Hebert was killed in what some people insist on calling an accident. Others are convinced it was murder.

Pretty juicy stuff, right? Charlotte doesn't think so. She's trying her best to forget all the rumors—she has more important things to worry about these days. Like vacuuming, window washing ... and her new job at the old Devilier house. The gorgeous historic home is being transformed into luxury apartments, and Maid for a Day is in charge of the cleanup. Should be easy enough, Charlotte thinks—until she finds a barely-cold corpse in one of the closets.

The police are sure the dead man is Drew Bergeron. Funny, considering Drew supposedly died years ago—and Charlotte distinctly remembers attending his funeral. Talk about messy. Suddenly all that gossip about the Heberts and Bergerons seems incredibly timely—and Charlotte wishes she'd listened just a little bit closer ...

**TITLE OF BOOK:** *Polished Off*
**BOOK NUMBER IN THE SERIES:** 3

**STORY GENRE (IF DIFFERENT FROM THE SERIES):** same

**STORY BLURB:** There's a bad case of spring-cleaning fever going around New Orleans' historic Garden District, and it's keeping Charlotte LaRue—proprietor of Maid for a Day—plenty busy. Especially when what's supposed to be a simple housecleaning job ends in a grim discovery—and things start to get real dirty real fast ...

Charlotte has just about had it with her sister Madeline. She's put up with her simpering sibling's selfish demands and snide comments for years, but when Maddie turns on her own son and his new bride, Charlotte's really steamed. She thinks Daniel and Nadia make a beautiful couple—and Nadia's little boy is just as cute as can be. And now that Nadia's abusive ex-boyfriend is out of the picture—no one's seen the cad in ages—the new family's future seems as bright as a freshly Windexed mirror.

But years of polishing, scrubbing, and dusting have taught Charlotte that it's only a matter of time before things get messy. Sure enough, when she pays a visit to a wealthy client's lavish mansion, an urn breaks open—and human bones spill out. A little snooping turns up a driver's license belonging to Nadia's no-good ex. Could the bones be his, too? It would certainly explain why he's been MIA for such a long time. Charlotte suddenly has a lot more than cleaning on her mind—like how to get Nadia and Daniel off the short list of suspects that also includes powerful mayoral candidate Lowell Webster, as well as Charlotte's own client, spoiled socialite Patsy Dufour. And before she knows it, Charlotte's up to her elbows in the kind of dirty business that doesn't pay the bills...

**TITLE OF BOOK:** *Wiped Out*

**BOOK NUMBER IN THE SERIES:** 4

**STORY GENRE (IF DIFFERENT FROM THE SERIES):** same

**STORY BLURB:** Running Maid for a Day keeps Charlotte LaRue plenty busy, of course. But her latest job involves more than dusting and mopping. She must also contend with the rumblings of a feuding New Orleans gardening club. Things certainly aren't coming up roses in Barbara Colley's expertly paced, character-driven whodunit.

Summer's off to a sweltering start, and Charlotte is already feeling the heat. One of her best clients has just up and moved, leaving Charlotte with a big chunk of free time in her normally hectic schedule. Her son, Hank, is thrilled. He thinks it's high time his mother retired. But Charlotte has other ideas—and a new client to boot. Gardening enthusiast Mimi Adams is planning to host the next meeting of the Horticultural Heritage Society, a popular club among New Orleans' A-list. Mimi wants Charlotte to be there.

Charlotte had expected some good gossip at the meeting, but these society ladies are downright ferocious. They've got their claws out, with free-floating talk of extramartial affairs (did Mimi really sleep with Rita's husband?) and a bitter argument over the club's recent presidential election (Mimi won … or did she?). A few days later, Mimi's dead. Poisoned, according to the doctor. But who planted it, and where? Was it in the bitter brownies at the meeting? Or in the red wine? As Charlotte takes a closer look at Mimi's "friends," neighbors, and scheming husband, she realizes she has a whole plot full of suspects to weed through … and she'd better start digging.

**TITLE OF BOOK:** *Married to the Mop*
**BOOK NUMBER IN THE SERIES:** 5
**STORY GENRE (IF DIFFERENT FROM THE SERIES):** same
**STORY BLURB:** Though she's short two employees, Charlotte LaRue answers a desperate plea the weekend before Mardi Gras. A woman named Emily Rossi is hosting a huge bash for out-of-town guests and just lost her maid to a family emergency. It seems an acquaintance of hers from the society set highly recommended Charlotte's services—so she makes Charlotte an offer she can't refuse …

And Charlotte soon learns why. Emily's husband, Robert, just happens to be the most ruthless crime boss in the country. The number-one suspect in the murder of his own father, he's taken over the reins of the "family business."

As usual, Charlotte keeps her nose to the grindstone—but that doesn't stop her from seeing the dysfunctional Rossi clan in all its glory. Robert's mother is seemingly senile, his daughter hates him, he quarrels with his brothers, and Charlotte suspects him of abusing his wife. She also gets a front-row seat to an explosive display of Robert's hair-trigger temper when he finds some of his priceless Faberge eggs missing.

Nevertheless, Charlotte agrees to help at the costume ball when one of the servers comes down with the flu. She's beginning to think the party is a cover for Robert's illegal activities, when the man himself is found dead in the library. And there's Emily, standing over her husband with a bloody knife in her hand.

The case seems cut-and-dried—to anyone but Charlotte, that is. Although Emily looks guilty as sin, Charlotte has seen enough of the Rossi family's dirty laundry to suspect everyone. And the Faberge eggs continue to disappear. If there's a crack in the killer's plan, Charlotte will find it, because she won't stand for anything—least of all, murder—being swept under the rug. But she'd better tread carefully if she doesn't want to spend Fat Tuesday in the bayou, sleeping with the catfish ...

**TITLE OF BOOK:** *Scrub-a-Dub Dead*

**BOOK NUMBER IN THE SERIES:** 6

**STORY GENRE (IF DIFFERENT FROM THE SERIES):** same

**STORY BLURB:** Maid for a Day Charlotte LaRue knows that sweeping murder under the rug is anything but simple in The Big Easy—especially since no smudge or stain is safe from her scrutiny ...

Doing a favor for a friend in need has Charlotte cleaning rooms at the New Orleans Jazzy Hotel. The historic Garden District mansion is serving as a home-away-from-home for Shreveport's chapter of the Red Scarf Sorority, a group of socially elite women in their forties.

While picking up beautiful red silk scarves from the floor of a room she's cleaning, Charlotte is startled by the sudden arrival of its ranting and raving occupant, who insists that Charlotte ignored the Do-Not-Disturb sign on the door and threatens to have her fired. Charlotte is stunned into silence, until the Red Scarf Sorority comes to the rescue. The women manage to calm Tessa Morgan, who just had a run-in with her estranged husband's much younger mistress, Lisa—and learned that they plan to marry. After some of the women jokingly suggest making Lisa permanently disappear, Charlotte takes her leave. The situation gets even messier when Charlotte runs into an old flame and learns that he is Tessa's stepfather—and that Lisa may be blackmailing him.

The next day Charlotte gets back to work only to learn that Lisa has been murdered, strangled by what could have been a red scarf. The hotel is awash in suspects, and soon Tessa is being dragged away in handcuffs. It seems Lisa had more enemies than friends, and Charlotte is convinced the police are on the wrong track with Tessa. It's time to start scouring through clues before the person who rubbed out Lisa makes a clean getaway ...

**TITLE OF BOOK:** *Wash and Die*

**BOOK NUMBER IN THE SERIES:** 7

**STORY GENRE (IF DIFFERENT FROM THE SERIES):** same

**STORY BLURB:** Charlotte LaRue, owner of New Orleans' Maid for a Day cleaning service, is swept into jeopardy when an uninvited guest arrives on her doorstep ...

As the saying goes, "No good deed goes unpunished." Charlotte LaRue knows she should take a broom and chase Joyce Thibodeaux off her front porch. Once married to Charlotte's tenant Louis Thibodeaux, Joyce is fresh out of detox for her alcoholism and has no place to go. She swears she's clean and sober and will find her own place in a few days. She pulls on Charlotte's heartstrings ... and soon she's staying in Charlotte's guest room.

Charlotte survived Hurricane Katrina, but Joyce proves to be an ill wind of a different kind. Soon a valuable gold watch left to Charlotte by her father is missing, and worse, a stranger is watching the house. Charlotte knows she has to show Joyce the door, but she never gets the chance. Instead her beloved parakeet, Sweety Boy, vanishes, her living room gets trashed, and Joyce ends up in the middle of the mess ... stone cold dead.

Now Charlotte is on the list of murder suspects along with Louis, who's been out of town on business ... or has he? Finding the answers means doing a little snooping herself. Grabbing her mop, she's starting with the hospital where Joyce last stayed: a place with skeletons in its closets and a bucketful of clues that just might lead to a killer ...

**TITLE OF BOOK:** *Dusted to Death*

**BOOK NUMBER IN THE SERIES:** 8

**STORY GENRE (IF DIFFERENT FROM THE SERIES):** same

**STORY BLURB:** As the owner of Maid for a Day, Charlotte LaRue has learned that behind closed doors, everyone's dirty laundry holds a few dark secrets—and in the end, they all come out in the wash ...

The city of New Orleans has long been a favorite backdrop for movie producers, and now one of Charlotte's best clients, Bitsy Duhe, is getting in on the action. A big Hollywood studio wants to use Bitsy's gorgeous Victorian house for a movie shoot, and they are willing to pay her handsomely for the honor. Bitsy consents, but only after Charlotte agrees to take care of her beloved home during the shoot and keep the place spotless as only Charlotte can. For Charlotte, the assignment is an exciting change of pace. On the first day, she meets the whole cast and crew, including one of Hollywood's hottest ingénues, Angel Martinique. But Charlotte quickly discovers that Angel's G-rated reputation is nothing like her off-camera diva-like behavior. Angel, it turns out, is no angel at all ...

Once the shoot begins, Charlotte has a front-row seat to all the backstage drama: the director who wants to control his favorite starlet's every move ... the make-up artist whose talents with cosmetics can't hide the mysterious bruises on her face ... the bodyguard who is clashing with everyone on the set ... and Angel's seemingly mild-mannered friend, Nick, whose shy demeanor hides a far more menacing side ...

Despite all the tension, the movie seems to be going well—until Nick is found dead in Angel's dressing room, a bloody letter opener lying just a few feet away. To Charlotte, it seems there is no shortage of suspects. But when the police investigation quickly zeroes in on Angel, Charlotte senses there's much more to her story than meets the eye. As Charlotte does a little digging into Angel's past, she comes up with a bit more dirt than she bargained for—enough to put her in the crosshairs of danger, if she doesn't watch her step ...

# CASE STUDY 5: SCIENCE FICTION/ FANTASY/FUTURISTIC

This author has a truly amazing website (terrybrooks.net) that includes everything you would ever want to know about his books and series. This is the ideal way to write and promote a series. The only complaint I have is that the site lacks new information. Nevertheless, the info that is there is fairly comprehensive. His back cover blurbs give potential readers a wonderful idea of what each story focuses on.

**SERIES TITLE:** The Heritage of Shannara by Terry Brooks
**SERIES GENRE:** Fantasy
**SERIES TIE:** Combination of Cast of Characters, Premise/Plot, Setting
  **MAIN STORY CHARACTERS:** Par and Coll Ohmsford, Cogline, Wren, and Walker Boh
  **MAIN PREMISE/PLOT:** Quest
  **MAIN SETTING:** The Four Lands
**SERIES BLURB:** The struggle between a handful of determined heroes and the insidious, pervasive evil that seeks to crush them.

**TITLE OF BOOK:** *The Scions of Shannara*
**BOOK NUMBER IN THE SERIES:** 1
**STORY GENRE (IF DIFFERENT FROM THE SERIES):** same
**MAIN STORY CHARACTER(S):** Par and Coll Ohmsford, Cogline, Wren, and Walker Boh
**STORY BLURB:** Three hundred years have passed since the death of Allanon, and the Four Lands are sadly changed. The Elves have vanished, and the Dwarves are enslaved. The Southland is no longer under the totalitarian rule of the Federation, and magic is strictly forbidden.

Yet Par Ohmsford, descendent of the fabled Shea, still has some of the power of the Wishsong. He and his brother Coll have come to Varfleet, where Coll recites the old legends while Par brings them to life with his Wishsong. A Seeker arrests them for using magic, but they escape with the aid of Padishar Creel, who claims to be the descendent of Panamon Creel.

In their flight to the Rainbow Lake, they are confronted by a hag-woman, but a man calling himself Cogline, the last Druid, drives her off. He tells them that she is a Shadowen—known only in rumors until then—and that the Shadowen are horrors that endanger all life. He also brings a message from the shade of the ancient Druid, Allanon, demanding that Par appear at the dread Hadeshorn, where Allanon will reveal more.

Then he leaves to summon the other Scions of Shannara—Wren, who lives in the Westlands and Walker Boh, somewhere in the Eastlands.

After further adventures with the Shadowen, all meet at the Hadeshorn. There Allanon's spirit reveals a terrible future where Shadowen have destroyed all life in the Four Lands. To prevent that, he orders Par to recover the long-lost Sword of Shannara, Wren to discover the vanished Elves, and Walker Boh to bring back the Druids and their ancient vanished stronghold of Paranor.

Each task is manifestly impossible.

**TITLE OF BOOK:** *The Druid of Shannara*

**BOOK NUMBER IN THE SERIES:** 2

**STORY GENRE (IF DIFFERENT FROM THE SERIES):** same

**MAIN STORY CHARACTER(S):** Cogline and Walker Boh

**MAIN SECONDARY CHARACTER(S):** Quickening, the King of the Silver River, Morgan Leah, Pe Ell, and Rimmer Dall

**STORY BLURB:** In the 300 years since the death of the Druid Allanon, the mysterious, evil Shadowen have seized control and are ruining the Four Lands. Using Cogline as messenger, the shade of Allanon summons the four scions of Shannara: Par, Coll, Wren, and Walker Boh. To Walker Boh he gives the duty of restoring the lost Druid's Keep, Paranor. For that, Walker needs the black Elfstone, but his search leads him only to a trap.

Meanwhile, the King of the Silver River, a fabulous being as old as mankind, creates a daughter named Quickening and sends her to help. She is joined by Morgan Leah and Pe Ell, an assassin who plans to eventually kill her.

They find Walker Boh dying after an attack by the Shadowen Rimmer Dall. Quickening heals him and tells him that the Elfstone is in the hands of another ancient being, the Stone King, who seeks to turn all the world to stone.

The journey will lead them to the far north, through the Charnal Mountains and beyond, into a perilous and unknown land. And no one knows what horrible monsters the Stone King has set to guard his citadel.

They form a strange company to undertake such a quest: Morgan Leah, whose once-magic sword has been broken; Walker Boh, with only one arm and no longer able to summon his magic; Quickening, who must depend on the men for her defense; and Pe Ell, who still intends to kill her.

Thus, the quest for the black Elfstone begins.

**TITLE OF BOOK:** *The Elf Queen of Shannara*
**BOOK NUMBER IN THE SERIES:** 3
**STORY GENRE (IF DIFFERENT FROM THE SERIES):** same
**MAIN STORY CHARACTER(S):** Wren
**MAIN SECONDARY CHARACTER(S):** Garth and Tiger Ty
**STORY BLURB:** "Find the Elves and return them to the lands of men!" the shade of the Druid Allanon had ordered Wren.

It was clearly an impossible task. The Elves had been gone from the Westlands for more than a hundred years. There was not even a trace of their former city of Arborlon left to mark their passing. No one in the Westlands knew of them—except, finally, the Addershag.

The blind old woman had given instructions to find a place on the coast of the Blue Divide, build a fire, and keep it burning for three days. "One will come for you."

Tiger Ty, the Wing Rider, had come on his giant Roc to carry Wren and her friend Garth to the only clear landing site on the island of Morrowindl, where, he said, the Elves might still exist, somewhere in the demon-haunted jungle.

Now she stood within that jungle, remembering the warning of the Addershag: "Beware, Elf-girl! I see danger ahead for you ... and evil beyond imagining." It had proved all too true. The jungle was dangerous enough. But the demons that dwelled there were truly evil beyond imagining.

She stood with her single weapon of magic, listening as the evil demons gathered for another attack. How long could she resist?

And if by some miracle she reached the Elves and could convince them to return, how could they possibly retrace her perilous path to reach the one safe place on the coast?

**TITLE OF BOOK:** *The Talismans of Shannara*
**BOOK NUMBER IN THE SERIES:** 4
**STORY GENRE (IF DIFFERENT FROM THE SERIES):** same
**MAIN STORY CHARACTER(S):** Par and Coll Ohmsford, Cogline, Wren, and Walker Boh
**MAIN SECONDARY CHARACTER(S):** Rimmer Dall
**STORY BLURB:** The descendents of the Elven house of Shannara had all completed their quests. Walker Boh, using the power of the Black Elfstone, had restored the lost Druid's Keep, Paranor, and become the last Druid himself. Wren had found the missing Elves and brought them back from the island of Morrowindl to the Four Lands. Now she was Queen of the Elves. And Par had found what quite possibly was the legendary Sword of Shannara.

But their work was not yet done—the Shadowen still swarmed over the Four Lands, poisoning all with their dark magic. And the leader of the Shadowen, Rimmer Dall, was determined that the scions of Shannara would not share with each other the knowledge that would end the sickness. Against Walker Boh then, he would dispatch the Four Horsemen. To Wren Elessedil, he would send a friend who would betray her. And for Par Ohmsford, whose wishsong was growing steadily more uncontrollable, he had devised the most terrible fate of all ...

The charges given by the shade of the Druid Allanon were doomed to fail—unless the Shannara children could escape the traps being laid for them, and Par could find a way to use the Sword of Shannara.

---

## CASE STUDY 6:
## HISTORICAL/WESTERN/
## TIME-TRAVEL/REGENCY

---

The author's website (carriebebris.com) has everything readers need to follow this series—including a series blurb! Incidentally, the blurbs beautifully fit the tone and genre of the series (and stay true to Jane Austen's originals).

**SERIES TITLE:** The Mr. & Mrs. Darcy Mystery Series by Carrie Bebris

**SERIES GENRE:** Regency Mystery

**SERIES TIE:** Recurring Characters

**MAIN SERIES CHARACTER(S):** Elizabeth Bennet and Mr. Darcy

**SERIES BLURB:** The Mr. & Mrs. Darcy Mysteries feature newlyweds Elizabeth Bennet and Mr. Darcy from Jane Austen's *Pride and Prejudice* as reluctant sleuths who become embroiled in intrigues surrounding their friends and family. Successive books bring the Darcys into contact with characters from other Austen novels, but you do not need to have read Austen's originals to enjoy the Darcy Mysteries. The newlywed Darcys' courtship hasn't ended, and their adventures have just begun.

**TITLE OF BOOK:** *Pride and Prescience (Or, a Truth Universally Acknowledged)*

**BOOK NUMBER IN THE SERIES:** 1

**STORY GENRE (IF DIFFERENT FROM THE SERIES):** same

**STORY BLURB:** When Caroline Bingley marries a rich, charismatic American, her future should be secure. But strange incidents soon follow: nocturnal wanderings, spooked horses, carriage accidents, an apparent suicide attempt. Soon the whole Bingley family seems the target of a sinister plot, with only their friends the Darcys recognizing the danger. A jilted lover, an estranged business partner, a financially desperate in-law, an eccentric supernaturalist—who is behind these events? Perhaps it is Caroline herself, who appears to be slowly sinking into madness …

**TITLE OF BOOK:** *Suspense and Sensibility (Or, First Impressions Revisited)*

**BOOK NUMBER IN THE SERIES:** 2

**STORY GENRE (IF DIFFERENT FROM THE SERIES):** same

**STORY BLURB:** When Harry met Kitty … Persuaded by Mrs. Bennet to sponsor a London social season for Elizabeth's sister Kitty, the Darcys reluctantly return to the glittering ballrooms and parlors of the fashionable world. There Kitty meets Harry Dashwood, the handsome young owner of Norland, and they quickly fall in love. But for the Bennet sisters, it seems the course of true love simply cannot run smooth. No sooner do Harry and Kitty announce their engagement than Harry begins to change. His disreputable behavior, unexplained absences, mysterious gatherings, questionable new companions, and sinister activities lead all to wonder: Who is the true Mr. Dashwood? Is he the respectable gentleman Kitty thought she knew or the dishonorable rogue now reflected in the mirror? A clue from Harry's family tree sends the Darcys once more on a quest to discover the truth before history can repeat itself. For, if Harry and Kitty are to have a future, the past must first be put to rest.

**TITLE OF BOOK:** *North by Northanger (Or, The Shades of Pemberley)*
**BOOK NUMBER IN THE SERIES:** 3
**STORY GENRE (IF DIFFERENT FROM THE SERIES):** same
**STORY BLURB:** After the excitement of recent adventures, Elizabeth and Fitzwilliam Darcy retire to the peace and quiet of Pemberley as they await the birth of their first child. Such tranquility, however, cannot last. First, a mysterious letter from the late Lady Anne Darcy is discovered—propelling Elizabeth on a quest to learn more about Darcy's deceased mother and an unsettled matter she left behind. Then a summons to Northanger Abbey involves the young couple in an intrigue that threatens not just the Darcy family name, but Darcy's freedom as well. And just when it seems their situation could not grow worse, Darcy's overbearing aunt, Lady Catherine de Bourgh, takes up residence at Pemberley. Add to all this rumors of treasure and hints of deceptions old and new, and it becomes apparent that Pemberley is filled not with peace, but with secrets and spirits of the past—and that their exposure could profoundly affect the generation of Darcys to come.

**TITLE OF BOOK:** *The Matters at Mansfield (Or, The Crawford Affair)*
**BOOK NUMBER IN THE SERIES:** 4
**STORY GENRE (IF DIFFERENT FROM THE SERIES):** same
**STORY BLURB:** Mr. Darcy's aunt, Lady Catherine de Bourgh, is eager to arrange a lucrative and socially advantageous match for her daughter, Anne. Of course, her ladyship has not taken into account such frivolous matters as love or romance, let alone the wishes of her daughter. Needless to say, there is much turmoil when the bride-to-be elopes. Their pursuit of the head-

strong couple leads the Darcys to the village of Mansfield, where the usually intricate game of marriage machinations becomes still more convoluted by lies and deception. There the Darcys discover that love and marriage can be a complex and dangerous business—one that can lead to murder.

**TITLE OF BOOK:** *The Intrigue at Highbury (Or, Emma's Match)*

**BOOK NUMBER IN THE SERIES:** 5

**STORY GENRE (IF DIFFERENT FROM THE SERIES):** same

**STORY BLURB:** Mr. and Mrs. Darcy are looking forward to a relaxing stay with dear friends when their carriage is hailed by a damsel in distress outside of the village of Highbury. Little do the Darcys realize that gypsies roam these woods, or that both their possessions and the woman are about to vanish into the night. The Darcys seek out the parish magistrate, who is having a difficult evening of his own. Mr. Knightley and his new wife, the former Miss Emma Woodhouse, are hosting a party to celebrate the marriage of their friends, Mr. Frank Churchill and Miss Jane Fairfax. During dinner, Mr. Edgar Churchill, uncle and adoptive father of the groom, falls suddenly ill and dies. The cause of death: poison. When the Darcys and the Knightleys join forces to investigate the crimes, they discover that the robbery and Edgar Churchill's death may be connected. Together they must work to quickly locate the source of the poison and the murderer's motive—before the killer can strike again.

**TITLE OF BOOK:** *The Deception at Lyme (Or, The Peril of Persuasion)*

**BOOK NUMBER IN THE SERIES:** 6

**STORY GENRE (IF DIFFERENT FROM THE SERIES):** same

**STORY BLURB:** In Jane Austen's *Persuasion*, the Cobb—Lyme's famous seawall—proved dangerous to a careless young woman. Now it proves deadly.

Following their recent intrigue at Highbury, Fitzwilliam and Elizabeth Darcy visit the seaside village of Lyme on holiday. Family business also draws them there, to receive from a fellow officer the personal effects of Mr. Darcy's late cousin, a naval lieutenant who died in action.

Their retreat, however, turns tragic when they come upon a body lying at the base of the Cobb. The victim is Mrs. Clay, a woman with a scandalous past that left her with child—a child whose existence threatened the inheritance of one of her paramours and the reputation of another. Did she lose her balance and fall from the slippery breakwater, or was she pushed?

Mrs. Clay's death is not the only one that commands the Darcys' attention. When Mr. Darcy discovers among his cousin's possessions evidence that the young lieutenant's death might have been murder, he allies with Captain Frederick Wentworth (hero of *Persuasion*) to probe details of a battle that took place across the sea ... but was influenced by conspiracy much closer to home.

## CASE STUDY EXAMPLE OF SERIES, STORY, AND PLANT ARCS

Although the Harry Potter series is fairly long—seven books—I chose to study it because this is a series readers of all ages, cultures, and preferred genres are familiar with. No other series qualifies like this one. Because it's so widely read, this example should be more easily understood—most readers already know the stories and therefore can concentrate on the arcs within them. You'll see the series, story, and plant arcs in a way you may have never considered before. I have tried to condense these as much as possible but they do, nevertheless, make for intense reading. When you finish, you can visualize the entire series laid out, story for story, and can appreciate how the development progresses naturally over the course of all seven books and how the series arc is resolved more than satisfactorily in the final installment. This example is meant to help you develop the arcs in your own series.

While I've mentioned elsewhere in the book that I typically organize Overall Series Arcs, Individual Story Arcs, and Series Plant Arcs in a three-column format, for ease of reading, I've presented them here in paragraph form.

## HARRY POTTER AND THE SORCERER'S STONE
### YEAR 1 IN THE SERIES

## OVERALL SERIES ARCS

Voldemort terrorized the wizarding world for eleven years—what stopped him? After killing Harry's parents, he couldn't kill Harry. His power broke and he was "gone," but most people believe he's still out there, too weak to carry on. How did baby Harry survive when no one else had before? What is the significance of the lightning bolt scar he received from this encounter?

Harry remembers a blinding green flash of light and a burning pain in his head, followed by a cruel laugh. At the end of Book 1, Voldemort tells Harry that his mother died protecting him. Her love left a mark that gave Harry protection. This is only part of the reason why Voldemort couldn't kill Harry that night and numerous times afterward. The full story isn't revealed until the final book in the series.

Harry's longing for a family who wants him (unlike the Dursleys) is a constant source of agony for him.

The first book establishes early on that Professor Snape, Potions master (who covets the job of Defense Against the Dark Arts) hates Harry. The explanation for this isn't fully explained until Book 7.

In Book 1 Professor Quirrell reveals that Snape attended Hogwarts the same time Harry's father did and that they loathed each other.

In Book 1, Dumbledore tells Harry that Snape hated his father because Harry's father saved Snape's life ... and perhaps this debt caused Snape to protect Harry. These revelations build with each subsequent book until the final, where the full truth is revealed.

Harry receives a Christmas present with an unsigned note that says Harry's father left an Invisibility Cloak in the gifter's possession, which is now being returned. The cloak becomes increasingly important throughout the series until its necessity and purpose become very clear in the final book.

Beginning in the first book, whenever Harry's scar hurts or burns, he deduces that it means danger is coming. Eventually, he connects this pain with Voldemort himself.

In Book 1 Harry "talks" to a snake at a zoo. The significance of this becomes clear in Book 2 and later books in the series, until the horrifying, full truth is realized in Book 7.

Harry guesses at the end of Book 1 that Voldemort will keep trying to get a body. He finally succeeds in Book 4, and all hell breaks loose.

Book 1 alludes to the prejudices against nonmagical families. This develops considerably throughout the series until we find out exactly what Voldemort has in mind for his new wizarding world order in Book 7.

## INDIVIDUAL STORY ARCS

Eleven-year-old Harry Potter is desperate to leave behind his life with the Dursleys. When he learns that he's a wizard, as were his parents, and he gets numerous letters informing him that he's been accepted into Hogwarts School of Witchcraft and Wizardry, his uncle won't allow him to read them until Hagrid delivers a letter to Harry personally on his birthday. He is astounded to hear himself referred to as a legend, i.e., "The Boy Who Lived."

Professor Quirrell took a year off from teaching to get firsthand experience in Defense Against the Dark Arts—and he's never been the same. The turban he always wears has a funny smell.

When Harry and Hagrid visit Gringotts Bank on orders from Dumbledore, Hagrid takes something out of vault 713, and that same vault is robbed (though the vault is now empty) later that day.

Harry gets a chocolate frog with a Dumbledore card, which tells him that Dumbledore works on alchemy with Nicholas Flamel.

The first day of term at Hogwarts, Dumbledore tells the student body that the third-floor corridor is forbidden. Harry and his friends discover why later when they find a three-headed dog standing on a trapdoor in one of the rooms. They conclude that the dog must be guarding whatever was in the small package Hagrid took from vault 713.

When a troll gets into the castle on Halloween, Professor Snape goes to the third floor instead of the dungeons with the rest of the teachers. When Snape comes back, he's injured. Is he after what the dog is guarding?

During Harry's first Quidditch match, his broomstick tries to buck him off. Harry, Ron, and Hermione assume Professor Snape is trying to jinx his broom.

Hagrid tells Harry and his friends that he bought the three-headed dog in a pub, and that whatever is in the package Dumbledore had him take out of vault 713 is between Dumbledore and Nicholas Flamel ... but none of them can remember who Flamel is. Hagrid later obtains a dragon egg—against the law—from a cloaked stranger in Hogsmeade. Eventually, he has no choice but to allow Charlie Weasley to take the dragon to Romania.

During detention in the Forbidden Forest, Harry witnesses a cloaked creature drinking the blood of a unicorn, which will keep anyone alive even if near death. But those who slay such an innocent creature must pay a price: They live a cursed half-life. ... However, the blood can also keep you alive until something else brings you back to full strength ... like the Sorcerer's Stone.

On Christmas night Harry becomes bewitched by the Mirror of Erised when it shows him the deepest, most desperate desire of his heart: his parents. Dumbledore catches him in front of it and tells him the mirror is to be moved the next day.

Another chocolate frog card of Dumbledore reminds Harry who Nicholas Flamel is, and the friends discover that he's the only known maker of the Sorcerer's Stone, which produces the Elixir of Life and makes the drinker immortal. Realizing someone was after it, Dumbledore moved it to Hogwarts.

Harry overhears Professors Snape and Quirrell arguing and believes that Snape is trying to get Quirrell to help him steal the Sorcerer's Stone. This leads Harry to believe that Snape wants the Sorcerer's Stone for Voldemort, but everyone says that as long as Dumbledore is present, the school is safe.

The night Hagrid won his dragon egg, he also mentioned to the stranger that his three-headed dog would go to sleep if music were played. Harry realizes Snape will try to steal the stone while Dumbledore is away ... tonight. Harry and his friends go to the third floor. But when Harry breaks past the barriers guarding the stone, he finds that it wasn't Snape who was trying to steal the stone—it was Professor Quirrell. This means Snape was trying to save Harry and protect the stone.

The Mirror of Erised is the key to obtaining the Sorcerer's Stone—Harry sees himself finding it. And he does.

Quirrell removes his turban, and growing out of the back of his head is a snake-like face—Voldemort, who can take a solid form only when he shares another body. He drank the unicorn blood to strengthen himself, but the Elixir of Life will give him back a body of his own.

When Harry touches Quirrell/Voldemort, the professor is burned because of the love inside Harry's skin (the mark of his mother's love that prevented Voldemort from killing him when he was a baby). Harry keeps hold of him until he's destroyed. Voldemort flees, a mere ghost.

Dumbledore and Flamel destroy the Sorcerer's Stone.

## SERIES PLANT ARCS

Dumbledore's Put-outer is first mentioned, but its full significance is not revealed until Book 7.

Speaking the name *Voldemort* is shocking and forbidden in the wizarding world. Instead, everyone calls him "He Who Must Not Be Named" or simply "You Know Who." This concept is fully explored in Book 7.

Godric's Hollow, where Harry and his parents lived, is mentioned in the first book and finally visited in the final book.

In Book 1 Sirius Black loaned Hagrid his flying motorcycle to bring Harry to the Dursleys the night his parents were killed. In Book 3 we learn how Sirius Black is connected to the death of Harry's parents.

Mrs. Figg, Harry's babysitter, is mentioned in the first book, but she becomes more than she seems in Book 5.

Hagrid reveals in Book 1 that he's not allowed to do magic because he was expelled from Hogwarts when he was in his third year. The specifics of this event aren't revealed until Book 2.

Gringotts Bank is run by goblins and is supposedly the safest place in the world to hide something, with the exception of Hogwarts. In Book 1 it's revealed that a dragon guards the highest security vaults. Harry and his friends face that dragon in Book 7.

Griphook, the goblin who works for Gringotts, is mentioned in Book 1, and he helps Harry and his friends rob the bank in Book 7.

Book 1 contains the comment "You never get such good results with another wizard's wand," and this truth becomes pivotal in Book 7.

Ron's rat Scabbers' origin is mentioned in Book 1 and becomes a plot thread in Book 3.

Dumbledore's defeat of the dark wizard Grindelwald is mentioned in Book 1 and several times throughout the series, but becomes critical to Book 7's plot in the developing and resolution of this series arc.

In Book 1 it is established that Charlie Weasley works with dragons in Romania. Charlie's job (and dragons) comes into play once again in Book 4.

In the first book, the Sorting Hat gives Harry a choice about which house he's placed in. This becomes very important in Book 2.

In Book 1 it's mentioned that Fred and George know the secret passages of the school better than anyone else. We find out why they're so familiar with them in Book 3.

In Book 1 it's mentioned that a bezoar can save a person from most poisons. This becomes necessary information in Book 6.

In Book 1 Harry catches the golden snitch in his mouth during a Quidditch game, and this fact is crucial in Book 7.

## HARRY POTTER AND THE CHAMBER OF SECRETS
### YEAR 2 IN THE SERIES

## OVERALL SERIES ARCS

In Book 2 Ron's younger sister, Ginny, has a crush on Harry. This attraction becomes mutual and grows in later stories.

In Book 2 we learn that Dobby the house-elf adores Harry and believes that, since Harry's triumph over Voldemort, house-elves live better lives. Dobby will do anything to help Harry (and does continuously through the series) ... even unto death.

In Book 2 we learn that Tom Riddle (Voldemort's real name) lived in a Muggle orphanage. He was Muggle born, with a Muggle father and witch mother. His mother died just after he was born. His father abandoned Harry and his mother before Harry was born because his father found out his wife was a witch. Tom was named after his father, and his middle name, Marvolo, was his grandfather's name. His origins grow more important as the series progresses.

Tom Riddle tells Harry at the end of Book 2 that he "decided to leave behind a diary to preserve his sixteen-year-old self in its pages"—a mere shadow of the truth. We'll learn the exact nature of Tom Riddle's diary in Book 7. The venom in the basilisk fang is used to destroy Tom Riddle's diary in Book 2. This method becomes crucial in Book 7.

Voldemort points out to Harry at the end of Book 2 how alike he and Harry are—they're both half-bloods, orphans, raised by Muggles, and Parselmouths. This fact becomes increasingly evident and the reasons for these similarities are clarified as the series goes along.

Tom Riddle tells Harry at the end of Book 2 that he "decided to leave behind a diary to preserve his sixteen-year-old self in its pages"—a mere shadow of the truth. We'll learn exactly what Tom Riddle's diary is in Book 7. The venom in the basilisk fang is used to destroy Tom Riddle's diary in Book 2. This method becomes crucial in Book 7.

The sword of Godric Gryffindor is used in Book 2 to destroy the basilisk. Its significance is revisited in Book 7.

In Book 2 Draco Malfoy calls Hermione a Mudblood which means "dirty blood"—a foul name for someone who's Muggle-born, as opposed to a pure-blood wizard.

It's revealed in Book 2 that Hogwarts was founded over a thousand years ago by the greatest witches and wizards of the age: Godric Gryffindor, Helga Hufflepuff, Rowena Ravenclaw, and Salazar Slytherin. A rift grew between Slytherin and the others because Slytherin wanted to be more selective about the students admitted into Hogwarts. He believed magical learning should be kept within all-magic families. This conflict develops throughout the books.

In Book 2 Dumbledore reveals Voldemort is hiding in the forests of Albania. This becomes important in later books.

At the end of Book 2 Dumbledore explains Tom Riddle's comments about his and Harry's similarities: Voldemort inadvertently transferred some of his powers to Harry the night he gave Harry his scar. This is developed more throughout the series, culminating in the full truth in the final book. The Sorting Hat considered putting Harry in Slytherin because of the likenesses Harry shares with Voldemort, but he ended up putting him where Harry asked to be put. Harry proves he is a true Gryffindor by pulling Godric Gryffindor's sword out of the hat. Again, this incident takes on greater meaning in Book 7.

## INDIVIDUAL STORY ARCS

Harry spends the summer without any contact with his friends from Hogwarts. On his twelfth birthday, he's supposed to spend the night locked in his room, pretending not to exist, since the Dursleys are entertaining company.

Dobby the house-elf appears and admits he's been intercepting Harry's mail all summer to make Harry believe his friends have forgotten him so he won't want to go back to school. He visits to extract a promise that Harry won't return to Hogwarts for the next school term. If Harry does go back to school, he'll be in mortal danger. A terrible plot is in the works at Hogwarts.

Dobby tells Harry the magical family he serves is unkind to him, but he doesn't say who they are. He says a house-elf's family must set him free or he will die in servitude to them.

Ron and his twin brothers show up in a flying car. They break Harry out of his room and take him to their home (the Burrow) to live until school starts. When Harry tells them about Dobby's visit, Ron's brothers reveal that Lucius Malfoy, the father of Harry and Ron's schoolmate Draco, was a big supporter of Voldemort. When Voldemort disappeared, Mr. Malfoy denied he was ever in league with him.

Do the Malfoys have a house-elf? House-elves come with big manors and castles owned by old, rich wizarding families.

Mrs. Weasley reads up on how to degnome a garden using a reference book by Gilderoy Lockhart, a celebrity wizard who's written many books on his encounters with dark creatures and becomes the next Defense Against the Dark Arts teacher at Hogwarts.

Harry attempts to travel with the Weasleys via the Floo Network to Diagon Alley, but he ends up going a grate too far to the Knockturn Alley Dark Arts shop Borgin and Burkes, where he witnesses Mr. Malfoy selling items that would embarrass him if the Ministry found them in his home.

In Diagon Alley, Gilderoy Lockhart is having a book signing and announces he'll be teaching Defense Against the Dark Arts at Hogwarts this year.

Mr. Malfoy and Mr. Weasley have a confrontation about how poor the Weasleys are—secondhand books—and because of the Weasleys love of all things Muggle. Mr. Malfoy picks up a stack of these tattered books and hands them to Ginny.

On September 1st, Harry and the Weasleys head to the train station in the flying car. Ron's parents accompany Ginny to the platform, as this is her first year, but when Ron and Harry try to follow, they find that the entrance to Platform 9¾ is sealed. They miss the train and decide to take the car. At Hogwarts, the car crashes into the Whomping Willow. Ron's wand snaps in half. The car backs out of the tree and dumps them and their things out on the lawn before disappearing into the Forbidden Forest.

If Professor Snape had his way, Harry and Ron would be expelled, but they're only given detention.

In their first Herbology lesson of the year, the students are given the task of repotting Mandrakes, which are used to make a powerful restorative to return people who have been petrified to their original states.

Lockhart unleashes pixies on the class in Dark Arts class, then, as if he doesn't have a clue what to do, asks Harry and his friends to get the pixies back into their cages. Later, Hagrid tells them that Lockhart was the only person Dumbledore could get for the Dark Arts job. He implies that Lockhart is a fraud.

Ron's detention entails polishing silver in the trophy room with Filch, the caretaker. Harry has to help Lockhart answer fan mail. While doing this, Harry hears a chilling voice say "Come to me, let me kill you." He hears the voice again on Halloween and realizes that whatever's behind the voice is going to kill. He and his friends follow the voice and find Mrs. Norris, Filch's cat, hanging above a pool of water. She's been petrified. The words "The Chamber of Secrets has been opened. Enemies of the Heir, beware" have been painted on the wall nearby. When Harry and friends are joined by the rest of the school, Draco shouts, "You'll be next, Mudbloods!"

Ginny seems horribly upset about what happened to Mrs. Norris. She worries Harry, Ron, and Hermione will be expelled.

Hermione asks a professor about the legend behind the Chamber of Secrets. Built as a hidden chamber under the castle, Slytherin sealed it until his own true heir arrived—the one who could unseal it and unleash a monster that only the Heir could control. He would use this horror to purge the school of those unworthy to study magic.

Harry and his friends investigate the place where Mrs. Norris was petrified and find a line of spiders fighting to get out. They speculate about whether Draco is the Heir of Slytherin. Did Lucius Malfoy open the chamber before, and has he now taught his son how to do it? Hermione comes up with the idea of concocting Polyjuice Potion to temporarily transform them into Slytherin students. Disguised, they'll ask Draco himself whether he is the Heir. The potion will take a month to brew and they decide to make it in the bathroom haunted by Moaning Myrtle since no one goes in there.

During a Quidditch match, a bludger has been tampered with and pursues Harry ruthlessly. It breaks his arm. While Harry's in the hospital, Dobby comes and tells him he's the one who sealed the train station barrier so Harry couldn't get on the train and come to Hogwarts. He also bewitched the bludger to injure Harry, hoping to send him home where he could be protected. Dobby can't let him stay at Hogwarts when the chamber is opened.

Dobby says the rag he's wearing is the mark of a house-elf's enslavement. Only if he's presented with clothes will he be freed from servitude.

A boy holding a camera in front of his face is petrified. This devastates Ginny, who's having nightmares about it.

During the first Dueling Club meeting, Draco casts a snake spell. Harry confronts the snake and instructs it to back down—and it does. Ron and Hermione inform him later that he's a Parselmouth (a speaker of snake language)—a rare gift, the mark of a Dark Wizard, and what Slytherin was famous for. Is Harry Slytherin's descendent? Would the Sorting Hat have put him in Gryffindor if he had had Slytherin blood? But the Sorting Hat wanted to put him in Slytherin.

Another boy is petrified, and next to him stands a school ghost. Nearby, a line of spiders scuttles away.

In Dumbledore's office, Harry meets Fawkes, Dumbledore's pet. Phoenixes can carry extremely heavy loads, their tears have healing powers, and they're extremely faithful to their owners.

Harry and his friends use the Polyjuice Potion and transform into Draco's best friends. Draco tells them he doesn't know who the Heir is, or he'd help him. His father won't tell him about the last time the chamber was opened fifty years ago—only that the person was expelled and is probably still imprisoned in Azkaban.

Moaning Myrtle's bathroom is flooded and a diary owned by T.M. Riddle is thrown at her. Riddle received an award for special services to the school fifty years ago. Obviously someone chucked the diary, but why? If the chamber was opened fifty years ago by someone who was expelled, and Riddle got an award for special services to the school fifty years ago, did he receive the award for catching the Heir of Slytherin?

Harry's school bag splits open and the diary falls out in front of Draco and a terrified-looking Ginny. Harry notices later that the rest of the books that fell out are drenched in ink from the bottle that broke, but the diary is as clean as it was before. Harry tries to write in the diary and Tom Riddle greets him. Tom tells him that the diary holds the memories of events that were covered up at Hogwarts. Riddle says the chamber was opened while he was a student, and a student was killed. Riddle reveals that it was Hagrid who opened the chamber in an attempt to hide a monstrous creature—a giant spider—he'd let into the school. Hagrid was expelled fifty years ago.

Harry hears the voice again and it gives Hermione an idea. Hermione is found petrified, with a mirror next to her.

Harry and Ron visit Hagrid under the Invisibility Cloak, but before they can ask him what happened fifty years ago, Dumbledore and the Minister of Magic come to take Hagrid to Azkaban. Then Mr. Malfoy arrives to announce that the school governors have decided to suspend Dumbledore; he agrees to step aside but adds that the only way he'll truly have left the school is when those loyal to him are gone—help will always be given to those who ask for it. Hagrid hints to the still-hidden Harry and Ron that the spiders will lead them to answers. Harry and Ron follow the spiders into the Forbidden Forest, where they encounter Aragog, Hagrid's monstrous pet from fifty years ago. Aragog insists that he wasn't the monster in the chamber that Hagrid set free. The monster in the chamber is an ancient creature that spiders fear above all others. Who did open the chamber, if not Hagrid?

A nervous Ginny tries to talk to Harry and Ron, implying she knows something about the chamber, but she runs away when her older brother appears.

Harry and Ron visit Hermione and find a scrap of paper in her fist that contains a page about the basilisk. Besides venomous fangs, the stare of the serpent will cause instant death. Hermione wrote "pipes" on the page. Harry understands that the basilisk is the monster in the chamber and that it's been using the pipes to get around the school. Harry can hear its voice because he speaks Parseltongue. No one has died because none of them have looked the creature straight in the eye: One saw it through his camera, another through the ghost. Hermione must have used the mirror to look around corners and saw the snake through it. Mrs. Norris saw it in the water's reflection. Pipes ... plumbing ... The entrance to the Chamber of Secrets must be in Moaning Myrtle's bathroom.

An announcement is made—another attack. Harry and Ron overhear that a student was taken into the chamber by the monster and a message was left. The student was Ginny.

Lockhart is assigned to rescue Ginny. Harry and Ron go after him. He admits that the feats in his books have been more than exaggerated. He used Memory Charms to make the doers of the actual feats forget they'd done them so he could take the credit. Harry takes Lockhart's wand and forces him to accompany them into Myrtle's bathroom, where they ask her how she died. Fifty years ago, she saw a pair of huge yellow eyes and became a ghost.

Harry finds a snake scratched into the side of the sink. He speaks Parselmouth, the sink moves, and a huge pipe is revealed. In the tunnels below, Lockhart steals Ron's damaged wand and his Memory Charm backfires on him, causing a cave-in that separates Harry from Ron and Lockhart.

Harry enters the chamber and finds Ginny, unmoving. Riddle steps out and says she won't wake. He gets Harry's wand and tells Harry that Ginny poured her soul into the diary. He grew stronger and more powerful and was able to control her. Ginny was responsible for opening the chamber and writing the messages. She finally grew suspicious of the diary and tried to throw it away. Harry found it—Harry, the very person Riddle wanted to meet. Riddle is Voldemort, the greatest sorcerer in the world. Harry insists Dumbledore is the greatest. Fawkes is summoned to the chamber by Harry's loyalty. The phoenix drops the Sorting Hat at Harry's feet.

Tom summons the basilisk and tells it to kill Harry. Fawkes blinds the serpent and sweeps the Sorting Hat into Harry's arms. Inside is the Sword of Gryffindor. Harry uses it to kill the monster, but one poisonous fang sinks into his arm. Fawkes heals him with tears. Fawkes then drops the diary in his lap. Harry plunges the fang into it. The venom burns a hole in it, and Riddle is destroyed. Ginny wakes. Fawkes carries the four of them out of the chamber.

Mr. Malfoy comes to the school with his house-elf Dobby. Dumbledore says Voldemort was acting through the diary. Harry realizes that Mr.

Malfoy gave the diary to Ginny along with the tattered books he handed her the day they were in the bookstore in Diagon Alley.

After removing his sock and putting it in the diary, Harry follows Mr. Malfoy and Dobby. When he thrusts both at Malfoy, Malfoy takes them and throws them aside. Dobby catches the sock—he's a free elf!

Harry has again prevented Voldemort from returning.

## SERIES PLANT ARCS

Mundungus Fletcher is a thief who makes his first appearance in Book 2 but becomes a recurring character throughout the books, serving various roles as needed.

In Book 2 the ghoul in the attic of the Weasley home is mentioned, and this becomes more important in Book 7.

In Borgin and Burkes, a cursed opal necklace is mentioned in Book 2—the same necklace that becomes important in Book 6? It's never said in the book whether this is the same necklace that cursed Katie Bell in Book 6 when she touched it.

The twin of the Vanishing Cabinet, which becomes pivotal in Book 6, is also mentioned here.

The Whomping Willow is mentioned first in Book 2, and the story of why it was placed on Hogwart's grounds is explained in Book 3.

Aragog, the Acromantula, is first mentioned in Book 2, and his death is part of the plot in Book 6.

## HARRY POTTER AND THE PRISONER OF AZKABAN
### YEAR 3 IN THE SERIES

## OVERALL SERIES ARCS

The development of the Patronus begins in Book 3 and continues throughout the series.

Dumbledore tells Harry at the end of Book 3 that he did a brave thing by saving Peter Pettigrew's life, and that Peter owes his life to Harry. He explains that when one wizard saves another, it creates a bond between them. A time will come when Harry will be glad he saved Peter's life. This event comes full circle in Book 7.

## INDIVIDUAL STORY ARCS

Five weeks into summer, on his thirteenth birthday, Harry receives a note from his best friend. Ron's father won the annual *Daily Prophet* Grand Prize Galleon Draw, and the whole family is spending a month in Egypt. Ron sends a picture of the family, including Scabbers, Ron's pet rat. They're also buying Ron a new wand.

Harry receives a permission form to allow third-year students to visit the village of Hogsmeade on certain weekends during the school year. It must be signed by a parent or guardian, but how will he get his aunt or uncle to sign it?

In a Muggle news report in the Dursleys' kitchen, Harry hears about a man named Sirius Black who's escaped prison and is extremely dangerous.

Harry's Aunt Marge is coming to visit for a week. Harry makes a deal with his uncle—he'll go along with whatever they want from him during her visit if his uncle will sign the permission form for Hogsmeade. During the last night of Aunt Marge's visit, she insults Harry's parents and he loses control of his magic. She swells up like a huge balloon. Harry grabs his trunk and rushes out of the house, believing he'll be expelled. As he's trying to figure out what to do, he sees a hulking dog watching him. Startled, he trips over his trunk and almost gets run over by the Knight Bus, emergency transport for the stranded witch or wizard. Harry says he wants to go to Diagon Alley in London.

The bus conductor, Stan, reads the *Daily Prophet*, which contains a story about Sirius Black's escape from Azkaban. He murdered thirteen people thirteen years ago. Stan says Sirius was a big supporter of You-Know-Who. He's the only person who's ever escaped from Azkaban.

The Minister of Magic is waiting for Harry at the Leaky Cauldron, relieved that Harry's all right. They've dealt with his aunt, and Harry won't be expelled. On the Minister's suggestion, Harry takes a room at the Leaky Cauldron. He wonders why the Minister came to handle this himself and why he seems worried about Harry.

When he sees a book about death omens in the bookstore, Harry wonders if the dog he saw before the bus appeared is a death omen.

Hermione and Ron's family arrive the day before school starts. They're staying overnight at the Leaky Cauldron and taking ministry cars to the train station the next day. Hermione wants to buy a pet. Ron brings Scabbers to the pet store. Scabber's left ear is tattered and he's missing a toe. Ron is told that an ordinary rat doesn't live more than three years—but Scabbers is far older than that and he's been through the mill. A cat tries to attack Scabbers. Hermione buys that cat, Crookshanks.

That night, Harry overhears Mr. and Mrs. Weasley arguing. Mr. Weasley insists that Harry has a right to know so he can be on his guard. Harry can't go wandering off by himself this year. He might have died when he took off from the Dursleys' house, before the ministry found him. Sirius Black is mad, and he was clever enough to escape Azkaban—which is supposed to be impossible. Sirius has been loose for three weeks, and the ministry is no closer to catching him. The only thing they know for sure is that Sirius is after Harry, and, if the criminal broke out of Azkaban, he can break into Hogwarts. Murdering Harry might bring Voldemort back to power. Azkaban guards will be stationed around Hogwarts' entrances this year. Harry thinks that, if Dumbledore is the only person Voldemort was ever afraid of, then Sirius—reportedly Voldemort's right-hand man— will be just as frightened of him.

The next morning they board the Hogwarts Express. Mr. Weasley starts to tell Harry about Sirius and asks Harry to promise not to go looking for him. Harry doesn't know why he'd look for someone who wants to kill him.

The train stops en route, unexpectedly, and dementors search the compartments. Intense cold sinks into everyone. Harry hears screaming and passes out. Professor RJ (Remus) Lupin, the new Defense Against the Dark Arts teacher, is standing over Harry when he comes to. Ron and Hermione tell Harry that when the dementor didn't leave, Lupin muttered something and a silvery thing (a Patronus) shot out of his wand. It chased the dementor away.

Professor Snape's expression is one of loathing when Dumbledore introduces Lupin to the student body.

At breakfast Ron notices Hermione's conflicting schedule. She'll be in three different classes at the same time.

During Divination, Professor Trelawney sees "the Grim" in Harry's teacup. It's an omen of death.

In Transfiguration class they learn about Animai—wizards who can transform into animals.

In Care of Magical Creatures they meet a Hippogriff—half horse, half bird. Buckbeak allows Harry to fly on his back. When Draco Malfoy is injured by the Hippogriff, his father complains to the school governors.

During Potions class Harry hears that Sirius Black has been spotted not far from Hogsmeade. Draco overhears and tells Harry that, if it was him, he'd hunt Black down himself; he'd want revenge. Harry wonders what he would want revenge for.

In Defense Against the Dark Arts they learn about boggarts—shape-shifters that take the shape of whatever they think will frighten a person most. Harry thinks that the boggart will appear as Voldemort, since that's what scares him most, but then he remembers the dementor on the train. When Lupin sets the boggart free and it turns on Harry, Lupin throws himself in front of Harry. The boggart turns into a silvery-white orb. Harry wonders why Lupin stopped him from taking a turn with the boggart.

While Hermione and Ron are in Hogsmeade during the first visiting weekend, Harry and Lupin talk about why he stopped Harry from facing the boggart—Lupin thought Voldemort would appear and cause panic. Snape comes in with a potion he made for Lupin because he's been feeling "off-color." Later Harry and his friends wonder if Snape wants to poison Lupin.

The Gryffindor portrait canvas on the door of the common room has been slashed, and the occupant is missing. The Fat Lady ran through other portraits to escape Sirius Black, who got very angry when she wouldn't let him in.

How did Sirius get in the castle? Enchantments have been placed on it, gaining entry via apparition is impossible, and dementors are guarding every entrance. The castle is searched and there's no sign of Sirius. Snape suggests that he could have entered the school with inside help. Dumbledore doesn't believe anyone would aid him.

Snape teaches one of Lupin's classes, telling the students that Lupin is ill. They learn how to distinguish werewolves from true wolves. Snape seems to have it in for Lupin. Why?

Hermione's cat is working overtime trying to catch Scabbers.

During a Quidditch match Harry sees the silhouette of a black dog. A familiar chill fills him, and he sees countless dementors beneath him. He hears a screaming woman, his mother. She's going to be murdered, but she's trying to protect him. A shrill laugh sounds, and Harry falls fifty feet off his broom. When he wakes, he's told Dumbledore had never been so angry. He slowed Harry's fall before he hit the ground, then turned his wand on the dementors that had come onto the grounds. He shot something silver at them and they left. Everyone thought Harry was dead. His broomstick hit the Whomping Willow and was destroyed.

..................................................

Harry can't help noticing that he's seen the Grim at least twice now, and both were followed by near-fatal accidents.

..................................................

Lupin is back, looking very ill. After class he reveals to Harry that they planted the Whomping Willow the same year he arrived at Hogwarts.

..................................................

Lupin says the dementors affect Harry worse than the others because his past contains true horrors. Dementors are incapable of a single cheerful thought. Most prisoners at Azkaban go mad in weeks, but Sirius Black escaped after thirteen years. Lupin says there are defenses against dementors and he'll teach them to Harry.

..................................................

After Ron and Hermione leave on another Hogsmeade weekend, Fred and George Weasley give Harry the Marauder's Map—designed by Moony, Wormtail, Padfoot, and Prongs. The map shows every detail of Hogwarts. Ink dots move around, labeled with names of those in the castle. It also includes secret passageways—including one beneath the Whomping Willow and one that leads into Hogsmeade. Harry uses this passageway to go to Hogsmeade, and he and his friends overhear the conversation of two professors, Hagrid and the Minister of Magic. They discuss Sirius Black in his younger days, when he was in school and his best friend was James Potter. Sirius was Best Man at James and Lily's wedding, and they named him godfather to Harry. The Potters knew Voldemort was after them. Dumbledore advised them to go into hiding using the Fidelius Charm, which involves magically concealing a secret inside a chosen person. That makes the secret impossible to find out unless the Secret Keeper divulges it. Sirius was their Secret Keeper. Barely a week later, he betrayed them. Hagrid rescued Harry just as Sirius showed up and loaned him his flying motorbike to get Harry to his aunt and uncle's. Peter Pettigrew, another of James Potter's school friends, caught Sirius the next day. Sirius blew him to pieces. All that was left was a finger. After hearing this, Harry's friends worry that he'll go after Sirius.

..................................................

Hagrid receives notice that Buckbeak will be put on trial to determine whether he should be executed after attacking a student.

For Christmas Harry gets a new Firebolt broomstick, but who sent it to him? The Gryffindor headmistress confiscates the broom until it can be checked for jinxes. Did Sirius Black send it?

Harry's anti-dementor lessons with Lupin begin with the use of a boggart. Harry practices the Patronus charm on one. A Patronus is a guardian that acts as a positive force or shield between the wizard and the dementor. Summoning a Patronus is highly advanced magic, and even qualified wizards have trouble producing one.

Harry hears his parents' deaths at Voldemort's hands as he attempts to produce a Patronus.

Lupin reveals that he and Harry's father were friends at Hogwarts. He also knew—or thought he knew—Sirius Black.

Harry produces a silvery, indistinct Patronus.

Harry asks Lupin what's beneath a dementor's hood. Lupin says a dementor only lowers its hood when it delivers the Dementor's Kiss, sucking the soul out of its victim. The ministry plans to have a dementor perform this on Sirius Black.

Harry's Firebolt is returned, jinx free. Harry and Ron rush back to the common room to apologize to Hermione; they've been ignoring her ever since she turned the broomstick in to McGonagall, and they find Neville unable to get into the common room. He's lost the password he'd written down.

Ron finds blood on his bedsheet and Scabbers is gone. Two cat hairs are nearby. Ron and Hermione's friendship seems to be at an end.

In the middle of the night Ron insists Sirius Black slashed his bed hangings and stood over him holding a knife. The new Gryffindor portrait occupant verifies that he let Sirius in because he had the password written on a piece of paper—the one Neville lost. The castle is searched, and Sirius seems to have escaped once more.

Using the Marauder's Map and his Invisibility Cloak, Harry visits Hogsmeade with Ron. They go to the Shrieking Shack, the most haunted building in Britain. Draco Malfoy shows up to taunt Ron about Hagrid. Buckbeak will be beheaded, he's sure, thanks to his father's efforts. Harry frightens Draco under his Invisibility Cloak, but it slips off and his head is revealed. Harry knows he has to get back to the castle before Draco does, but he's too late.

Snape says Harry is like his father: arrogant, flouting the rules. Harry says he knows that his father saved Snape's life and Snape sneers. James and his friends played a joke on Snape that would have resulted in his death if James hadn't gotten cold feet at the last moment.

Snape demands that Harry give him the map, which refuses to reveal its secrets to him. Snape hands the map over to Lupin, since it's his area of expertise. Lupin takes it and informs Harry privately that he knows it's a map, and that Harry should have handed it in, knowing Sirius Black could have used it to get into the school. His parents gave their lives for him, and this seems a poor way to repay them.

Buckbeak is to be executed. Hermione and Ron make up.

Harry sees Crookshanks with a black dog. But if the cat can also see it, can it be a death omen?

Harry and his friends use the Invisibility Cloak to be with Hagrid while Buckbeak is executed. They find Scabbers hiding there. When the executioner comes with the Minister of Magic and Dumbledore, Harry, Ron, and Hermoine go out the back way. Scabbers bites Ron trying to escape. They see Crookshanks, and Ron saves Scabbers from the cat's attack. The black dog comes. The Whomping Willow hits Harry and Hermione while the dog drags Ron out of sight into its base. Crookshanks runs under the branches and presses on the knot on the trunk. The tree goes utterly still. They follow a tunnel toward Hogsmeade and come out in the Shrieking Shack. They find Ron, who tells them the dog is an Animagus—Sirius Black. Sirius begs them to listen to the whole story, but Lupin rushes in, demanding to know where "he" is. Sirius points at Ron. Lupin asks why "he" didn't show himself until now ... unless he was the Secret Keeper and therefore the one who actually betrayed Lily and James Potter.

Hermione says she's been covering for Lupin, who's a werewolf, and he's been helping Sirius all the time.

Lupin had been bitten by a werewolf when he was young. Though no cure exists, the potion that Snape brews for him makes him safe to be around when transformed. Without it, he becomes a full-fledged monster once a month. Attending Hogwarts as a student seemed impossible for Lupin, but Dumbledore planted the Whomping Willow and built the tunnel and the Shrieking Shack for him to hide in when he turned.

Lupin says the Marauder's Map told him that Sirius was here with Harry and his friends, along with Peter Pettigrew, another Animagus—Scabbers. There were three unregistered Animagi at Hogwarts: James Potter (a stag), Sirius Black (a dog), and Peter Pettigrew (a rat). They made life bearable for Lupin by becoming Animagi. Snape was interested in where Lupin went every month, and Sirius thought it would be amusing to tell him to use the knot on the tree trunk to get inside. Snape met a full-grown werewolf when he reached the shack, and James pulled him out, saving his life. That's why Snape doesn't like any of them.

Snape appears. He saw Lupin and Sirius on the map in Lupin's office, which proves that Lupin's been helping his old friend into the castle. Harry and his friends knock Snape unconscious. Sirius reveals that he knew where to find Peter from the photograph of Ron and his family in the *Daily Prophet*. In the photo Scabbers (Peter) is on his shoulder, missing a toe. Peter cut off his toe and left it at the scene the day all the Muggles were killed, just before he transformed into a rat. This ensured that everyone believed Sirius was to blame for betraying Lily and James. Crookshanks recognized Peter for what he was and helped Sirius by giving him the Gryffindor password and trying to capture Scabbers. Peter left blood on the sheets to fake his own death. Sirius had convinced Lily and James to make Peter their Secret Keeper—a bluff to make Voldemort go after Sirius instead. Peter gave Voldemort the information on where Lily and James were hiding.

Sirius and Lupin turn Peter back into a human. Peter didn't go after Harry all this time because, with Voldemort hiding or half dead, he had no motivation. He had planned to wait for Voldemort to regain his strength before rejoining him.

Sirius transformed into a dog in Azkaban to keep his sanity. He also used his dog form to escape, as dementors have difficulty sensing animal emotions. Sirius says he would never have betrayed James and Lily, and Harry believes him. But he won't let Sirius and Lupin kill Peter—they'll take him up to the castle and give him to the dementors.

On the way back through the tunnel, Sirius says he's Harry's godfather. Once Sirius's name is cleared, if Harry ever wants a different home, he can come and live with Sirius.

They emerge on Hogwarts' grounds into the light of a full moon. Lupin didn't take his potion tonight, and he transforms. Peter dives for Lupin's wand, but Harry prevents him from getting it. However, Harry can't stop him from transforming into a rat and scurrying away.

Sirius tries to lead the werewolf away from them, but Harry follows. Dementors are everywhere, encircling Sirius. Harry tries to produce a Patronus, but a dementor lowers its hood.

Suddenly Harry sees a silvery light growing brighter on the other side of the lake. It drives back the dementors, and then gallops away. The figure is familiar to him, as is the person the Patronus returns to. Harry collapses.

He awakens in the hospital and is told Sirius is locked away and any moment the dementors will perform the kiss. Dumbledore comes in and Harry tells him they have the wrong man. Dumbledore believes him but says that they need more time. Hermione understands immediately what he means. Dumbledore says that Sirius is locked in an office on the seventh floor. If all goes well, they can save more than one innocent life tonight. It's five minutes to midnight—three turns ought to do it.

. . . . . . . . . . . . . . . . . . . . . . . . . . . . . . . . . . . . . . . . . . . . . . . . . . . . . . . . . . . . . . . . . . . . . . . . . . . . . . . . . .

Dumbledore locks them in the hospital wing, and Hermione takes out a tiny hourglass on a chain, which she turns over three times. Harry feels like he's flying backwards very fast, and then everything comes back into focus. Hermione tells him they've gone back in time three hours. The device is a Time-Turner. It's how she's managed to attend all of her lessons this year. She repeats hours several times and is able to attend several simultaneously scheduled classes at once. Dumbledore sent them back to change something. Three hours ago, they were at Hagrid's, just before Buckbeak was executed. They can save him. Then they'll fly the Hippogriff up to rescue Sirius—the two can escape together. But awful things can happen when wizards meddle with time. They can't be seen by anyone, especially themselves.

. . . . . . . . . . . . . . . . . . . . . . . . . . . . . . . . . . . . . . . . . . . . . . . . . . . . . . . . . . . . . . . . . . . . . . . . . . . . . . . . . .

They steal Buckbeak, waiting until the Minister and executioner have seen him so Hagrid won't be blamed for letting Buckbeak go. They rush into the forest to wait until they can rescue Sirius. They watch the Whomping Willow and see themselves enter it after Sirius drags Ron inside. Lupin comes, then Snape. They wait for everyone to come back up, and Harry talks about the large silver something that forced the dementors to retreat. Only a very powerful Patronus could have done that. But who conjured it? Harry saw the person; he thinks it was his dad.

. . . . . . . . . . . . . . . . . . . . . . . . . . . . . . . . . . . . . . . . . . . . . . . . . . . . . . . . . . . . . . . . . . . . . . . . . . . . . . . . . .

Everyone emerges from the willow, and Harry realizes that he has to let Peter escape again—they can't be seen. When Lupin the werewolf runs in their direction, they rush to Hagrid's house to hide. Later Harry goes outside again so they'll know when it's time to rescue Sirius. He expects to see who sent the Patronus, but no one comes to save Sirius and his other self. The dementor lowers its hood. Harry realizes that it wasn't his father he'd seen earlier—he saw himself. He conjures a powerful, real Patronus—a stag that drives the dementors away. He conjured the Patronus this time because he knew he'd done it before.

Hermione arrives with Buckbeak, and they rescue Sirius. Man and beast fly away. Harry and Hermione rush back to the hospital. They tell Dumbledore they did it, and he locks them in the hospital wing. When Snape realizes Sirius is gone, he's furious and assumes Harry had something to do with his escape. Dumbledore assures him that Harry's been locked up and the doctor can testify that he hasn't left his bed since Dumbledore locked them in.

The dementors are removed from Hogwarts, and Lupin resigns from his teaching post. He gives Harry the map and his invisibility cloak.

Harry wonders if Peter has gone to Voldemort yet. But a worse realization is that he must return to the Dursleys when he'd been so close to having a home and family. Living with Sirius would have been like getting his own father back. But Sirius and Buckbeak have successfully gone into hiding.

Hermione has handed in the Time-Turner and dropped a few classes next year.

Ron plans to arrange for Harry to come to the Quidditch World Cup with him and his family this summer. Cheered at the thought, Harry is on the train home when he gets an owl from Sirius, who tells him he sent the Firebolt—thirteen birthdays worth of presents from his godfather. Sirius has also signed the permission form so Harry can visit Hogsmeade with his friends on weekends next year.

## SERIES PLANT ARCS

The dementors, guardians of the wizarding prison Azkaban, are introduced in Book 3 but will make other appearances in later books as well. Even Muggles can feel a dementor's presence, though they can't see them, as shown in Book 5.

Book 3 mentions that the stagecoaches at the Hogsmeade train station are pulled by "invisible horses." This issue is revisited and clarified in Book 5.

Cedric Diggory, Hufflepuff Seeker, is first mentioned in Book 3, and he becomes a major character in Book 4.

Cho Chang, Ravenclaw's Seeker, is first mentioned in Book 3 and becomes Harry's first love in Book 5.

Toward the end of Book 3, Professor Trelawney unknowingly utters a real prophecy to Harry: The Dark Lord's servant, chained these twelve years, breaks free and rejoins his master. The Dark Lord will rise again. When Harry tells Dumbledore about Trelawney's prophecy, the headmaster says that this is her second real prediction. We learn in Book 5 that she made another prophecy when Harry was just a baby.

A Patronus—a guardian that acts as a positive force or shield between the wizard and the dementor—has other uses, as later books will reveal.

## HARRY POTTER AND THE GOBLET OF FIRE
### YEAR 4 IN THE SERIES

## OVERALL SERIES ARCS

In Book 4 we are told that Dumbledore trusts people and gives them second chances—Snape is one such person. But what did Snape do for his first chance? Dumbledore says the reason he believes Snape stopped supporting Voldemort is a matter between him and Snape. The truth isn't revealed until the final book.

In Book 4 Moody asks Harry if he's ever considered a career as an Auror before. Harry moves closer toward this occupation throughout the rest of the series.

Percy Weasley has always been ambitious, but in Book 4 it's said that he would never betray his family for his career. Ron himself isn't so sure about this. His brother's career with the Ministry of Magic means everything to him, and this becomes an issue for the rest of the series.

In Book 4 Voldemort says he's gone farther along the path that leads to immortality than anyone before him. We find out how far he's gone in Books 6 and 7.

In Book 4 Voldemort hints that Dumbledore invoked an ancient magic to ensure Harry's protection as long as he's in his relations' care. Voldemort can't touch him at the Dursleys. This theme continues throughout the last books in the series. When Mrs. Weasley asks Dumbledore if they can take Harry straight to the Burrow with them this summer at the end of Book 4, Dumbledore says Harry has to go back to the Dursleys' first because of this protection.

At the end of Book 4 Dumbledore says to Snape, "You know what I must ask you to do. If you're ready..." Snape says he is. We don't find out what this means until later in the series.

At the end of Book 4 Dumbledore tells Harry that the Prior Incantatem spell took place because Harry and Voldemort's wands share the same core. When a wand meets its brother, neither works properly against the other. If forced to do battle, one of the wands regurgitates spells it's performed in reverse. This develops more in later books.

At the end of Book 4 the Minister refuses to accept that Voldemort is back. He believes they're trying to start a panic to destabilize all that the government has worked for these past thirteen years. Snape shows the Minister the Dark Mark on his arm to prove that Voldemort is back. The mark was faded all these years, and, as it had been Voldemort's means of summoning his followers before, the fact that it's bright and clear proves Voldemort has returned. The Minister still doesn't believe.

Dumbledore advises Fudge in this book to remove the dementors from control of Azkaban, since they were Voldemort's most dangerous supporters.

Dumbledore says he needs to send envoys to the giants to persuade them to stand against Voldemort.

All of these plot threads are developed in later books.

In Book 4 Harry and Ron overhear Hagrid and Madame Maxime, another half-giant. At the end of Book 4 Hagrid says Dumbledore has given him a job over the summer that he's not supposed to talk about.

## INDIVIDUAL STORY ARCS

Fifty years ago all three Riddles were found dead by their maid. Their gardener, Frank Bryce, was arrested. No one had been seen near the house that day except a dark-haired, pale teenage boy. Only Frank saw him, and no one believed him. But the medical reports came back, and the Riddles had been in perfect health, outside of the fact that they were all dead with frozen looks of horror on their faces. Did they die of fright? With no proof of murder, Frank was released. He returned to his cottage on the Riddles' grounds. Frank's devotion to the property is an obsession. When he sees a light at the old house one night, he assumes the local boys are having fun with him. Inside the house he overhears voices talking about something that needs milking and feeding. They'll stay here until the Quidditch World Cup is over because it can't be done without Harry Potter. But Harry is so well protected. "Wormtail" says that Bertha Jorkins's disappearance won't go unnoticed. The other voice says one more death will clear the path to Harry Potter. His faithful servant will be at Hogwarts and Harry will be his. Frank sees a gigantic snake, 12 feet long, and it passes him, hissing. Can this man talk to snakes? The snake indeed tells the man that Frank is listening. He's brought in and sees the thing that was talking to the snake. Frank screams, there's a flash of light, and he dies.

Harry wakes from a nightmare, the scar on his forehead burning. He remembers an old man, a snake, Wormtail, and the voice of Voldemort. Wormtail and Voldemort had been talking about someone they'd killed, and they'd been plotting to kill Harry. The last time the scar had hurt, Voldemort had been close by. Harry writes to his godfather, Sirius Black, about it. Sirius is on the run, in hiding, because the wizarding and Muggle worlds believe him guilty of murder.

Harry is hoping the Weasleys, the family of his best friend Ron, will invite him to stay with them soon.

A letter from Mrs. Weasley arrives. They want to take Harry to the Quidditch World Cup and have him as their guest for the rest of the summer.

When Harry gets to the Burrow, he's told about Fred and George's Wizard Wheezes—the joke supplies that they've invented. They're planning to sell them at Hogwarts to make money. They want to open a joke shop.

Percy Weasley works at the Ministry of Magic for Mr. Bartimus Crouch, head of the Department of International Magical Cooperation.

Percy hints that there's another big event coming up after the World Cup.

Ludo Bagman, head of the Department of Magical Games and Sports, got the Weasleys good tickets for the Cup.

Ludo lost a member of his department over a month ago. Bertha Jorkins went to Albania and never came back.

The Weasleys and Harry use a Portkey (any charmed object that transports a wizard from one place to another at a prearranged time) to get to the site of the Cup. They meet up with Amos and Cedric Diggory, who's Captain and Seeker for Hufflepuff house Quidditch team at Hogwarts.

In the Quidditch stadium they meet Winky, a house-elf who's a friend of Dobby's. She worries that setting Dobby free wasn't such a good thing since Dobby now requires that he be paid for his work—a shameful thing for a house-elf. Winky is sitting in the stands because her master, Mr. Crouch, told her to save him a seat.

After the match Harry wakes up and immediately surmises that something is wrong. People are screaming and running. Black-hooded figures are levitating Muggles. Mr. Weasley says he's going to help the Ministry and that Harry and the Weasley siblings should get into the woods and stick together. They find Draco Malfoy there. Harry loses his wand. He finds Winky trying to get away from the chaos. He and his friends hear footsteps, then someone whispers "Morsmorde." Something vast, green, and glittering erupts from the darkness into the sky—it's Voldemort's sign, the Dark Mark. Mr. Crouch and the other Ministry wizards demand to know which of them conjured the Dark Mark. But then Winky is found nearby, stunned. She has a wand—Harry's! Winky insists she didn't conjure the Mark. Did she pick up Harry's wand when he dropped it? The Prior Incantato spell is used to discover the last spell the wand performed—it was the Dark Mark. As punishment, Winky is set free from her servitude.

Voldemort's Mark hasn't been seen for thirteen years. He and his supporters used to send it into the air whenever they killed. The Death Eaters, Voldemort's supporters, got scared tonight when they saw the Mark and Disapparated immediately.

Harry remembers that three days ago he woke up with his scar hurting. Now Voldemort's mark has appeared in the sky.

The day Ron and Harry set off for school, Mr. Weasley gets an urgent message from the Ministry. Mad-Eye Moody, a retired Auror (Dark Wizard catcher) heard an intruder in his yard who tried to break into his house. Moody filled half the cells in Azkaban. He has enemies everywhere and he's getting paranoid and seeing Dark Wizards everywhere.

On Platform 9¾ Bill Weasley says he wishes he was back at Hogwarts because this year is going to be an interesting one, and he hopes to get time off to come and watch. Even Mrs. Weasley says that she'd invite Harry for Christmas, but she expects all the students will want to stay at school this year. They'll find out what's going on at the feast that night.

Hermione learns that there are house-elves working in the Hogwarts kitchen and decides to begin an elf rights campaign.

Dumbledore announces at the feast that the Inter-House Quidditch Cup won't take place this year. Instead, Hogwarts is hosting the Triwizard Tournament, a friendly competition between the three largest European schools of wizardry—Hogwarts, Beauxbatons, and Durmstrang. One champion will be selected to represent each school. The selection of champions will take place on Halloween. The prize is the Triwizard Cup and a thousand Galleons. They're imposing an age restriction on contenders—seventeen years or older can put forth their names for consideration. Harry wonders what it would be like to be the Hogwarts champion, and if Cho Chang, the girl he likes, would glow with admiration for him.

Dumbledore introduces their new Defensive Against the Dark Arts teacher, Mad-Eye Moody, who drinks only from his own flask. Moody teaches them three illegal, heavily punishable Unforgivable Curses: the Imperius Curse, which gives total control over an enemy (this one controlled a lot of wizards when Voldemort was all-powerful and made it difficult to decide who was being forced and who acted of their own free will. The spell can be fought but takes serious strength of character); the Cruciatus Curse, which produces painful torture; and Avada Kedavra, the killing curse. This one produces a flash of blinding green light and a rushing sound. There is no countercurse or block. Only one person has been known to have survived it: Harry. He recognizes what happened in his memories of his parents' deaths as the killing curse.

Neville Longbottom seems particularly disturbed after class. Moody says Professor Sprout told him that Neville is good at Herbology, and Moody gives him Magical Water Plants of the Mediterranean.

Hermione starts S.P.E.W.—Society for the Promotion of Elfish Welfare. Fred and George tell Hermione that the house-elves in Hogwarts's kitchen are happy and think they have the best jobs in the world.

Harry gets a letter from Sirius. He's coming to Hogsmeade. He advises Harry to go straight to Dumbledore about his scar's pain. Dumbledore brought Moody out of retirement after reading the signs that something dangerous was about to happen. Harry is distressed that he made Sirius think he had to come back. What if Sirius gets caught?

The delegation from Beauxbatons arrives with their headmistress, Madame Maxime, who's as large as Hagrid.

Durmstrang also arrives, and one of their students is Victor Krum, a favored Seeker at the Quidditch World Cup. Their headmaster is Karkaroff.

Ludo Bagman and Mr. Crouch also arrive for the official opening of the tournament.

The champions will be tested by three tasks spaced through the school year. An impartial selector will choose the champions: the Goblet of Fire. Anyone who wants to submit must write his name on parchment and drop it into the goblet. On Halloween the goblet will return the name of those it judges to be the most worthy to represent their schools. Once a champion has been selected, that person is obligated to see the tournament through to the end. Placing your name in the goblet constitutes a binding, magical contract.

Karkaroff turns deathly pale, fear and fury on his face, when he sees Moody.

Fred and George take an aging potion and try to put their names in the goblet. They're hurled out of the circle.

Hagrid tells Hermione that he won't join S.P.E.W.—taking a house-elf's work away will make him unhappy. Paying him would be insulting.

The school champions are announced on Halloween night: Victor Krum for Durmstrang, Fleur Delacour for Beauxbatons, and Cedric Diggory for Hogwarts. But the goblet isn't done. Another name shoots out: Harry Potter. Harry immediately says he didn't put his name in and didn't ask an older student to put it in, but he's forced to join the other champions. He can't duck out, age limit or no age limit. Moody says only a skilled wizard could have hoodwinked the goblet. It's Moody's job to think the way Dark Wizards do ... as Karkaroff well knows.

The first task will take place on November 24. The champions aren't permitted help from teachers. They'll face the challenges armed with only their wands.

Harry is afraid. Someone wants him to compete—why? To get him killed? Voldemort wants him dead, but he's in some distant country, feeble and powerless. Yet in Harry's dream, Voldemort had been plotting his murder. No one believes that Harry didn't somehow trick the goblet. Ron is especially furious. Hermione alone knows he couldn't have entered by himself. She says Ron is jealous because Harry always gets the attention. She advises him to tell Sirius.

As one of the champions, Harry is interviewed by Rita Skeeter, a notorious reporter for the *Daily Prophet*. She publishes a front-page piece about Harry, most of which isn't true, including that Harry and Hermione are in love. This seems to confirm to Ron that Harry is enjoying the attention.

Hagrid takes Harry to see the dragons that will be the first task. Fear is sinking into Harry. He feels like his whole life has been leading up to this and will be over with the first task.

Harry tells Sirius everything, and his godfather tells him that Karkaroff was a Death Eater. Moody caught him and put him in Azkaban. He was released because he named names. The fact that Moody was attacked the night before he started at Hogwarts could mean that someone wanted to prevent him from coming because he would make it difficult for them. Death Eaters are becoming more active lately, and a Ministry of Magic witch went missing. Bertha Jorkins disappeared in Albania, where Voldemort was last rumored to be. She would have known the Triwizard Tournament was coming up. The Tournament is a good way to attack Harry and make it look like an accident.

Harry plays fair and tells Cedric about the dragons, since the other champions already know. Moody advises Harry to use a summoning charm to get his Firebolt. The task is to collect the golden egg by getting past the dragon that is guarding it. Harry loses his fear when he's on his broomstick. He's the quickest champion to get his egg. He and Krum tie for first place.

Ron seems to realize the danger involved in the Tournament and that whoever put Harry's name in the goblet is trying to do him in. They make up.

The second task will take place on February 24. The golden eggs contain clues to the nature of the second task and how they can prepare for it. When Harry opens the egg, a horrible, piercing wailing fills the air.

Harry finds Dobby and Winky working in Hogwarts's kitchen. Winky is disgraced and having trouble adjusting. She continues to be loyal to her master. That's part of the house-elves enslavement—that they keep secrets and silence, upholding the family honor. Harry tells Dobby to come and see him sometime.

Gryffindor's headmistress, Professor McGonagall, informs Harry that the Yule Ball, held on Christmas Day, is a traditional part of the Triwizard Tournament. Harry has to find a date. Harry wants to ask Cho Chang, but when he asks her, she says she's already going with Cedric Diggory, but she seems truly regretful. Harry asks Parvati Patil. Ron will go with her sister. Hermione says she's going with someone but won't tell who it is. They find out at the ball. She's with Victor Krum, and Ron is insanely jealous.

Percy Weasley attends in Mr. Crouch's place as his new assistant. Mr. Crouch isn't well.

Harry and Ron go outside to get away from the ball and overhear Snape and Karkaroff arguing. Karkaroff says something's been getting clearer for months now. Snape advises Karkaroff to flee, but tells him he has decided to stay at Hogwarts.

As the second task nears, Hermione keeps trying to get Harry to work on the clues in his egg. Cedric advises Harry to take a bath with the egg.

Quoting Draco Malfoy, Rita Skeeter publishes a damaging article about Hagrid's dangerous teaching and his giant connections. Hermione is determined to get back at Skeeter for this.

Harry takes the egg to the Prefects' bathroom. Moaning Myrtle advises him to open the egg under the water, where Harry hears the song about the merpeople in the Black Lake on school grounds and deduces that he'll have to go into the lake to get back something important to him that's been taken. But how can he breathe that long?

Ludo Bagman reveals that Crouch is missing. Harry sees Crouch's name on the Marauder's Map—at one o'clock in the morning. On his way to investigate under his Invisibility Cloak, he overhears Snape saying to Filch and Moody that someone broke into his office and stole potion ingredients.

When Moody comments that Dumbledore believes in second chances but that some spots don't come off, Snake grasps his left forearm as if he's in pain.

Upon seeing the map, which Snape has seen in the past, Snape insists that Harry is nearby under the cloak, but Moody says that Dumbledore is interested in who's got it in for Harry. Could Snape have something against the boy? Snape backs down.

Alone with Moody, Harry tells him about seeing Mr. Crouch on the map—could he have stolen from Snape's office? Moody says he's obsessed with catching Dark Wizards, true, but he's nothing compared to Barty Crouch. Later Harry wonders why Moody is keeping such a close eye on Karkaroff and Snape. Clearly he believes one of them put Harry's name in the goblet. Harry writes to Sirius about it.

Harry and his friends search for a charm to help him spend an hour underwater. The night before the second task, Ron and Hermione are summoned to McGonagall's office. Dobby wakes Harry the next morning and tells him the second task starts in ten minutes. Harry still has no idea what to do for the task. Dobby says that the merpeople have Ron, and Harry has an hour to get him back from the bottom of the lake. Dobby gives Harry gillyweed to make him breathe underwater. Harry chews it up and suddenly feels like he can't breathe—but when he goes underwater, he discovers that he has gills and webbed hands and feet. Ron is tied at the bottom with Hermione, Cho, and Fleur's little sister. He cuts Ron free, but none of the other champions are coming. When Harry tries to take Hermione, too, the merpeople step in and say Harry can take only his own hostage. Cedric comes and retrieves Cho, then Krum comes for Hermione. There's no sign of Fleur. Harry pulls his wand on the merpeople, who back away and let him take Ron and Fleur's sister. On the surface, Ron says he shouldn't have taken the song from the egg seriously. Nothing would have happened to any of them. They just wanted to make sure he got back with his hostage in the time limit.

Fleur is hysterical about her sister and grateful to Harry for retrieving her. Fleur had been attacked by the grindylows and couldn't get to her sister.

Unfortunately Harry was well outside the time limit for the competition. But since he was first to return, and he was adamant about getting all of the hostages to safety, he's rewarded points for moral fiber and comes in second behind Cedric.

The third and final task will take place on June 24. The champions will be told the details beforehand.

Rita Skeeter writes another slam piece, this time about Hermione, painting her as a scarlet woman. But Hermione wonders how Rita could have known things that were said in private. Hermione has a new cause—figuring out how Rita knows so much.

Snape accuses Harry of stealing ingredients from his private store, including Polyjuice Potion.

Sirius is in Hogsmeade, as the black dog Animagus. Harry, Ron, and Hermoine follow him to the cave he's been staying in, where Sirius tells them Crouch used to be the Head of the Department of Magical Law Enforcement. He ordered very harsh measures against Voldemort's supporters. Crouch's own son was caught with a group of Death Eaters who were trying to find Voldemort and return him to power. Crouch gave his son to the dementors. He was 19 and died a year after. Crouch and his wife were allowed a deathbed visit. The wife died shortly afterward of grief.

Sirius says when he was in school with Snape, he hung around a gang of Slytherins who turned out to be Death Eaters.

In Hogwarts's kitchen Winky is drinking six bottles of butterbeer a day. Mr. Crouch trusted her with his most important secret.

The house-elves are offended when Hermione says they have as much right as wizards to get wages, holidays, and proper clothes.

The champions find a maze in place of the Quidditch field. The Triwizard Cup is located in the center of the maze. The first champion to touch it receives full marks, but there will be obstacles, creatures, and spells to break.

Harry and Krum find Barty Crouch staggering out of the Forbidden Forest. He's bloody, exhausted, and crazed. He says he needs to see Dum-bledore and warn him—he's done a stupid thing. It's all his fault. Bertha died, as did his son. The Dark Lord is stronger. Harry rushes to get Dumbledore, but when they return, Crouch is gone and Krum has been stunned. Krum says Crouch attacked him. Moody appears and says he'll search for Crouch. Dumbledore advises Harry not to send any owls until morning. Harry had just been thinking of telling Sirius what happened.

Harry has another dream similar to the one he had with the snake, Voldemort, and Wormtail. Voldemort punishes Wormtail for his blunder, which almost ruined everything. "He's dead," but Harry Potter remains. Harry's scar burns badly when he wakes. He goes to Dumbledore and overhears the headmaster with the Minister of Magic, Cornelius Fudge. Dumbledore believes there's a connection between Bertha Jorkins's and Barty Crouch's disappearances.

Harry sees a shallow stone basin in Dumbledore's office. There's a silvery gas inside it. He looks down and sees a room in the swirl. He dips his head into the substance and suddenly he's in the room, inside someone's memory. Mr. Crouch extracts the names of Death Eaters from Karkaroff. He pronounces Snape a Death Eater, but Dumbledore defends him, saying he was a Death Eater but that he was cleared by the council because he's been spying for them, no longer loyal to Voldemort.

Harry is taken out of the memory into another one: Ludo Bagman inadvertently passed information to Voldemort's supporters. Bagman has not been accused of Dark activity since his trial, nor has Snape.

Another memory: Mr. Crouch's son is accused of capturing an Auror, Frank Longbottom, and subjecting him to the Cruciatus Curse, and for having knowledge of the whereabouts of Voldemort and planning to restore him to power. Crouch's son begs him not to send him back to Azkaban—to no avail.

Dumbledore catches Harry in his memories and tells him it's a Pensieve. When he has too many memories in his head, he siphons the excess and uses the basin to examine them later.

Dumbledore believes Harry's scar hurts when Voldemort is near and when he's feeling strong emotion. Voldemort and Harry are connected by the failed curse.

Harry and his friends see Malfoy acting suspicious, appearing to use a walkie-talkie or something like it, but those sorts of things don't work at Hogwarts. So what's he doing?

In the maze Harry finds the lack of obstacles in his path disturbing. He hears Fleur scream and follows the sound but can't find her. Later, he hears Cedric shouting, then Krum's voice uttering the Crucio Curse. Harry rushes to help and stuns Krum. Harry and Cedric realize Krum must have done the same to Fleur earlier. They move on through the maze separately. They reach the Triwizard Cup at the same time and decide to take it together. They're transported to a graveyard. The Cup is a Portkey. A figure appears, carrying what looks like a baby. Harry's scar suddenly explodes with pain worse than ever before. Voldemort's voice says to kill the "spare" and Cedric is killed by the Avada Kedavra curse.

Harry is tied to a headstone with the name Tom Riddle (Voldemort's real name). It's the grave of Voldemort's father.

Wormtail lights a fire under a huge cauldron of water, then adds the baby, a bone from Voldemort's father, his own hand, and Harry's blood. Voldemort is resurrected. Voldemort activates the Dark Mark on Wormtail's left arm, and some of his followers return, including Lucius Malfoy. The others are too cowardly to return, one has left him forever, and his other, most loyal, is at Hogwarts. It's through his efforts that Voldemort has returned at last.

Voldemort tells Harry that his mother's sacrifice was old magic that prevented Voldemort from touching him. His curse rebounded on him and he was ripped from his body, alive but unable to help himself. Without a body, he couldn't use a wand. None of his servants tried to find him and perform the magic to restore him to a body. Then Wormtail sought him out, but before he found him, he met up with Bertha Jorkins and brought her to Voldemort. She told him about the Triwizard Tournament. He had to get Harry because his blood would be the most powerful for his rebirth—his mother's protection would also be in Voldemort's veins. His faithful servant made sure Harry's name was drawn from the goblet and that Harry won the Tournament. He turned the Cup into a Portkey to bring him to the graveyard, beyond the reach of Dumbledore's protection. Harry escaped him in the past by lucky chance, but now Voldemort will prove he can't stand against him by allowing Harry to fight him.

Harry can't run because his leg was injured while going through the maze, but he's given his wand and he decides he's going to die fighting, like his father. Harry and Voldemort cast spells at the same time, and their wands connect. Ghostly shapes come out of the web—Cedric, telling Harry to hold on and not break the connection, the old man in Harry's dream, Bertha, and Harry's mother and father. His mother says they'll give him some time, but when the connection is broken he has to get to the Portkey, which will take him back to Hogwarts. Cedric asks him to take his body back to his parents. Harry runs to Cedric's body when the connection breaks, and he summons the Portkey. They return and Harry tells Dumbledore that Voldemort is back. Moody takes Harry to his office and asks about Voldemort's return. He tells him he put his name in the goblet and made sure he got through to the end. Karkaroff fled when he felt the Dark Mark burn on his arm. Moody says he scorns the faithless followers who fled at the sight of the Mark at the World Cup. He alone delivered Harry to his master—told Cedric about opening the egg underwater so he'd tell Harry, planted the book with Neville so he'd use gillyweed, staged it so that Dobby would get it for him. He put the Imperius Curse on Krum so he could stop the others from getting to the Cup.

Polyjuice Potion was used to transform an imposter into Moody. When it wears off, Harry recognizes the imposter as Barty Crouch's son. His mother persuaded his father to rescue him from Azkaban. They gave him Polyjuice Potion with his mother's hair and she took some of his. They took on each other's identity. His mother died in Azkaban, and his father staged his mother's death while Winky nursed his son back to health. Hidden and controlled, all he could think about was returning to Voldemort. Winky talked his father into letting Crouch, Jr. attend the Quidditch World Cup under an invisibility cloak (Winky pretended she was saving a seat for her master). Crouch, Jr. was fighting his father's control. He stole a wand sticking out of a boy's pocket and cast the Dark Mark. When Winky was discovered by Barty Crouch, Barty knew his son was nearby under the cloak. When everyone was gone, he used the Imperious Curse on his son and took him home, dismissing Winky because she let him acquire a wand and almost escape. But then Voldemort came to him, and they used the Imperius Curse on Barty. Barty fought it and escaped in an attempt to tell Dumbledore everything. Crouch, Jr. says he stunned Krum, killed his father, and covered him with the cloak.

Dumbledore asks Harry to come to his office, where Sirius is waiting for him. Harry tells them everything.

Fudge allows a dementor to perform the kiss on Mr. Crouch's son—and now Crouch, Jr. can't give evidence that Voldemort has returned and that he's been working for him all along.

Fudge gives Harry the Triwizard earnings. Harry doesn't want the gold.

Sirius reveals himself to Mrs. Weasley and Snape, Dumbledore vouches for his innocence and asks all of them to join in the fight against Voldemort. They have to alert the old crowd.

When Dumbledore gives Snape a task, Harry wonders what Dumbledore asked him to do, and how he can be so sure the former Death Eater is on their side. He'd been their spy—has he taken up the job again and made contact with Voldemort? Maybe Snape was never truly loyal to Dumbledore.

At the Leaving Feast Dumbledore tells the whole school that Voldemort killed Cedric.

The Daily Prophet fails to write about Cedric or what happened. The Minister is forcing silence. And Rita won't be writing anything at all for a while—not unless she wants Hermione to reveal her secret: She's an unregistered Animagus. Hermione shows them a beetle in a jar.

Harry gives his winnings to Fred and George for their joke shop. They're all going to need a few laughs in the dark days to come.

Dumbledore and Snape burst in. This man isn't Moody. Moody's in a trunk in the office.

## SERIES PLANT ARCS

In Book 4 Gregorovitch, the wandmaker, is mentioned. He becomes very important in Book 7.

In Book 4 Dumbledore speaks of needing a bathroom while roaming the halls of the castle and finding one that he hasn't seen since. In fact, this is the Room of Requirement that becomes important in Book 5 and later books.

Hermione's and Ron's romance begins very mildly in Book 4 and grows throughout the rest of the series.

Dumbledore's brother Aberforth and his love of goats is mentioned in Book 4. In Book 7 Aberforth actually enters the series.

Fleur, one of the Triwizard Tournament champions, meets Bill Weasley in Book 4. In Book 5 they begin dating and are married in Book 7.

## HARRY POTTER AND THE ORDER OF THE PHOENIX
### YEAR 5 IN THE SERIES

## OVERALL SERIES ARCS

In Book 5 Harry's Aunt Petunia, his mother's sister, says she overheard "that awful boy" telling her sister about dementors who guard Azkaban. The identity of the boy isn't revealed until Book 7.

The tension between goblins and wizards is at an all-time high with the return of Voldemort in Book 5, but this is made most evident in Book 7.

In Books 3 and 5 it's hinted that the Minister of Magic has connections with the Muggle Prime Minister. We're privy to a meeting between them in Book 6.

In Book 5 it's said that Sirius's brother, Regulus Black, died fifteen years ago. Regulus and his death become especially important in Book 7.

Sirius tells Harry that he ran away when he was sixteen and went to the Potters. His parents had a pure-blood mania. Sirius's younger brother believed it, too, and became a Death Eater. But he panicked, tried to back out, and Voldemort had him killed.

In Book 5 Harry takes Sirius aside and tells him the truth about the vision he had when Mr. Weasley was attacked by the snake, including how he wanted to hurt Dumbledore when their eyes met. Is there a snake inside him? The truth is revealed in Book 7.

## INDIVIDUAL STORY ARCS

Mrs. Figg, a neighbor of the Dursleys, asks Harry over for tea whenever she meets him on the street.

Voldemort is back, and Harry's tension has been mounting every day of the summer. He's had no news at all, not even from his friends. If anything had happened, it would surely be on the Muggle news. Harry is aware that his friends' letters could be intercepted, but no one has even let him know when they'll come for him.

Harry hears a loud, echoing crack—someone Apparating or Disapparating. Who was near him when the noise came?

Harry has been dreaming about long, dark corridors, dead ends, and locked doors. His scar often prickles uncomfortably.

Dementors attack Harry and his cousin. Harry produces a Patronus to drive them away. Mrs. Figg shows up and tells him not to put his wand away because more dementors might come. She also says she's going to kill Mundungus Fletcher, who's supposed to be protecting Harry. Mrs. Figg is a Squib, a nonmagical witch.

It was clearly Mundungus who Disapparated near Harry. In addition to protecting Harry, he was supposed to prevent him from using magic at all.

Harry receives notice that he's been expelled from Hogwarts because he performed magic in the presence of a Muggle. A note quickly follows from Mr. Weasley, who says Dumbledore is trying to sort it all out and he shouldn't leave the Dursleys or surrender his wand.

Another owl comes, and the Ministry has only suspended Harry. He'll have a hearing on August 12 and the decision about being expelled will be made then.

When Harry's aunt and uncle find out the Dark Wizard who killed Harry's parents has returned, they tell him to get out. Another owl arrives, this one a howler for Petunia, that says, "Remember my last." She insists that Harry has to stay. Harry doesn't know who sent her the howler.

The next night Mad-Eye Moody and R.J. Lupin have come with several others to take Harry to headquarters. He's introduced to Tonks and Kingsley Shacklebolt, among others. They fly to #12 Grimmauld Place in

London, the headquarters of the Order of the Phoenix—the secret society Dumbledore founded to fight against Voldemort the last time.

When they get inside, Ron and Hermione tell Harry that Dumbledore made them swear not to tell Harry anything. Harry is furious about being kept in the dark.

Hermione and Ron haven't been able to attend the meetings in the house, but Fred and George have invented Extendable Ears to eavesdrop on them. The Order is keeping tabs on known Death Eaters, as well as recruiting. Some are standing guard over something else besides Harry.

Fred and George tell Harry they haven't secured premises for their joke shop yet, but they've started a mail-order service.

Snape is here for a major meeting, giving top-secret reports. Bill is also here—he's been seeing Fleur Delacour.

At the name of Percy Weasley, everyone goes silent. Percy's been promoted at the Ministry—Junior Assistant to the Minister. Fudge is trying to limit Ministry workers' contact with Dumbledore, whose name is mud because Fudge believes he's trying to make trouble by saying Voldemort is back. Anyone in league with Dumbledore will be fired. Fudge wants Percy to spy on his family and Dumbledore. Percy's loyalty is to the ministry, and he takes what the *Daily Prophet* says seriously. In those pages Harry has become a standing joke as they turn him into someone no one will believe.

The headquarters for the Order is Sirius's parents' house. Since he's the last Black alive, it's his. He offered it to Dumbledore for headquarters—the only useful thing he's been able to do since he went into hiding.

Sirius wants to tell Harry what Voldemort's been up to, but Mrs. Weasley insists that Harry isn't James, as if Sirius thinks he's got his best friend back. Mr. Weasley says Dumbledore realizes that Harry will have to be filled in to a certain extent, now that he's staying at headquarters. They tell him Voldemort's been lying low. They know he plans to build up his army again—witches and wizards and dark creatures. Fudge is making sure no one believes Voldemort is back—he seems to think Dumbledore is trying to overthrow the Ministry. Voldemort is trouble they haven't had to face for fourteen years. Many members of the Order are Ministry workers and they'd lose their jobs if they spoke out openly. Plus, they need spies on the inside. Once Dumbledore's credibility is diminished and he's out of the way, Voldemort will have a clear field. Apart from gaining followers, Voldemort is looking for something he didn't have last time: a certain weapon.

Mrs. Weasley, Ron, and Hermione have been decontaminating the house. Grimmauld Place is ideal for headquarters because every security measure known to wizard-kind is on it. It's Unplottable, so Muggles can't get to it. As Secret Keeper for the Order, Dumbledore has made it impossible for anyone else to find it either, unless he tells them where it is.

Harry worries about his upcoming hearing at the Ministry and asks Sirius if he can live with him here at headquarters if he's expelled. Sirius says they'll see.

Harry and Mr. Weasley arrive early at the Ministry and learn that his hearing has been moved up and the meeting place changed. Dumbledore arrives to present himself as witness for the defense. Not once does he meet Harry's eyes. When Harry claims he conjured the Patronus because of the dementors, Fudge insists it's a convenient story, since Muggles can't see dementors. But Dumbledore produces a witness to the fact—Mrs. Figg. Harry's past misdeeds are recounted and dismissed summarily by Dumbledore.

Fudge and his biggest supporter, Dolores Umbridge, Senior Undersecretary, react with amusement when Dumbledore reminds them they have no authority to punish Hogwarts students.

More than half of the court is in favor of clearing Harry of all charges. Before Harry can talk to Dumbledore and thank him, Dumbledore disappears.

After leaving the courtroom, Harry encounters Fudge with Lucius Malfoy, who Harry knows is a Death Eater.

Mr. Weasley tells Harry that Lucius has been giving generously to a variety of causes and organizations for years, thereby getting in with the right people.

The night before they leave for Hogwarts, Harry dreams about the locked door.

Sirius joins them—in his Animagus form of a dog—to get to the train station.

They meet Luna Lovegood, daughter of the editor of *The Quibbler* magazine. Luna is in Ginny's year at school, but she's in Ravenclaw. Cho Chang visits Harry on the train. Draco Malfoy has been made a prefect and comes to taunt them, saying that Harry needs to watch himself or he'll be "dogging" his footsteps. Had he recognized Sirius as a dog on the platform?

Hagrid isn't there to take first-year students across the lake to the castle. Is he not back from the mission Dumbledore gave him at the end of last term?

This year reptilian-like horses with giant bat wings pull the carriages that take the older students to the castle. No one but Harry and Luna can see them.

There's a new teacher at the front of the start-of-term feast, and Harry recognizes her as Dolores Umbridge, one of the witches who attended his hearing at the Ministry. She's the new Defense Against the Dark Arts teacher. After Umbridge's speech Hermione realizes that the Ministry will be interfering at Hogwarts.

Harry realizes he should have expected the other students' behavior toward him. He'd emerged from the Triwizard maze last term clutching the dead body of a fellow student, claiming to have seen Voldemort return to power. He had never explained the terrible events in that graveyard to his fellow students. Many now look at him in fear, distrust, and concern.

Harry learns that Seamus's mother didn't want him to return to Hogwarts because of what the *Daily Prophet* has been saying about Harry and Dumbledore: that Harry's a liar and Dumbledore an old fool. Neville says he and his grandmother believe Harry.

Harry can't help but wonder if Dumbledore is mad at him because of what everyone's been saying about him all summer—which is Harry's fault. Why else is Dumbledore avoiding him?

Cho tries to talk to Harry. She doesn't seem to hate him for coming out of the maze alive when Cedric, her boyfriend, didn't. Harry is hopeful that their relationship will develop.

In Potion classes, Snape is as unfair to Harry as he always has been, though he's working with the Order now. Ron wonders what evidence exists that Snape really left Voldemort.

In Umbridge's first class she makes it plain that their study of the Dark Arts will be academic only. They won't be learning how to practice and use any defensive spells. Harry says if they're being attacked, it won't be risk free. Umbridge demands to know who would attack children, and Harry says Voldemort. She insists that the rumor is a lie. Harry refuses to back down, and he's given a detention for which he must write lines. But when he writes "I must not tell lies" on the paper, the words are cut into the back of his hand. The ink on the paper is in his own blood. After a week of detentions, the words are etched permanently into his hand and enflamed.

The *Daily Prophet* reports that Sirius Black is hiding in London. Draco's father must have recognized Sirius as a dog on the platform. Also, a wizard was arrested for trespassing and attempted robbery at the Ministry of Magic.

Percy writes to Ron and warns him to stay away from Harry. He hints that Dumbledore might not be in charge at Hogwarts much longer.

Sirius tells Harry that Umbridge loathes part-humans. Harry says she's not letting them use magic at all. Fudge obviously doesn't want them trained in combat. He's afraid they'll form a wizard army with Dumbledore to take on the Ministry. It's only a matter of time before Fudge has Dumbledore arrested. Sirius implies that Hagrid should have been back by now and no one knows what happened to him.

Umbridge has been appointed High Inquisitor at Hogwarts—with unprecedented control at the school, including the right to inspect her fellow instructors to make sure they're suitable.

Harry and his friends discuss the fact that they're not going to learn any defense from Umbridge. Maybe they should teach themselves so they can be prepared for attacks and make sure they can defend themselves. Harry can teach them. He knows what it's like to face Voldemort. At the first Hogsmeade weekend, many students show up for the meeting at the Hog's Head, including the Weasleys, Luna, Cho and a friend of hers, and Neville. They all want Harry to teach them. They decide to meet once a week … but where to meet?

Hermione asks everyone who's interested to write their names on a parchment she's prepared. If you sign, you're agreeing not to tell Umbridge or anyone else what they're up to. Immediately following the meeting, Umbridge disbands all organizations and clubs at the school. Those who form or join one will be expelled. Harry wonders if someone at the meeting told Umbridge, and Hermione says she put a jinx on the parchment. The tattler will vividly display his or her treachery.

Hedwig is injured while coming back from delivering a message. Someone attacked her. McGonagall reminds Harry that communication channels in and out of Hogwarts are being watched.

Sirius contacts Harry again (via the fireplace in the common room) and says Mundungus overheard the students talking about forming a defensive group led by Harry. Sirius thinks it's a brilliant idea. But Umbridge nearly intercepts Sirius's communication, and it's clear that she's the one who hurt Hedwig.

Harry's scar hurts, and he knows it's because Voldemort is angry. He wants something done, and it's not happening fast enough. Ron wonders if Harry is reading Voldemort's mind. No, he's just getting flashes of his mood. Is Voldemort trying to get the weapon? Or has the Order thwarted him from getting it? What is this weird connection between himself and Voldemort?

Harry dreams of the door at the end of the passageway and wants to enter it.

Dobby visits Harry, and Harry asks him if he can find a place for twenty-eight people to practice spells without being discovered by teachers—especially Umbridge. Dobby knows just the place: The Room of Requirement. Only a person who has real need of it can enter. When it appears, it's always equipped for the seeker's needs. They decide to have the first meeting the next night. During the meeting they decide to call themselves Dumbledore's Army or the D.A. Hermione writes it on their list of names. Over the next two weeks Harry's accomplishments in teaching his fellow students motivate him. Hermione enchants fake Galleons to tell each member of the D.A. the date and time of their next meeting. The coin has been enchanted so it will grow hot when Harry changes his, and the coins of the others will automatically mimic his.

Hagrid returns, and Harry and his friends use the Invisibility Cloak to see him. He's bloody and wounded. He and Madame Maxime went to look for giants. Hagrid gave gifts of magic from Dumbledore, but the Death Eaters brought better gifts.

At Hagrid's first lesson he's obviously been attacked by something again. He introduces thestrals, the winged creatures that pull the carriages. Hagrid says the only people who can see them are those who have seen death. The thestrals are incredibly fast and have an amazing sense of direction.

After a D.A. meeting on Christmas, Harry and Cho kiss.

That night Harry dreams of the corridor. He's slithering along when he sees a man at the end of the hall, sitting in front of the door. He strikes. The man slumps back. Harry wakes with his scar blinding him with pain.

He knows Mr. Weasley's been attacked. He was there—he saw it. He *did* it! When McGonagall takes him to Dumbledore, Dumbledore won't look at Harry.

Dumbledore raises the alarm. Mr. Weasley is found and taken to St. Mungo's Hospital. The other Weasley children are woken, Sirius is informed they're on their way to Grimmauld Place, and Dumbledore prepares a Portkey for them. As Harry puts his hand on it, his eyes meet Dumbledore's and his scar burns white-hot. He feels hatred so strong, he wants to strike him.

When Harry tells Sirius what happened to Mr. Weasley, he alters the story slightly to make it sound like he was on the sidelines when the snake attacked, but Ron knows better. Harry can't escape his guilt. He attacked Mr. Weasley. But he doesn't have fangs, and he was in bed in the castle.

Mrs. Weasley sends a communication that Mr. Weasley is alive. She'll have news soon. Hours later she arrives and says he'll be all right now. She hugs Harry, thanking him for saving Mr. Weasley's life. Harry is terrified of sleeping, in case he becomes the snake again and attacks someone else. At the hospital the kids eavesdrop and the adults say that the snake was sent as a lookout to get a clearer picture of what Voldemort is facing. Mrs. Weasley says it's as if Dumbledore has been waiting for Harry to see something like this. He's seeing things from inside Voldemort's snake. What if Voldemort is possessing him? Harry wonders if this is why Dumbledore avoids him. Maybe *he's* the weapon Voldemort wants to use. If Voldemort is possessing him, is he giving him a clear view into the Order right now?

Harry avoids everyone until Ginny says that she knows what it's like to be possessed by Voldemort—with Tom Riddle's diary. She couldn't remember huge blocks of time. But Harry's not experiencing that. He can't be the weapon.

Snape comes to headquarters to tell Harry that Dumbledore wants him to learn Occlumency—the magical defense of the mind against external penetration. Voldemort is highly skilled at extracting feelings and memories from other people's minds.

....................................................................

Mr. Weasley is released from the hospital, cured.

....................................................................

Back at school Harry asks Cho to go to Hogsmeade with him on Valentine's Day.

....................................................................

During Harry's first Occlumency lesson, Snape reveals that Harry's mind is connected to Voldemort's mind. When Harry's asleep, he can share Voldemort's thoughts and emotions. He visited the snake's mind because that's where Voldemort was at the moment. Snape will teach him to close his mind since Voldemort recently became aware of the connection between them. He could try to make Harry do things. During the lesson Harry recognizes the corridor in his dreams—it leads to the Department of Mysteries, where Mr. Weasley had been the night he was attacked. When Harry asks Snape if Voldemort wants something from there, Snape reacts with surprise and hostility.

....................................................................

That night Harry dreams Voldemort is ecstatically happy. This coincides with the mass breakout (including Bellatrix Lestrange) of Death Eaters from Azkaban. But the Ministry is saying Sirius Black did it to rally the Death Eaters.

....................................................................

Harry throws himself into D.A. meetings. Neville works harder than ever because Bellatrix is the one who used a damaging curse on his parents, causing them to be institutionalized for life.

....................................................................

Harry's dreams have intensified, and the Occlumency lessons seem to make them worse.

....................................................................

On Valentine's Day Hermione asks Harry to meet her at the Three Broomsticks at noon. When Harry mentions this to Cho, she turns frosty. They part unpleasantly.

....................................................................

Hermione is at the pub with Rita Skeeter, now unemployed, and Luna. Hermione has asked Rita to write the story of Voldemort's return from Harry's point of view. *The Quibbler* will publish it. When Umbridge sees

Harry's interview, she assigns Harry more detentions and bans him from Hogsmeade.

Cho apologizes after this, and even Seamus's mother seems to believe that Voldemort has truly returned.

During an Occlumency lesson with Snape, Harry sees into his own childhood. But then a woman screams from the corridor. Umbridge has sacked Trelawney. Dumbledore intervenes, insisting that Trelawney stay at the school even if she doesn't teach anymore. Dumbledore has already secured a new Divination teacher, Firenze the centaur. His herd banished him because he agreed to work for Dumbledore, and he can't return to the Forbidden Forest ever again.

During D.A. meetings, Harry teaches the others how to produce a Patronus. Dobby warns the group that Umbridge and her Inquisitorial Squad are on their way. Everyone flees. Harry is the only one who doesn't get away. Umbridge takes him to Dumbledore's office, where the Minister of Magic is waiting. Cho's friend was their informant. She has the marks of the jinx Hermione put on the parchment. She won't say a word now. The parchment is produced, and Dumbledore says that he was recruiting an army of students. Tonight was supposed to be the first meeting. Dumbledore will be sent to Azkaban, but Dumbledore informs the Minister that he has no intention of going along quietly. Dumbledore hexes everyone in the room in order to warn Harry that he must study Occlumency extra hard. Then Dumbledore disappears.

Umbridge is made Head of Hogwarts. She tries to get Harry to talk with Veritaserum in his tea. During this meeting she says that only her own fireplace isn't being monitored.

Fred and George decide a bit of mayhem is in order, which they stage before quitting school. They invite everyone to come to their shop in Diagon Alley, Weasleys's Wizard Wheezes.

Harry looks into the memories Snape siphoned into the Pensieve, and sees James and Sirius tormenting Snape when they went to Hogwarts. Harry's mother, Lily, defends Snape. She seems to hate James. So how did they get married? And how could his father and Sirius have been so mean? He feels sorry for Snape. When Snape catches Harry in his memories, he discontinues Occlumency lessons for good.

Harry has to know the truth. While his friends create a distraction, he goes into Umbridge's office and contacts Sirius. He asks him about what he witnessed in Snape's memories. Sirius says he's not proud of their behavior. They were jerks back then. Lily and James started dating their seventh year. But Snape and James had never gotten along. Harry tells Sirius that Snape discontinued Occlumency and Sirius is furious—nothing is more important than Harry learning how to close his mind.

Harry dreams he enters the door at the end of the corridor. He's in a circular room with shelves full of glass spheres. He hurries toward row 97.

During Quidditch Hagrid asks Harry and Hermione to come with him to the Forbidden Forest. The reason Hagrid is always so beat up becomes instantly clear. He's brought back his half-brother Grawp, a giant, from the mountains. He's worried that if he's sacked, there'll be no one to teach Grawp how to speak English.

Harry has a vision that Voldemort has captured Sirius. Hermione is worried that this is just what Voldemort wants him to believe, so they create another diversion so Harry can use the fireplace in Umbridge's office to contact Sirius. Kreacher tells them Sirius went out and no one else is there. Umbridge catches Harry, Hermione, Ron, Ginny, Luna, and Neville.

When Umbridge calls Snape for more Veritaserum, he says she's used it all. Harry gives Snape a veiled message: "He's got Padfoot at the place where it's hidden." Umbridge is prepared to use an illegal curse to get the information she needs from Harry, but Hermione stops her by saying they were trying to contact Dumbledore to tell him that the weapon they can use against the Ministry is ready. Umbridge orders Hermione and Harry to show her where it is. Hermione leads them into the Forbidden Forest. The centaurs surround them, then they carry Umbridge off.

When they get out of the forest, Ron, Ginny, Luna, and Neville have overtaken the Inquisitorial Squad and retrieved their wands. Luna suggests they get to London on thestrals.

At the Department of Mysteries they find an archway with a tattered black veil. There's a faint whispering from the other side. They get away from it quickly.

Harry finds the black door, the circular room full of globes, row 97, but Sirius isn't there. Ron finds an orb with Harry's name on it. Death Eaters arrive. Lucius Malfoy says Voldemort lured Harry here with the vision of his godfather. Now he wants him to hand over the prophecy—before it's destroyed. The only person who can retrieve a prophecy is the one about whom the prophecy is made. Someone made a prophecy about Harry, and it's the reason Voldemort wants to kill him in the first place.

The Order of the Phoenix rush in. The prophecy is smashed. Sirius avoids a curse from Bellatrix's wand and falls into the archway with the black veil. He is gone—presumably dead. Furious, Harry chases Bellatrix into the Atrium. Voldemort appears and Harry tells him the prophecy is gone. Harry Potter has thwarted him again!

Dumbledore deflects Voldemort's killing curse, and the two wizards duel. Voldemort enters Harry, possessing him, but all Harry can think is that he'll never see Sirius again. The grief fills him, and Voldemort leaves him.

The Minister arrives just in time to see Voldemort with his own two eyes. He can no longer deny that he's back.

The Minister gives orders for Umbridge to be removed from Hogwarts and Dumbledore reinstated as headmaster.

In Dumbledore's office Harry says it's his fault Sirius is dead. He fell for Voldemort's trick. Snape obviously passed his message on to the Order.

Dumbledore says he realized fifteen years ago that the scar was the sign of a connection forged between Harry and Voldemort. When the scar began to warn Harry when Voldemort was near or feeling powerful emotion,

Dumbledore thought he saw a shadow of Voldemort in Harry's eyes. He tried to protect him by avoiding him.

Dumbledore insists that Harry return to the Dursleys. When they took him in, his mother's dying protection was sealed by her only remaining relative, Petunia. While Harry can still call the Dursley home his own, he can't be harmed by Voldemort. He must return there once a year.

Harry asks about the prophecy, and Dumbledore tells him it's because of the prophecy that Voldemort tried to kill him when he was a baby. Instead, his curse backfired. He's been determined to hear the full prophecy and the knowledge of how to destroy Harry.

Trelawney uttered the prophecy to Dumbledore sixteen years ago. "The one with the power to vanquish the Dark Lord approaches … and the Dark Lord will mark him as his equal, but he will have power the Dark Lord knows not … and either must die at the hand of the other for neither can live while the other survives." When Voldemort tried to kill Harry, he instead gave him powers that allowed Harry to escape. Snape, then a Death Eater, eavesdropped on that prophecy and told Voldemort the part he heard.

Dumbledore rescues Umbridge from the centaurs, and the *Daily Prophet* announces the return of Voldemort.

All of Harry's friends and the Order gather at the train station to ensure that Harry is treated well by the Dursleys—or else.

## SERIES PLANT ARCS

The Black family house-elf Kreacher makes an appearance in Book 5. Kreacher wonders how Harry stopped the Dark Lord. Each time he pretends to be cleaning while Harry and the Weasleys decontaminate headquarters, he sneaks something off to his cupboard so it can't be thrown out. Kreacher loathes everyone now inside the "noble house of Black." He can't be set free since he knows too much about the Order. While cleaning the house, they find a heavy locket that none of them can open. Kreacher smuggles this extremely important item out of the rubbish sack. Kreacher will make more appearances in the last two books in the series.

In Book 5 Phineas Nigellus—Sirius' great-great grandfather, least favorite headmaster of Hogwarts ever—makes an appearance. His importance grows in Book 7.

Tonks is introduced in Book 5. She's Sirius's cousin, the daughter of Bellatrix and Narcissa Black's sister. Tonks takes on a larger role as the series progresses.

Mad-Eye Moody shows Harry a photograph of the original Order of the Phoenix. Aberforth, Dumbledore's younger brother, is in it. In Book 5 Harry meets Albus Dumbledore's brother, Aberforth. He's the owner of The Hog's Head in Hogsmeade. Aberforth enters the story fully in Book 7.

After Mr. Weasley is attacked by the snake in Book 5, Dumbledore tells Harry that celebrated wizards are given renown by having portraits in various wizarding places. They're free to move between the portraits. This fact is expanded on throughout the rest of the series.

In Book 5 Sirius gives Harry an enchanted mirror that becomes important in Book 7. He has the other half, and Harry can use it if he ever needs him.

## HARRY POTTER AND THE HALF-BLOOD PRINCE
### YEAR 6 IN THE SERIES

## OVERALL SERIES ARCS

In Book 6 Harry tells Ron and Hermione about the prophecy. He was scared about it at first, but he always knew he'd have to face Voldemort in the end. This happens in Book 7.

In Book 6 it's revealed that the wandmaker Ollivander disappeared. His shop is empty, with no sign of a struggle. We find out what happened to him in Book 7.

Book 6 marks the "the beginning of the end" with the topic of Horcruxes. This is what the entire series has been leading up to, and Book 6 touches on them. They are fully developed and resolved in Book 7.

**BELOW ARE THE HORCRUX SERIES PLOT ADVANCEMENTS THAT TAKE PLACE OVER THE COURSE OF THE STORY:**

Harry notices that Dumbledore's hand is blackened and shriveled. He's wearing a large ring with a black stone that's cracked in the middle on his uninjured hand. When Harry asks him about the injury, Dumbledore says he'll explain another time.

This year Harry will be taking private lessons with Dumbledore.

Harry gets a note from Dumbledore that their private lessons will start on Saturday. During the lesson they use the Pensieve to relive a memory of a wizard employed by the Department of Magical Law Enforcement. They see Tom Riddle's mother, Merope, a Squib, and Tom Riddle's grandfather and uncle. Merope's father is wearing the black stone ring that Dumbledore was wearing the last time Harry saw him. Merope's father says they are the last living descendents of Salazar Slytherin. Merope looks longingly out the window at a Muggle neighbor she's in love with.

Merope's father and brother were arrested for their illegal use of magic, and Merope used a love potion to make the Muggle she loved fall in love with her. A few months after their marriage, the Muggle returned to his home without his wife, claiming he'd been hoodwinked. He left Merope pregnant. As for the ring Merope's father wore, Dumbledore says he acquired it a few days before he fetched Harry from the Dursleys. That was when he injured his hand.

Over the next few weeks Harry notices that Dumbledore's seat in the Great Hall is almost always empty. Is he leaving the school to do something with the Order?

During another private lesson with Dumbledore, Harry sees a memory of Merope, who chose death in spite of a son who needed her. They watch a memory of the first time Dumbledore met Merope's son, eleven-year-old Tom Riddle, in the orphanage. The matron tells Dumbledore that Tom bullies the other children. He's strange. When Tom realized he had been doing magic, he told Dumbledore that he could make things move without touching them, make animals do what he wanted without training them, and cause bad things to happen to those who annoy him. If he wanted to, he could make them hurt. Always he knew he was different and special. Dumbledore warned him that certain behaviors wouldn't be tolerated at Hogwarts or in the wizarding world. Tom tells Dumbledore he can talk to snakes.

Harry and Dumbledore venture into another memory of a teenage Voldemort, taking the black stone ring from his mother's brother.

In another memory Voldemort and Slughorn are talking, but a thick white fog prevents them from seeing or hearing their conversation beyond Voldemort's question about Horcruxes. Dumbledore says Slughorn tampered with the memory because he's ashamed of what he remembers. The true memory remains hidden beneath the altered one. Dumbledore gives Harry the task of persuading Slughorn to divulge the real memory—it'll be the most crucial of all.

After a Potions class Harry asks Slughorn about Horcruxes, and he immediately guesses that Dumbledore tasked him with getting at the real memory. Slughorn denies any knowledge of Horcruxes.

Harry and Dumbledore look at two more memories. In the first, Voldemort graduated Hogwarts with top marks. Everyone expected him to do spectacular things, but instead he went to work for Borgin and Burkes. This wasn't his first choice—he wanted to remain at Hogwarts as the Defense against the Dark Arts teacher. But he saw his job as a useful recruiting ground for building an army. Voldemort was gifted at his job, as he could persuade people to part with their treasures. A client showed him her two greatest treasures: Helga Hufflepuff's golden cup and Salazar Slytherin's locket. The client died two days later. The cup and the locket were missing. Voldemort resigned his post and disappeared.

The second memory is Dumbledore's, when Voldemort came to see him years later and again requested a job. He no longer looked the same. His eyes were snakelike, nearly scarlet. Voldemort bragged to Dumbledore that he'd pushed the boundaries of magic further than anyone before. Since Dumbledore refused to give him the position, they'd never been able to keep a Defense Against the Dark Arts teacher for longer than a year.

Harry takes the luck potion he won in a Potions class and goes to Hagrid's vegetable patch, where he finds Slughorn. Harry tells Slughorn about Hagrid's dead acromantula. The venom is valuable. Slughorn agrees to meet Harry there with a bottle to toast the poor beast's passing.

Harry pretends to drink while the other two get drunk. When Hagrid passes out, Harry tells Slughorn how his parents died. His mother gave her life, yet Slughorn won't give him a memory. Harry is the Chosen One. He has to kill Voldemort, and the only way to do it is with that memory. Slughorn says he's ashamed of the great damage he did that day. He gives Harry the memory.

Harry rushes to Dumbledore's office, and they view the memory: Voldemort asks Slughorn about Horcruxes. Slughorn tells him that a Horcrux is an object in which a person has concealed part of his soul. The soul is split and part is hidden inside the object. Then, even if the body dies, the soul remains undamaged. Existence in that form is worse than death. Voldemort asks how to split the soul. It can be done through an act of supreme evil—committing murder. Voldemort asks if you can split the soul more than once—the answer is seven times, since that's the most powerfully magical number.

With this memory Dumbledore's theories are confirmed. Voldemort was trying to make himself immortal. That's why he survived when the killing curse he sent at Harry rebounded on him. He created many separately concealed Horcruxes.

Dumbledore was convinced that Tom Riddle's diary was a Horcrux. Riddle emerged from the diary not as a mere memory but a thinking, acting being, a fragment of soul that lived in the book. However, Riddle was remarkably blasé about a precious fragment of his soul concealed in what was used as both a weapon and a safeguard. That fragment is no more. It's clear that he's less human, and his soul has been mutilated beyond the realms of "usual evil." Voldemort says the number seven is powerfully magical. The Horcruxes could be hidden anywhere in the world. Dumbledore says Voldemort made six Horcruxes. The first part of his soul, however maimed, still resides inside his regenerated body—that's the last piece that must be attacked in order to kill him. Harry destroyed the diary, and Dumbledore destroyed the black ring. Four Horcruxes remain. Voldemort likes to collect trophies with powerful magical histories. Harry guesses Slytherin's locket and Hufflepuff's cup. He probably set out to track down objects owned by Gryffindor and Ravenclaw, too. Dumbledore doesn't know if he found an object for Ravenclaw, but Gryffindor's sword remains safe in his office inside the glass case. Harry says that must be why Voldemort came back to Hogwarts—to try to find something from Gryffindor and Ravenclaw. He didn't get the sword, so that leaves one more Horcrux. Dumbledore wonders if it is Voldemort's snake Nagini. In any case, when Voldemort entered Harry's parents' house, he was at least one Horcrux short of his goal. He intended to make the final Horcrux with Harry's death.

Harry asks if Voldemort feels it when a Horcrux is destroyed. Dumbledore doesn't think so. He's so immersed in evil, his soul so detached, that he doesn't feel as normal people do. With all the Horcruxes destroyed, Voldemort can be killed since he'll become mortal—maimed and diminished in soul. Even still, it won't be easy to kill him.

Voldemort singled out Harry because the prophecy proclaimed him the most dangerous, and in doing so it made Harry the person who would be in most danger. By focusing on Harry, Voldemort gave Harry unique weapons to use against him. But Harry has never been seduced by the Dark Arts—because he's protected by his ability to love. When Voldemort tried to possess Harry at the Ministry last year, he endured mortal agony because of the love and purity inside Harry.

Dumbledore says he's found a Horcrux—Slytherin's locket—and tells Harry he can come along with him to retrieve it. He thinks it's hidden in the cave where young Tom Riddle once terrorized two children from the orphanage. At the edge of a black lake, they find a boat and cross to a small island. There a stone basin is set on a pedestal. Harry sees dead bodies in the water. Dumbledore deduces that once they take the Horcrux, the bodies won't be peaceful anymore. The only way to get the Horcrux from the basin is to drink the potion. The potion will do something that will prevent them from taking the Horcrux—cause extreme pain or incapability or forgetfulness. It'll be Harry's job to make sure Dumbledore drinks every drop. Dumbledore drinks four goblets full before collapsing. Harry forces him to continue drinking even when he's screaming in horror.

They take the locket and return to Hogsmeade. Harry realizes the locket isn't the same one as in the Pensieve memories. It's not Sytherin's locket. There's a folded parchment inside it, addressed to the Dark Lord and written by someone who says Voldemort's secret has been discovered. The real Horcrux has been stolen and will be destroyed, if possible. The note is signed R.A.B. Dumbledore weakened himself for nothing. This isn't the Horcrux.

Harry tells Ron and Hermione everything. He knows he has to continue where Dumbledore left off in finding and destroying the Horcruxes. He can't let anyone stand between him and Voldemort again.

In Book 6 Hagrid reveals that Dumbledore is angry with Snape. He overheard Snape say Dumbledore took too much for granted and maybe he doesn't want to do it anymore. Dumbledore told him flat out that he'd agreed to do it and that was that. We find out exactly what is meant by these statements in Book 7.

## INDIVIDUAL STORY ARCS

Fudge, the Minister of Magic, arrives in the office of the Muggle prime minister to inform him that the bridge that broke cleanly in half, the "hurricane," the dismal, chilly mist in the middle of July, and the murders of last week are directly related to the return of Voldemort, a wizard who can't be killed. They're at war. Voldemort is amassing an army and moving into the open. The head of their Department of Magical Law Enforcement is lost, probably murdered by Voldemort. Fudge has been sacked. His successor, Rufus Scrimgeour, will be coming to meet the prime minister soon.

. . . . . . . . . . . . . . . . . . . . . . . . . . . . . . . . . . . . . . . . . . . . . . . . . . . . . . . . . . . . . .

Bellatrix follows her sister Narcissa (Cissy) to Snape's home. Bellatrix says it's a mistake to trust Snape, but Cissy insists that Voldemort trusts him. Cissy will do anything to save her son, Draco. Her husband, Lucius, is in jail. She's forbidden to speak about the plan to anyone, but Snape already knows it. He says if Draco succeeds in his task, he'll be honored above all others. Snape believes Draco should try first and, if he fails, Snape will take over. He'll protect Draco. But is he willing to make the Unbreakable Vow? Bellatrix serves as their Bonder. The vow is sealed.

. . . . . . . . . . . . . . . . . . . . . . . . . . . . . . . . . . . . . . . . . . . . . . . . . . . . . . . . . . . . . .

Dumbledore has sent Harry a letter stating that he'll be coming to escort him to the Burrow, where Harry will be staying for the rest of his holiday. Dumbledore also would like Harry's assistance in a matter. Dumbledore says that Sirius's will has been discovered. He left Harry everything he owns, including Grimmauld Place. Harry offers the house to the Order for their continued use as a headquarters, but Dumbledore says they're worried that an enchantment that ensures only a pure-blood relative can own it has been set upon it, which would mean the house would go to Bellatrix. The only way to test the enchantment is to see if Harry has inherited the Black family house-elf, Kreacher. Dumbledore summons Kreacher and Harry gives him an order. He obeys, so he's passed into Harry's ownership. Dumbledore suggests that Harry send Kreacher to the Hogwarts kitchen, where the other house-elves can keep an eye on him.

. . . . . . . . . . . . . . . . . . . . . . . . . . . . . . . . . . . . . . . . . . . . . . . . . . . . . . . . . . . . . .

Dumbledore mentions to the Dursleys that Harry comes of age in a year's time. With Voldemort at large once again, Harry is in even greater danger. The magic Dumbledore evoked fifteen years ago still gives Harry powerful protection as long as he calls the Dursleys' home his own. The moment he turns seventeen, the magic will lift and he'll be vulnerable. Until then, he needs to return once more to this house before his seventeenth birthday to keep the protection vital.

..........................................................................................

Harry Apparates at Dumbledore's side to a village where an old colleague is staying. Dumbledore hopes Horace Slughorn, who's fascinated by Harry Potter, will join his staff this year. Slughorn admits he knew Harry's parents. His mother was one of the brightest he's ever taught. She was one of his favorites. Slughorn agrees to come out of retirement to become a Hogwarts teacher.

..........................................................................................

Dumbledore tells Harry that Slughorn used to handpick favorites at Hogwarts. He formed a club of them. He'll try to collect Harry for his club.

..........................................................................................

Harry asks about the Inferi mentioned in the *Daily Prophet*. Dumbledore says they're corpses that have been bewitched to do a Dark Wizard's bidding. Voldemort is using them.

..........................................................................................

Dumbledore advises Harry to confide in Ron and Hermione about everything. Dumbledore tells him to keep his Invisibility Cloak with him at all times from this moment on—at the Burrow and the school.

..........................................................................................

Tonks is at the house with Mrs. Weasley. She looks ill.

..........................................................................................

Mrs. Weasley tells Harry that Mr. Weasley's been promoted to head of the office for the Detection and Confiscation of Counterfeit Defensive Spells and Protective Objects.

..........................................................................................

Mr. Weasley tells Harry that Fred and George are in Diagon Alley and that their joke shop is a hit.

..........................................................................................

The next morning Harry learns that Bill Weasley and Fleur Delacour are getting married.

..........................................................................................

Hermione suggests that Tonks has been grieving over Sirius's death.

..........................................................................................

They receive their O.W.L. results. Harry receives seven O.W.L.s but only receives an Exceeds Expectations in Potions, so he can't become an Auror. Snape told them last term that he takes only Outstanding students to go on to N.E.W.T. level.

..........................................................................................

While in Diagon Alley to get their books, Harry and Hermione see Draco Malfoy with his mother. They go to Fred and George's shop. Harry sees

Draco hurrying up the street alone—obviously having dodged his mother. Beneath the Invisibility Cloak, Harry and his friends follow Malfoy into Knockturn Alley. He goes into Borgin and Burkes, which sells a variety of sinister objects. Draco is near the same black cabinet that Harry once hid in to avoid Draco and his father. They overhear Draco asking if Borgin knows how to fix it; it can't be moved. Borgin has to tell him how to fix it. Draco threatens him and tells him to make sure "that one" stays since he'll need it—don't sell it. Draco wants something repaired and wants to reserve something in the shop.

Harry believes that, with his father in prison, Draco has replaced him as a Death Eater.

Under the cloak Harry follows a Slytherin student into Draco's compartment on the train to Hogwarts and overhears Draco say that he might not be at Hogwarts next year. He's been given a mission.

After everyone else leaves the compartment at the Hogsmeade station, Draco stays behind and puts the Petrificus Totalus spell on Harry and breaks Harry's nose. He throws the cloak over Harry.

Suddenly the cloak flies off and Tonks is there. She fixes his nose. She's been stationed in Hogsmeade to give the school extra protection. She sends her Patronus ahead to let someone at the school know she is with Harry. Snape meets them at the gates and comments on Tonks's new, weak Patronus.

At the start-of-term feast Dumbledore introduces their new Potions professor—Slughorn. Snape will be taking over Defense Against the Dark Arts.

McGonagall tells Harry that Slughorn accepts Exceeds Expectations to continue Potions at N.E.W.T. level. Harry's ambition to be an Auror is restored. Ron and Harry borrow books from Slughorn. Slughorn tells them about a potion he's brewed: Felix Felicis—liquid luck. All your endeavors will succeed until it wears off. The liquid luck will be the prize to the person who brews the best Draught of Living Death during class. Draco is feverish in his work—he wants that lucky day. Why?

When Harry opens the book he took from the cupboard, he sees that the previous owner scribbled all over the pages, making notations and crossing things out. Harry decides to follow the changes the owner specifies in the recipe. He's the clear winner for the potion. Slughorn says that, like his mother, he's a dab hand at Potions. When Harry looks at the book later, he sees that the previous owner called himself the Half-Blood Prince. Harry's best class becomes Potions, thanks to the Half-Blood Prince. Harry pours over the book, which contains handwritten hints and shortcuts that help him earn a glowing reputation with Slughorn, but there are always jinxes and hexes scribbled in the margins. He's attempted some of them and wants to try the sectumsempra, which is noted to be for enemies.

Lavender Brown has a crush on Ron. Hermione notices and turns cold toward a suddenly strutting Ron. Yet Hermione confounds Ron's competition during Quidditch tryouts to make sure Ron gets chosen for the Gryffindor team.

When Harry and his friends visit Hagrid, he tells them Aragog—his gigantic, talking spider—is dying.

After a day in Hogsmeade Harry and his friends are following Katie Bell and a friend back to the school. The two girls are fighting over a package and it falls to the ground. Katie rises into the air, letting out a terrible scream. Harry looks in the package without touching it and recognizes the ornate opal necklace that he'd seen once at Borgin and Burkes. The label said it was cursed. Katie must have touched it. Her friend tells them she came out of the bathroom at the Three Broomsticks holding it, saying it was a surprise she had to deliver for someone at Hogwarts. She didn't say who gave it to her. Harry realizes that Draco knew about the necklace, too. Was that what he wanted when he went in Borgin and Burkes just before the term started? McGonagall says Draco wasn't in Hogsmeade today—he had detention with her. But Harry believes Draco had an accomplice.

Slughorn plans a Christmas party around Harry's schedule, and those he's invited can invite their own guests. Hermione casually says Ron can come with her. Harry wonders what it would be like if the two of them started going out … and then split up.

Harry sees Ginny kissing Dean, and he's jealous. But she's out of bounds, since she's Ron's sister.

Ron and Hermione are no longer talking, Ron and Lavender are always kissing, and Harry is being cornered by girls who suddenly find him fascinating. Hermione warns him that Romilda Vane is trying to decide how to slip him a love potion so she can go to Slughorn's Christmas party with him. Harry wants to invite Ginny, but he can't get involved with her. He decides to ask Luna as a friend. Romilda gives Harry a box of chocolate cauldrons. He doesn't dare eat them.

Draco crashes Slughorn's Christmas party. He looks ill. Harry follows Draco and Snape and overhears their conversation. Draco says he didn't have anything to do with what happened to Katie Bell. Snape says he swore to his mother he'd protect him. He made the Unbreakable Vow. Snape asks what Draco's plan is. He can help him. But Draco refuses.

During Christmas at the Burrow, Lupin says he's been living with his fellow werewolves, but most are on Voldemort's side, such as Fenrir Greyback—the most savage werewolf alive.

Harry mentions to Lupin that Tonks's Patronus has changed. Lupin says sometimes a great shock or emotional upheaval can cause the change.

Percy arrives with the new Minister of Magic. Scrimgeour wants to make Harry the Ministry's mascot to convince everyone that they're winning the war against Voldemort.

During Potions class Slughorn sets a task for each student to come up with an antidote to the poison they make. The Half-Blood Prince's solution to any poison is a bezoar from the stomach of a goat.

Ron accidentally eats the chocolate cauldrons Romilda Vane gave to Harry, thinking they're a birthday present for him. They were filled with love potion. Harry takes Ron to Slughorn, who cures him and then pours them a toast for Ron's birthday from his last bottle of mead. He meant to give it to Dumbledore for Christmas. Ron is the first to swallow and he crumples. Harry gets a bezoar from Slughorn's bag. Ron was poisoned. It must have been the mead. Was it meant for Ron, Harry, Slughorn, or Dumbledore, since Slughorn intended to give it as a gift? Is there a connection between this and the cursed necklace? Clearly neither got to the person they were supposed to kill.

.................................................

Harry's still keeping an eye on Draco, noting his whereabouts on the Marauder's Map. Sometimes Draco vanishes altogether from it. Harry calls on Kreacher and Dobby to tail Draco to find out where he's going, who he's meeting, and what he's doing.

.................................................

Hermione and Ron become friends again.

.................................................

Kreacher and Dobby report that Draco has been making regular visits to the Room of Requirement and posting guards outside. Since they don't know what the room becomes when Draco enters, Harry doesn't know what to ask it to transform into and let him in. How can he find out what Draco's doing? None of Harry's attempts gain him entrance.

.................................................

Moaning Myrtle tells Harry that a boy came to see her but hasn't come back for months. He's sensitive, bullied, lonely, not afraid to show his feelings by crying.

.................................................

During Potions, Draco looks thinner. Obviously the mission, whatever it is, is going badly.

.................................................

Hagrid sends a letter saying Aragog is dead. He asks Harry to attend the funeral. Ron realizes that this is the perfect opportunity for Harry to use the luck potion to get Slughorn to give Harry the real memory Dumbledore needs, not the one Slughorn manufactured to make himself look better.

.................................................

Ron and Lavender have broken up, as have Ginny and Dean. Harry wants to ask Ginny out, but he doesn't want to lose his best friend in the process.

.................................................

Harry sees Draco in the bathroom with Moaning Myrtle. He says no one can help him. He can't do it; it won't work. If he doesn't get it to work soon, he'll be killed. Draco is crying. When he looks up in the mirror, he sees Harry and draws his wand. Harry yells "Sectumsempra," and blood spurts from Draco's chest. Snape comes and heals the wound while Harry watches, horrified at what he's done.

Snape tells Harry to get his schoolbooks. If he uses Occlumency against him, Harry knows he'll see the Half-Blood Prince's book in his mind. Harry asks Ron for his potions book and rushes to the Room of Requirement, where he can hide it. He sees a broken Vanishing Cabinet. He hides the book in the cupboard next to it, then puts a dusty wig with a tarnished tiara on the statue's head on the top of the cupboard.

Gryffindor wins the Quidditch Cup. Ginny runs to Harry and he kisses her. When they break apart, Ron's shock gives way to acceptance.

Hermione thinks she knows who the Half-Blood Prince is: Eileen Prince. She was captain of the Hogwarts Gobstones team. If her father's a wizard surnamed Prince and her mother is a Muggle, that would make her a Half-Blood Prince.

On the way to Dumbledore's office, Harry runs into Professor Trelawney, who's just been tossed out of the Room of Requirement. Someone, a male, was inside and whooping gleefully.

Trelawney says Dumbledore doesn't want to hear about the warnings she's seen in the cards: the lightning-struck tower, calamity, and disaster.

Trelawney tells Harry about the first time she met Dumbledore. Harry knows she made the prophecy, but she reveals something he didn't know: that they were interrupted by Snape, who'd been eavesdropping. The barman caught him. Harry realizes then that it was Snape who carried the prophecy to Voldemort. Harry confronts Dumbledore about it, and Dumbledore says what happened to Harry's parents is Snape's greatest regret. It's the reason he turned away from Voldemort and agreed to be Dumbledore's spy.

Harry tells Dumbledore about Trelawney being chucked out of the Room of Requirement and how Draco is celebrating—whatever he's been trying to mend must have been fixed. And now Dumbledore is about to leave the school. Dumbledore says the school has extra protection when he's gone. Dumbledore plans to take Harry with him to obtain the Horcrux he found. Harry gets his Invisibility Cloak and tells Ron and Hermione everything. He gives them the Marauder's Map and the rest of the luck potion. He tells them to summon the D.A.

When Harry and Dumbledore return to Hogsmeade with the Horcrux, Madame Rosmerta from the Three Broomsticks rushes out to tell them the Dark Mark has appeared over Hogwarts.

They get broomsticks and fly to the school. They dismount on the Astronomy Tower. Someone runs up the stairs of the tower and Harry is immobilized under his cloak by a spell Dumbledore puts on him. Dumbledore is disarmed by Draco, who says he's let Death Eaters into the school. Dumbledore says he's not a killer. Yes, he'd almost killed Katie Bell and Ron while trying to kill Dumbledore—feeble attempts. His heart couldn't have been in them. He must have had help. Madame Rosmerta is under the Imperious Curse. Dumbledore urges Draco to get on with his plan now, since Dumbledore can't defend himself without his wand.

Draco says he mended the Vanishing Cabinet in the Room of Requirement. There's a pair of cabinets. The other is in Borgin and Burkes. The passage they create was used by the Death Eaters to get into the school. Draco then put the Dark Mark over the tower so Dumbledore would hurry there. Dumbledore is convinced Draco won't go through with his plan, but Draco says he has to do it or Voldemort will kill his family. Dumbledore says he can help him by hiding him and his mother and, when the time comes, his father. Voldemort expected him to fail in his attempt. He didn't believe Draco could kill Dumbledore because Dumbledore is too powerful.

Death Eaters thunder up to the tower. They order Draco to kill Dumbledore, but his resolution is even weaker now. Snape appears and Dumbledore says his name in a soft, pleading way. Snape raises his wand and sends the killing curse at Dumbledore, who falls backward over the battlements.

Once the Death Eaters and Draco and Snape flee, Harry can move again. He has to catch Snape. He's running toward the gate with Draco where they can Disapparate just beyond. Harry catches up and tries to use the sectumseprum curse on Snape, who's furious that he dares to use his own spells against him. Snape, the Half-Blood Prince, invented those spells. Buckbeak attacks Snape, who runs through the gate and Disapparates.

Harry tells Hagrid that Snape killed Dumbledore. He shows him his body.

Bill was bitten by Fenrir, but he's alive. He wasn't bitten at the full moon and Fenrir hadn't transformed, so maybe he won't be a true werewolf. Fleur says she doesn't care if he's been bitten. She still loves him. Tonks turns up and says she doesn't care that Lupin is a werewolf. She loves him, too.

Harry tells everyone about the Vanishing Cabinets, about Snape and Draco, and how Dumbledore was killed. Everyone is stunned. They always believed Dumbledore knew something about Snape that they didn't, and that he had an ironclad reason for trusting him. There's no sign of Snape. Hermione says Eileen Prince is his mother.

Dumbledore will be laid to rest at Hogwarts. Harry's greatest protector is dead. During the funeral, bright white flames erupt around Dumbledore's body and, in its place, a white marble tomb forms.

Harry tells Ginny they can't be together anymore. He has things to do alone now. Voldemort will try to use her as bait—try to get to him through her.

Ron and Hermione follow Harry to the lake for privacy, and he says he's not coming back to Hogwarts next year. He'll go back to the Dursleys once more, like he promised Dumbledore, then he must track down the rest of the Horcruxes. Ron and Hermione say they're coming with him. But first they have to attend Bill and Fleur's wedding.

## SERIES PLANT ARCS

In Book 6 on the train to Hogwarts, Neville and Luna ask Harry if he's doing D.A. meetings this year. They enjoyed them and learned a lot from them. The D.A. is resurrected in Book 7.

In Book 6 during the first Hogsmeade weekend, Harry catches Mundungus with a bag of stolen things from Grimmauld Place. Exactly what he took will be revealed in Book 7.

Dittany healing potion is mentioned in Book 6. It becomes important in Book 7.

In Book 6 while drinking the potion to gain access to the Horcrux, Dumbledore says, "It's all my fault. I know I did wrong. Don't hurt them. Hurt me instead." We find out what he means in Book 7.

> Keep in mind that all series arcs and plants were introduced in the previous books in the series. In this final book, everything moves toward closure. For that reason, there are only story arcs here.

## HARRY POTTER AND THE DEATHLY HALLOWS
### YEAR 7 IN THE SERIES

## INDIVIDUAL STORY ARCS

Snape tells Voldemort that the Order of the Phoenix plans to move Harry Potter from his current place of safety next Saturday at nightfall. An entire party of Aurors will be used to transfer the boy. He'll be hidden at the home of one of the Order. The Death Eaters will have little chance to take him once he arrives there unless the Ministry has fallen by then. They can't touch him before the enchantment lifts from the Dursleys or once he arrives at his destination. The only time they can get at him is while he's traveling. Voldemort says he has to be the one to kill Harry. To do that, he needs to borrow a wand from one of them. He volunteers Lucius Malfoy's wand.

Voldemort brings up Bellatrix and Narcissa's niece Tonks, who just married the werewolf Lupin. Voldemort says the oldest wizarding families are diseased. To keep them healthy, they must prune until only those of true blood remain.

Harry is cleaning out his trunk and cuts himself on the enchanted mirror his godfather had given him when he was alive. Harry sees a flash of bright blue, like Dumbledore's eyes, in the mirror. But Dumbledore is dead. He has to face that. He fills an old rucksack with what he needs. The Order believes that when the protective charm breaks, the Dursleys will also be in danger of Voldemort, who plans to torture and kill them like he did Harry's parents. The Dursleys are put in protective custody.

An article in the *Daily Prophet*, written by Elphias Doge, remembers Albus Dumbledore. He arrived at Hogwarts at age eleven, a year after his father was convicted of attacking three Muggles. Dumbledore's notable friends include Nicholas Flamel, alchemist, and Bathilda Bagshot, noted historian. Dumbledore's mother died and left Albus guardian to a younger brother and sister. Another tragedy struck afterward, and his sister Ariana died. She'd been reported to be in poor health for a long time. Dumbledore and his brother Aberforth became estranged but in later years reestablished a cordial relationship. Dumbledore's notable achievements are discovering the twelve uses of dragon's blood and winning the legendary wizarding duel with Grindelwald in 1945.

In the *Daily Prophet*, Rita Skeeter is promoting her upcoming biography, *The Life and Lies of Albus Dumbledore*. She hints that Dumbledore dabbled in the Dark Arts in his youth and was a narrow-minded intolerant.

Harry's guard arrives: Hermione, Ron, Fred, George, Bill, Mr. Weasley, Mad-Eye Moody, Tonks, Lupin, Fleur, Kingsley, Hagrid, and Mundungus Fletcher. They're using broomsticks, thestrals, and Hagrid's motorbike.

The moment Harry's outside of range of the house, the protective charm on him will break. They're leaving early and putting protection on a dozen different houses so Voldemort won't know which one they're hiding Harry in. Harry's going to Tonks's parents. He'll use a Portkey once there to get to the Burrow. As an additional safeguard, seven different Harry Potters, through the use of Polyjuice Potion, will be heading to a different safe house. The pairs will be: Moody and Mundungus (aka Harry decoy #1), Mr. Weasley and Fred (decoy #2), Lupin and George (decoy #3), Bill and Fleur (decoy #4), Kingsley and Hermione (decoy #5), Tonks and Ron (decoy #6), and Hagrid and the real Harry.

..........................................................................................

Harry gets into the sidecar of what used to be Sirius's motorbike with his rucksack, broomstick, and Hedwig in her cage. Mr. Weasley's been tinkering with the bike. The purple button will give a bullet-burst of speed. The teams take off at exactly the same time. They're surrounded by Death Eaters almost immediately. Hedwig is caught by a curse and falls to the floor of the cage. When Hagrid presses the purple button, the sidecar breaks away from the bike. Hagrid pulls Harry onto the back of the bike. When Harry shouts "Expellaramus," the Death Eaters seem to realize that he's the real Harry. Voldemort appears and sends the killing curse at Harry, but Harry's wand acts of its own accord, dragging his hand like a magnet. Voldemort shouts in fury and disappears. Harry crashes the bike into a muddy pond. When he comes to, Tonks's parents come out. Hagrid is fine. They take the Portkey to the Burrow. Mrs. Weasley and Ginny rush outside to say no one else is back yet. Ron and Tonks's and Mr. Weasley and Fred's Portkeys came back without them. Lupin and George arrive. One of George's ears has been cursed off. Lupin says they were betrayed. The Death Eaters recognized Harry as the real one because they see Expellaramus as Harry's signature move. Hermione and Kingsley arrive, then Mr. Weasley and Fred, Tonks and Ron, and Bill and Fleur. Bill tells them Moody is dead and Mundungus Disapparated. Harry wants to leave the Burrow because his presence makes it dangerous for all of them, but after all they went through, it would make their efforts pointless.

Harry has a vision of Voldemort's fury at the wand maker Ollivander. The problem was supposed to be solved by using someone else's wand. But Lucius's wand was destroyed.

Mrs. Weasley has found out that Harry, Ron, and Hermione are dropping out of school. Harry tells her that Dumbledore left him with tasks to complete. Mr. Weasley helps them by transforming the ghoul in the attic into a Ron look-alike covered in blisters. Once Harry, Ron, and Hermione leave, the ghoul will live in Ron's room and, if anyone asks where he is, they'll show him the ghoul with a highly contagious spattergroit. Hermione has modified her parents' memories and moved them to Australia. Harry realizes the measures they've taken to protect their families are signs that they really are coming with him and they understand the danger involved.

Harry tells Ron and Hermione he plans to go to Godric's Hollow first. His parents' graves are there, and he feels he will find answers there. They have to trace the real locket R.A.B. took and find out if it was actually destroyed. Hermione's been researching how to destroy Horcruxes with the books she summoned from Dumbledore's office. One of them gives explicit instructions on how to make a Horcrux. Harry says Dumbledore believed that Voldemort already knew how to make a Horcrux when he asked Slughorn about them—he wanted to find out what would happen to a soul split into seven. The book says that stabbing a Horcrux with a basilisk fang is one of the few foolproof ways of destroying one. Ripping, smashing, or crushing won't work since those damages can be magically repaired. The fragment of soul depends on its container for survival. But the bit of soul can possess someone, if he or she gets too close.

The morning of Harry's birthday, he's wakened by Ron, who says Harry was muttering "Gregorovitch" in his sleep. Harry can't remember where he heard the name before. He only knows that he was having a vision of Voldemort looking for him.

The Minister of Magic shows up and tells Harry, Ron, and Hermione that Dumbledore's will has been found, and he left all three of them something. To Ron, Dumbledore left his Deluminator (the Put-Outer gets a fancy name in this book). To Hermione, Dumbledore left his copy of *The Tales of Beedle the Bard*. To Harry, Dumbledore left the snitch that Harry caught during his first Quidditch match at Hogwarts. Scrimgeour says a snitch is a good hiding place for a small object because they have flesh memories. They carry enchantments that allow the snitch to identify with the first person to lay hands on it. When Harry takes the snitch, nothing happens. Dumbledore also left Harry the sword of Gryffindor, but Scrimgoeur says it wasn't his to give away. The sword presents itself to any worthy Gryffindor, but the fact that it did so to Harry doesn't make it his property. Later Harry and his friends discuss the things Dumbledore left them. Why did he leave these things in particular? While he must have known the Ministry would examine them too closely for him to leave instructions, he could have tried to tell them something. The Deluminator only seems to turn lights on and off. The book is full of wizard fairy tales. Harry reminds his friends that he didn't catch the snitch with his hand, but with his mouth, and when he presses the snitch to his mouth, words appear on it: "I open at the close."

At the wedding Harry meets Luna Lovegood's father Xenophilius. Victor Krum attends. He's offended by Xenophilius's robes. He's wearing a triangle and eye symbol that Krum says is the sign of Grindelwald, the Dark Wizard Dumbledore defeated.

Harry suddenly remembers who Gregorovitch is: the wandmaker who made Krum's wand. Krum says he retired years ago. Harry wonders why Voldemort is looking for a celebrated wand maker. After what happened between Harry and Voldemort's wands the night Voldemort was resurrected, he must have gone looking for answers as to why that occurred.

Elphias Doge attends the wedding, and he and Ron's Aunt Muriel talk about Dumbledore and Rita's Skeeter's upcoming biography. Muriel says Dumbledore's mother was a terrifying Muggle. She was mortified that her daughter Ariana was a Squib. Back then, Squibs were often hushed up. No one ever saw Ariana. Doge insists that her health was delicate and Dumbledore was heartbroken by Ariana's death. Muriel adds that Aberforth broke his brother's nose during the funeral. Bathilda Bagshot was there and heard Aberforth shout that Ariana's death was his brother's fault. Dumbledore didn't defend himself. Muriel says she thinks it's Bathilda who told Rita everything. But Doge points out that the magical historian was an old friend of Dumbledore's—though she's quite gaga these days. She lived in Godric's Hollow, as did Dumbledore's family.

Kingsley's Patronus lands in the middle of the wedding to announce that the Ministry has fallen, Scrimgeour is dead. Death Eaters are coming. The protective enchantments around the Burrow have broken. Hermione calls Ron and Harry to her and they take hands. They Disapparate to Totenham Court Road, a Muggle area. She's brought everything they need. She enchanted a small beaded bag with an extension charm. There are wizards dressed as workmen in the next booth and they draw wands. Harry and his friends are too fast and they render them unconscious. But how were they found so fast in a Muggle area? Harry says they need to go some place safe— Grimmauld Place. They've put up jinxes against Snape, and they're able to get past the enchantments. Ron's father sends his Patronus to tell them the family is safe but not to reply because they're being watched. Harry's scar is hurting like mad, and he knows it's because Voldemort is angry. The Death Eaters have let Harry get away again.

In Sirius's old bedroom, Harry finds part of a letter from his mother to Sirius. She talks of Dumbledore still having James's Invisibility Cloak. But Harry wonders why Dumbledore, who could make himself invisible with spells, would need a cloak?

Harry finds another bedroom with a name on it: Regulus Arcturus Black. R.A.B.? Sirius's brother was a Death Eater. He tried to leave Voldemort and he was killed. They search the house for the real locket. Harry remembers that when they were cleaning the house two years ago, they discovered a locket that none of them could open. They'd tossed it in the rubbish, and Kreacher had nicked loads of things back from them. They check his cupboard, but they don't find it. Harry summons Kreacher from Hogwarts' kitchen and asks him if he stole the locket back. Kreacher admits he did, but it's gone now. Mundungus stole Master Regulus's locket. Kreacher tells them that Regulus joined Voldemort and then Voldemort needed a house-elf. Regulus told him to do whatever Voldemort told him to and then go home. Voldemort took Kreacher to a cave beside the sea—where Dumbledore and Harry had gone at the end of last term. Voldemort had tested the defenses surrounding the Horcrux there by borrowing a disposal servant. Kreacher was forced to drink the potion, then Voldemort put the locket in the basin and filled it with more potion. He left Kreacher on the island, but Kreacher obeyed his master and Apparated home.

Later Regulus asked Kreacher to take him to the cave he'd gone to with Voldemort. Regulus drank the potion, took the locket, and put the fake one with the note inside instead. Regulus ordered Kreacher to go home without him and destroy the real locket. Nothing Kreacher did to the locket hurt it. He'd failed his master. Regulus had forbidden him to tell anyone what had happened. Harry tells Kreacher they want to finish the work Regulus started, and to do that, they need to find the locket. He asks Kreacher to find Mundungus and bring him back to Grimmauld Place. Harry gives the fake locket, a Black family heirloom, to Kreacher, and the house-elf becomes Harry's loyal servant.

Lupin visits and says Death Eaters are staking out any place that has a connection with Harry. They ask Lupin how the Death Eaters found them in a Muggle area. It's worrying.

Voldemort has set into motion a Muggle-born Registration Committee. Unless you can prove you have at least one close wizarding relative, you'll be arrested for illegally obtaining magical power. Only wizards with Blood Status can attend Hogwarts.

Lupin tells them Tonks is pregnant. He offers them help with their mission. Tonks will be fine with her parents; Harry realizes he's going to leave his wife and unborn baby for this. Lupin admits he believes he made a grave mistake in marrying Tonks. He's made her an outcast, and what if he's passed his condition on to an innocent child? Harry calls him a coward, and Lupin stomps out.

Kreacher returns with Mundungus, and Harry asks him about the locket. He says a woman from the Ministry bought it from him: Dolores Umbridge.

Snape is named Hogwarts's Headmaster. Hermione puts Phineas Nigellus's Grimmauld portrait into her bag so he can't use the passageway between the headmaster's office and Grimmauld to spy on them.

Harry sees a vision of Voldemort finding Gregorovitch. The connection between Harry and Voldemort is something Harry hates, but it allows him to know what Voldemort is doing.

They come up with a plan to get into the Ministry. They use Polyjuice Potion to assume the identities of Ministry workers. Ron is forced to repair a weather condition in a Death Eater's office and informed that his "wife" is being interrogated today. Umbridge assigns Hermione in disguise to keep record in the courtroom. Harry goes to Umbridge's office under his Invisibility Cloak. Not finding the locket in the office, he goes down to the courtroom. Umbridge is wearing the locket. Harry Stupefies her and Hermione gets the Horcrux, duplicating it so Umbridge won't know it's missing. Ron informs them they have a few minutes before Death Eater's descend on them. They take hands to Disapparate, but something goes wrong. When Harry comes to, he's on the forest floor with Ron and Hermione. Ron was nearly splinched (some part of him was almost left behind during Disapparition). Hermione is using dittany to heal his arm. She says a Death Eater caught hold of her just as they Disapparated. He wouldn't let go, and so he arrived with them at Grimmauld. He recognized the place. She shook him off and brought them here in the woods where they held the Quidditch World Cup three years ago. Hermione puts up protective enchantments around their tent.

They examine the locket. There's no sign of magical damage. They all feel the evil emanating from it. They can't destroy it now, so they'll have to keep it safe, each taking turns wearing it, until they can figure out how to damage it permanently.

Harry has another vision of Voldemort telling Gregorovitch to give something to him. The wand maker insists it was stolen from him years ago. Harry wakes and believes Voldemort killed Gregorovitch after reading his mind to find out who stole it from him. Harry also saw the person in Gregorovitch's mind.

With no idea where the other Horcruxes are, they move around every night. Harry begins to suspect his friends are having conversations about him.

One night they hear voices outside their tent: Griphook and Gornuk, two goblins, Tonks's father, and Dean Thomas, a fellow Gryffindor. One of them mentions that Ginny and a couple friends tried to steal the sword of Gryffindor from the headmaster's office. Snape sent the sword to be kept in Gringotts. The goblins there realized it was a fake but didn't say anything to the Death Eaters. They say *The Quibbler* has been printing all the stuff the *Prophet*'s ignoring. On the front page of every issue of *The Quibbler* is a rally cry for those against Voldemort to support Harry.

Hermione takes the portrait of Phineas out and asks him if he saw the real sword. He says the last time he saw it, Dumbledore was using it to break open a ring. The sword of Gryffindor can destroy Horcruxes! Dumbledore tried to will it to Harry to use it on the locket. Realizing the Ministry wouldn't have let Harry have it, Dumbledore had a copy made and placed it in the glass case. So where's the real one?

Ron becomes furious at the growing list of things Harry doesn't know. They've achieved nothing in all the time they've been out. They thought Harry knew what he was doing, that Dumbledore told him something, and that he had a real plan. Harry tells Ron to go home. Hermione says she's staying, and Ron thinks she's choosing Harry. He storms out and Hermione rushes after him, but he Disapparates. Harry acknowledges that, with their protective enchantments, it'll be impossible for Ron to find them again.

Harry's anger that Dumbledore left him virtually nothing to go on is growing. Harry and Hermione continue to talk to Phineas's portrait to gather news. Harry deduces that Ginny, Neville, and Luna have re-formed the D.A.

Hermione shows Harry a symbol on the fairy tale book Dumbledore left her—the triangular eye, Grindelwald's mark.

Harry says he wants to go to Godric's Hollow, and this time Hermione agrees. Maybe Dumbledore put the real sword there for Harry to find—with Bathilda Bagshot. They use Polyjuice Potion and Apparate under the cloak. They meet up with Bathilda, and she leads them to her home. She and the house smell bad, like rotting meat. Harry finds a picture of the thief who stole something from Gregorovitch—it's the same person he saw in Rita Skeeter's book about Dumbledore. Bathilda leads Harry upstairs without Hermione. His scar prickles, and the Horcrux around his neck twitches. The body of Bathilda collapses and a snake pours out. Harry realizes Voldemort is coming. Harry grabs Hermione, and she performs a powerful spell that sounds like a bomb going off. They jump out the window and Disapparate. Harry hears Voldemort's scream of rage. Bathilda must have been dead for a while. Voldemort placed the snake inside her to wait in case Harry went there.

Hermione tells Harry that his wand was severed by the blasting spell. She can't mend it.

Hermione took Rita's book about Dumbledore from Bathilda's. The picture of the thief was Dumbledore's friend Grindelwald, who was Bathilda's great-nephew. Grindelwald became one of the Dark Wizards of all time, second only to Voldemort. There's a letter reproduced in the book written by Dumbledore to Grindelwald in which Dumbledore says wizards must rule over Muggles. His ideas helped Grindelwald rise to power. Grindelwald was at the Dumbledore house when Ariana died, and he fled the country within hours of her death.

While keeping watch over their campsite one night, Harry sees a bright silver light appear—a Patronus doe. Harry follows her to a small frozen pool. Inside the ice he sees the sword of Gryffindor. He tries to summon it but remembers the qualities of a true Gryffindor—daring, nerve, chivalry. He has to get into the water to get the sword. He uses Hermione's wand to crack the ice, then he dives. He gets the sword, but the locket tightens around his neck, strangling him. Arms close around him and pull him out. The locket is cut free of his neck. Harry sees Ron has come back.

Whoever cast the Patronus must have put the sword in the ice. Harry figures out how to use Parseltongue on the locket to open it, then Ron stabs it. The Horcrux is destroyed.

Ron tells them he wanted to return to them the minute he Disapparated—into a gang of Snatchers who earn their living by rounding up Muggle-borns and blood traitors. Ron got away with two wands. He stayed with Bill and Fleur in their Shell Cottage.

Harry asks him how he found them again. Ron says the Deluminator allowed him to hear their voices. When he clicked it, the light went out but another appeared and led him outside, where the light entered him. He knew then where he needed to go. He couldn't see or hear them once they were in the tent and the enchantments were up, but he knew they were nearby. Unfortunately, Harry and Hermione have been Disapparating under the cloak. Ron has been following them in this way ever since.

Ron tells them Voldemort's name has been jinxed. They use it to track people and it breaks protective enchantments. It's how the three of them were found so easily after the wedding.

Ron gives Harry one of the extra wands.

Hermione decides they should go see Xenophilius about Grindelwald's Mark because they've seen the symbol so often of late. On Xenophilius's wall, there's an Erumpent horn—it can explode at the slightest touch. There's also a headdress modeled upon the head of Rowena Ravenclaw. When they ask Luna's father about the symbol he wore at the wedding, he says it's the sign of the Deathly Hallows. The symbol isn't Dark, only a way to reveal oneself to other believers who might help with the quest. Believers seek the Deathly Hallows, based on the story in *The Tale of the Three Brothers* from *The Tales of Beedle the Bard*. The brothers were learned in the magical arts and made a bridge appear across treacherous waters. Death spoke to them, angry that he'd been cheated of three victims. But, cunningly he congratulated them on their magic and offered them each a prize. The first brother asked for the most powerful wand in existence, the Elder Wand. The second asked for the power to recall others from death. Death gave him a stone to bring back the dead, the Resurrection Stone. The third didn't trust Death and so asked for something to hide him from Death—Death's own Invisibility Cloak, the true cloak of invisibility, enduring eternally. Together, these three artifacts make up the Deathly Hallows. If united, they'll make the possessor master of Death. Xenophilius believes the Hallows actually exist. The Elder Wand is the easiest to trace—it's left a blood trail throughout wizarding history.

Was the Sorcerer's Stone the Resurrection Stone?

Hermione says she saw the Deathly Hallows symbol on the grave of Ignatius Peverell in Godric's Hollow. He and his brothers were the ones in the story, the original owners of the Hallows.

Harry goes up to Luna's bedroom and realizes that she isn't there and hasn't been for weeks. Xenophilius keeps looking out the windows. They draw their wands. He admits the Ministry took Luna. If he hands Harry over, maybe they'll give her back. He aims a spell at them that hits the Erumpent horn and it explodes. Death Eaters arrive, and Hermione uses a spell to make the second floor drop onto the first. They Disapparate. Hermione wanted the Death Eaters to know they were there so they wouldn't kill Luna's father. If the Death Eaters actually saw Harry, they wouldn't kill Xenophilius for calling them needlessly.

Harry remembers that Voldemort's grandfather on his mother's side claimed to be descended from Peverell. The ring he wore had their coat of arms. Maybe the black stone in that ring was the Resurrection Stone. Dumbledore must have put the stone inside the snitch.

Harry wonders if he can defeat Voldemort with the Deathly Hallows. He also remembers that Dumbledore had his father's Invisibility Cloak the night his parents died. He wanted to examine it … because he believed it was a Hallow?

All Harry needs is the Elder Wand. And then he realizes what Voldemort has been seeking. Voldemort hasn't been looking for a new wand, but an old one. The fact that Voldemort had used one of the Hallows to create a Horcrux proves he doesn't realize the Elder Wand's full power—that it's one of three. Dumbledore didn't tell Harry because it's a quest, and he had to discover this fact on his own.

On Potter Watch, the radio program that's telling the truth about what's going on, they hear that Ted Tonks and Gornuk were killed. Dean Thomas and Griphook escaped. Xenophilius Lovegood has been imprisoned, and Hagrid is on the run. Lupin urges everyone to stand behind Harry. They're all with him in spirit, and Harry should follow his instincts. Harry knows then that Lupin went back to Tonks.

Harry's scar hurts and in his mind he sees the thief. Voldemort has found him. But the thief claims he never had the wand.

Narcissa Malfoy says her son can identify Harry. But Draco isn't sure. Bellatrix comes in and sees the sword and demands to know how it got out of her vault at Gringotts. She says they're in danger. Harry, Ron, Dean, and Griphook are put in a cell in the basement with Luna and Mr. Ollivander. Hermione is kept behind and tortured. Hermione says the sword is a fake, and Bellatrix tells Draco to have Griphook verify this. Harry takes out the enchanted mirror and sees the bright blue eye. He begs for help. Harry asks Griphook to lie to Bellatrix about the sword and tell her it's a fake. Dobby Apparates into the cell after Griphook is taken back upstairs. He says he can Disapparate out with them. Harry asks him to take Luna, Dean, and Ollivander to Shell Cottage, and then come back. Upstairs, the Disapparation is heard, and Wormtail is sent to investigate. They tackle him and take his wand. Wormtail tries to strangle Harry, but suddenly he slackens and strangles himself to death. Dumbledore had realized Wormtail would have an unconscious impulse of mercy in the end.

They rush upstairs. Griphook tells Bellatrix the sword is a fake. She calls Voldemort. The chandelier falls to the floor when Dobby Apparates into the room. Dobby takes Bellatrix and Cissy's wands. Harry rescues Griphook and the sword, Ron rescues Hermione, and they Apparate out with Dobby. But, as they're leaving, Bellatrix throws a knife. Dobby jerks. They land at Shell Cottage. Dobby collapses, saying Harry's name as he dies. Hermione and Griphook are badly injured, but they'll be all right. Harry can sense Voldemort's dreadful rage at those left behind at Malfoy Manor, but Harry's grief for Dobby diminishes it. He digs a grave alone. He's learned to shut his mind to Voldemort through grief. Dumbledore would have said it was love. Harry knows that whoever sent Dobby to the cellar was the owner of the blue eye he saw in the mirror fragment.

A plan has formed in Harry's mind. He takes Ron and Hermione to talk to Griphook. He tells him he needs to break into Gringotts—the Lestrange vault. Griphook says it's impossible, and anyway the sword in the vault is a fake. The one Griphook now holds is the real one. Harry tells him he needs the help of a goblin to break in. Griphook says he'll think about it, but resentment fills his eyes when Harry takes the Gryffindor sword on his way out of the room. Hermione guesses that Harry thinks there's a Horcrux in the Lestrange vault.

Harry asks Ollivander if his wand can be repaired, and Ollivander shakes his head. Harry shows him the two wands he took from the Malfoys and asks who they belong to. The owners are Bellatrix and Draco. Ollivander says if Harry took Draco's wand, it may now be Harry's wand. If a wand has been won, generally its allegiance will change. Harry took Draco's wand by force.

Harry asks about the Elder Wand. Voldemort originally sought a wand to conquer Harry's but now seeks the Elder Wand because he thinks it'll make him invulnerable. Ollivander assures Harry that the Elder Wand isn't a fairy tale.

Harry tells Ron and Hermione later that Grindelwald stole the wand from Gregorovitch—and Dumbledore dueled Grindelwald to take the Elder Wand. It's at Hogwarts, buried with Dumbledore. Harry realizes it's too late to do anything. Voldemort is already there taking it, and he knows now that Dumbledore didn't want him to have the wand. He wants him to get the Horcruxes.

Griphook decides to help Harry break into Gringotts—in return for the sword of Gryffindor. Harry says they'll tell him he can have the sword after he's helped them get into the vault. They just won't tell him *when* he can have it. They have to use the sword on the Horcruxes first.

Lupin comes to visit. Tonks had the baby, a boy—Ted. Lupin asks Harry to be godfather.

Hermione uses Polyjuice Potion to become Bellatrix (she took her wand at Malfoy Manor), so she'll be convincing. Ron assumes a fake identity while Harry and Griphook are concealed under the cloak. They meet up with a Death Eater in Diagon Alley, who tells them the inhabitants of Malfoy Manor are confined to the house. In the lowest levels of Gringotts, they pass under a waterfall that washes away all enchantment. There's a dragon barring access to the vault. It's partially blind. They use Clankers to subdue it. They enter the vault and search it for Hufflepuff's cup. Harry uses the sword to retrieve the cup, but once he has it Griphook gets away with the sword. Harry releases the dragon from the chains, and he, Ron, and Hermione climb on its back. The dragon soars out into the sky.

Harry realizes that as soon as the goblins tell Bellatrix her vault was broken into, Voldemort will realize they're hunting Horcruxes. Harry sees a vision of just that. Voldemort knows he has to return to each of his hiding places, but his snake must remain close now. The stone at the house, the locket at the lake ... but he alone knows where he stowed the Horcrux at Hogwarts. He thinks Hogwarts is safe though because Snape is there, and it'll be hard for Harry to get into the school without being noticed.

Harry and his friends Apparate in Hogsmeade under the cloak. As soon as they arrive, an alarm goes off. The barman of the Hog's Head lets them in and, upstairs, they see a large oil painting of a blond girl. The barman is Aberforth. Harry sees that he has brilliant blue eyes. It's his eye he saw in the mirror. He was the one who sent Dobby. He says he bought the other part of the mirror from Mundungus to keep an eye on Harry.

Aberforth tells them when his sister was six, she was attacked by Muggles who saw her doing magic. They destroyed her, and the magic turned inward and drove her mad. His father went after the Muggles and got locked up for it. He couldn't tell anyone the truth because the Ministry would have institutionalized Ariana for good. The family moved. Ariana went into one of her rages and killed their mother. Albus was forced to come home, but then Grindelwald came and Albus neglected Ariana while they were hatching clever schemes. Aberforth told his brother off for it. Albus didn't like it, nor did Grindelwald. They pulled their wands. Grindelwald put a curse on Aberforth, and Albus tried to stop it. They dueled, and Ariana got in the way. She died and Grindelwald ran for it. Albus never got over his guilt for her death.

Harry tells Aberforth they have to get into the castle. Aberforth goes to the portrait and tells Ariana she knows what to do. She walks into the long tunnel painted behind her. Neville follows her back and enters the room, saying he let everyone know. They'll be Apparating into the bar and going into the castle through the passageway. The four of them enter the Room of Requirement through the portrait. Fred, George, and Ginny arrive, then Luna and Dean. Harry asks the D.A. members if they can help him find something from Ravenclaw that's missing. Luna suggests Ravenclaw's lost diadem. Professor McGonagall comes after a Death Eater summons Voldemort. She says she'll secure the school while Harry looks for the object. Snape escapes from the school. Kingsley, Tonks, Lupin, Bill, Fred, and Mr. and Mrs. Weasley arrive. Percy Weasley also comes, saying he'd been a fool and he's sorry.

Hermione and Ron have disappeared, saying something about a bathroom.

Voldemort appears at the front of the school and says he doesn't want to kill the teachers at Hogwarts or spill magical blood. Give him Harry Potter and no one else will be harmed. They have until midnight.

Harry finds the ghost of Ravenclaw. The Gray Lady tells him the diadem belonged to her mother, and she stole it from her. She told all of this to Tom Riddle.

Harry remembers hiding the Half-Blood Prince's potion book in the Room of Requirement—in a cupboard topped with a statue in a wig and tiara. That must be Ravenclaw's diadem.

Ron and Hermione have their arms full of basilisk fangs from the Chamber of Secrets. They'll destroy the Horcruxes with them. Hermione already used one on the cup.

They clear the Room of Requirement of D.A. members, and then go back into it to search for the diadem. Draco and his old school thugs come in to stop Harry, but he gets the diadem. Draco's friends' spell destroys the room, devouring themselves. Harry goes back to save Draco.

Another Horcrux is destroyed

Fred is killed in the ensuing battle.

They have to find Voldemort and the snake. Harry goes into Voldemort's mind and sees him in the Shrieking Shack. Voldemort doesn't believe he needs to be involved in the battle. He thinks Harry will come to him on his own. Harry knows Nagini is a Horcrux. Besides, he won't let his friends sacrifice their lives for him. Harry puts on his cloak and goes on alone. He sees the snake in an enchanted sphere.

Snape and Voldemort are talking. Voldemort says the Elder Wand doesn't work for him—he's performing only his usual magic with it, nothing extraordinary. But he thinks he understands—the wand can't serve him properly because he isn't the true master. It still belongs to the wizard who killed its last master—Snape killed Dumbledore, so he's the true master. Voldemort sends the snake to kill Snape. Believing the Elder Wand will now do his bidding, Voldemort leaves with the snake. Harry goes to Snape and reveals himself. Snape gives Harry a memory and then dies.

Voldemort's forces retreat, but Voldemort tells Harry that he's permitted his friends to die for him rather than face him. Voldemort will wait for one hour in the Forbidden Forest. If Harry doesn't come to him, the battle resumes with Voldemort at the frontlines, ready to punish all who have concealed Harry from him.

Harry and his friends return to the castle to discover that Lupin and Tonks are dead.

Harry looks at the memory Snape gave him in the Pensieve.

Memory 1: Harry's mother Lily and her sister, Petunia. A skinny boy is watching them, Snape at nine or ten years old. Petunia is scared but fascinated by Lily's magic. Snape reveals himself and informs Lily that she's a witch and he's a wizard.

Memory 2: Snape and Lily are talking about Hogwarts. Lily asks if it matters that she's Muggle-born, and Snape says it makes no difference.

Memory 3: Platform 9¾. Lily is trying to convince Petunia she can come to Hogwarts, too, but Petunia says she doesn't want to be a freak. Lily asks why she wrote to Dumbledore herself to ask him to take her. On the train, Lily cries and Snape tries to console her, saying she'd better be in Slytherin. The other boys in the compartment, James Potter and Sirius Black, taunt Snape. Lily is chosen for Gryffindor and, though she's happy, she looks sadly at Snape, who's in Slytherin.

Memory 4: Years later, Snape and Lily are arguing. Are they no longer best friends? Lily says she doesn't like who he's been hanging around with. They use Dark Magic. Snape is jealous of James Potter and his friends— but especially James.

Memory 5: Snape calls Lily a Mudblood. He can't wait to join Voldemort, can he? He's chosen his way, and she's chosen hers.

Memory 6: Snape has just overheard Trelawney's prophecy. He meets with Dumbledore and begs him to help. Voldemort thinks the prophecy refers to Lily Evans … and her son. Voldemort will hunt them down. Hunt *Lily* down. Dumbledore has to hide them and keep them safe. Dumbledore asks what Snape will exchange for this favor. Snape agrees to anything to save the woman he loves.

Memory 7: Snape, in Dumbledore's office, says he wishes he were dead instead of Lily. Dumbledore says if Snape truly loved Lily, he'll help Dumbledore protect her son.

Memory 8: Dumbledore says there's only one thing to be done if he and Snape want to save Draco from Voldemort's wrath. Snape must kill Dumbledore when the time comes to prevent Draco's soul from being damaged. Dumbledore tells Snape that there will come a time after his death that Voldemort will fear for the life of his snake and won't let it out of his sight. It'll be safe to tell Harry at that time—tell him that, when Voldemort's killing curse rebounded, a fragment of his soul latched itself onto Harry. Part of Voldemort lives inside Harry and while that part—a parasitic growth—remains attached to him, Voldemort can't die and Voldemort must be the one to kill Harry. Harry will arrange things in the end so that, when he sets out to meet his death, Voldemort will be completely vanquished.

Snape is shocked that Dumbledore was supposed to keep Lily's son safe, yet all along he's been raising Harry like a pig for slaughter. Dumbledore asks if Snape has come to care for Harry. Snape produces a Patronus—a silver doe just like Lily's Patronus. Everything he's done is for Lily.

Memory 9: Snape talks to Dumbledore's portrait after his death. Snape will have to give Voldemort the correct date of Harry's departure from the Dursleys. He's counting on Snape to stay in Voldemort's good books or Hogwarts will fall into the hands of Death Eaters.

Memory 10: Phineas tells Snape that Harry's camping in the Forest of Dean—he overheard them talking when Hermione opened her bag. Dumbledore's portrait says the sword of Gryffindor can only be taken under conditions of need and valor.

Harry understands at last that he's not supposed to survive. Along the way, he's to dispose of Voldemort's remaining links to life. When he presents himself to Voldemort, Harry won't defend himself. Neither will live. Harry's will to live has always been stronger than his fear of death. He puts on the Invisibility Cloak to leave the castle, but Neville walks into him. Harry asks him to kill Voldemort's snake.

As he walks into the Forbidden Forest, Harry remembers the snitch. "I open at the close." He presses it to his lips and whispers that he's about to die. The shell opens and the Resurrection Stone is inside. He turns it over three times, and his father and mother, Sirius, and Lupin appear, less substantial than living bodies but more than ghosts. They tell him it'll be over soon. They'll stay with Harry to the end. No one can see them but Harry. Harry comes up to a group of Death Eaters—Lucius and Narcissa Malfoy and Bellatrix. Hagrid is bound to a tree. Voldemort is in the center. Harry reveals himself and Voldemort kills him.

Harry wakes in a mist and hears something flapping and struggling. He sees the form of a small, naked child. It shudders where it has been left, unwanted. He's afraid and repulsed by it.

Dumbledore appears to congratulate Harry. Dumbledore is dead but Harry isn't … The fact that he didn't defend himself made all the difference. Harry let Voldemort kill him, so the part of Voldemort's soul that's in him would be destroyed. His soul is whole, completely his own.

Voldemort took Harry's blood when he was resurrected, and so tethered Harry to him while he lives. Harry was the seventh Horcrux—the one he never meant to make. Voldemort's soul was unstable when he killed Harry's parents and tried to murder an innocent child. Voldemort's body keeps Harry's mother's sacrifice alive, and, while the enchantment survives, so does Harry.

Dumbledore and Grindelwald shared an obsession over the Deathly Hallows. Dumbledore resented that he had to give up his life to care for his siblings. He wanted glory. But Aberforth shouted truths at him he didn't want to hear—that he couldn't seek the Hallows with his fragile sister in tow. Grindelwald lost control. Ariana lay dead on the floor, and Dumbledore was left with his shame and grief. Dumbledore had learned the hard way that he couldn't trust himself with power. But he had no choice but to duel Grindelwald and stop him from completing his terrible plans. Harry is the worthy possessor of the Hallows, but Dumbledore was afraid that, if presented outright with the objects, he would seize them at the wrong time for the wrong reasons. Now Harry is the true master of death ,and Voldemort can be finished for good.

Harry returns to himself in the Forbidden Forest and hears that Voldemort collapsed when the killing curse rebounded, and now both have returned. Voldemort is obviously wary of approaching him and sends Narcissa to verify his death. She asks Harry in barely a whisper if Draco is alive in the castle, and Harry says yes. Narcissa proclaims Harry dead. She knows the only way she can enter Hogwarts and find her son is as part of the conquering army. She cares nothing about Voldemort. Hagrid is made to carry Harry's body to the castle to show Voldemort's enemies what's become of their hero. Voldemort presents Harry's lifeless body and orders everyone in the castle to kneel before him if they want to be spared.

Voldemort is no longer keeping his snake in the enchanted sphere because he believes Harry is finished.

Harry's friends and loved ones rally around him even in death. Neville charges Voldemort but is thrown back. Still, he refuses to join Voldemort. He belongs to Dumbledore's Army. A window shatters above and the Sorting Hat lands in Voldemort's hands. He tosses it away. The giants and centaurs attack, and Harry takes that time to put on the cloak. Neville draws the sword of Gryffindor out of the Sorting Hat and uses it to slice off the snake's head.

Harry fights his way to Voldemort. Mrs. Weasley kills Bellatrix, and Voldemort turns on her. Harry reveals himself and that the last true master of the Elder Wand wasn't Snape, but Draco Malfoy. Draco disarmed Dumbledore the night he died. Harry overpowered Draco and took his wand from him, and this means that Harry is the true master of the Elder Wand. They both cast spells, and the Elder Wand flies through the air to the master it won't kill. Harry catches the wand and Voldemort takes the rebounded killing curse. He's finally dead. The Death Eaters flee.

Harry, Ron, and Hermione go to Dumbledore's office, and Harry speaks to Dumbledore's portrait. He dropped the Resurrection Stone in the forest—he's not sure where, but he won't look for it. He'll keep his cloak, but he was happier with his old wand. He uses the Elder Wand to repair his old wand. The Elder Wand will go back in Dumbledore's tomb.

Nineteen years later, Harry, an Auror, and Ginny are sending their children off to Hogwarts. They meet up with Ron and Hermione and their children. Everyone on the train stares at Harry's scar, but it hasn't pained him for nineteen years. All is well.

# INDEX

# WRITER'S DIGEST

## Is Your Manuscript Ready?

Trust 2nd Draft Critique Service to prepare your writing to catch the eye of agents and editors. You can expect:

- Expert evaluation from a hand-selected, professional critiquer
- Know-how on reaching your target audience
- Red flags for consistency, mechanics, and grammar
- Tips on revising your work to increase your odds of publication

Visit **WritersDigestShop.com/2nd-draft** for more information.

BUILD A FULLY DEVELOPED STORY FROM THE GROUND UP!

### *From First Draft to Finished Novel*

**BY KAREN S. WIESNER**

Karen Wiesner takes you steps closer to the publication of your story with instruction, checklists, and worksheets that touch upon everything from plot conflicts to the art of editing and polishing your manuscript. You'll get a thorough lesson in the fundamentals of character development, plot conflicts, adhering to submission guidelines, writing etiquette, and more. This must-have guide includes detailed examples from published novels that clearly illustrate the story-building principles you must master in order to see your work in print.

Available from WritersDigestShop.com and your favorite book retailers.

To get started join our mailing list: **WritersDigest.com/enews**

### FOLLOW US ON:

F̶i̶n̶d̶ ...ing and
a̶ ...̶digest

A̶ ...̶ebook page:
facebook.com/writersdigest